For Jan, who also believes in magic

Acknowledgments

Lyrics from "Post World War II Blues" by Al Stewart used with permission. Copyright © 1973 Gwyneth Music Limited. All rights reserved.

Lyrics used with permission from "God" by John Lennon. Copyright © 1970 and 1971 Northern Songs Ltd. All rights in the United States and Mexico controlled by Maclen Music, Inc., c/o ATV Music Corp. All rights reserved.

Lyrics from "Promentalshitbackwashpsychosisenema Squad" ("The Doo Doo Chasers"), words and music by George Clinton, Gary Shider, and Linda Brown. Copyright © 1979 by Malbiz Music, Inc. Search for holders of rights in progress at time of publication.

Lyrics from "Groovallegience," words and music by George Clinton, Walter Morrison, and Bernard Worrell. Copyright © 1979 by Malbiz Music, Inc., and Bridgeport Music, Inc. Search for holders of rights in progress at time of publication.

Lyrics from "Visions," words and music by Stevie Wonder, used with permission. Copyright © 1973 Jobete Music Co., Inc. & Black Bull Music. International copyright secured. All rights reserved.

Lyrics used with permission from "Do You Think I'm Disco" ("Do You Think I'm Sexy"). Copyright © 1978 Rod Stewart, WB Music Corp., and Nite Stalk Music. All rights reserved.

Lyrics used with permission from "It Takes a Lot to Laugh" by Bob Dylan. Copyright © 1965 Warner Bros. Inc. All rights reserved.

Lyrics used with permission from "Rock and Roll Nigger" by Patti Smith and Lenny Kaye. Copyright © 1979 Ninja Music. All rights reserved.

Lyrics used with permission from "New Day Woman" by Suzi Quatro, Len Tucker, and Alistaire McKenzie. Copyright © 1975 Rak Publishing Ltd. All rights reserved.

Lyrics used with permission from "Up Against the Wall, Red Neck Mother" by Ray Wylie Hubbard. Copyright © 1974 by Tennessee Swamp Fox Music Co. All rights reserved. International copyright secured.

Lyrics used with permission from "Willie, Waylon and Me" by David Allen Coe. Copyright © 1976 Showfor Music. All rights administered by Warner-Tamerlane Publishing Corp. All rights reserved.

Lyrics used with permission from "The Boxer." Copyright © 1968 by Paul Simon. All rights reserved.

Lyrics used with permission from "Sweet Survivor" by Peter Yarrow, Barry Mann, and Cynthia Weil. Copyright © 1978 by Peter Yarrow/Silver Dawn Music. All rights reserved.

Lyrics used with permission from "Honest Lullaby" by Joan Baez. Copyright © 1977, 1979 Gabriel Earl Music/ Joan Baez.

Lyrics used with permission from "Wasted on the Way" by Graham Nash. Copyright © 1982 Putzy-Putzy Music. All rights reserved.

Lyrics from "Do You Remember Rock and Roll Radio?" used with permission. Copyright © 1980 Bleu Disque Music Co., Inc., and Taco Tunes. All rights administered by Warner Bros. Music Corp. All rights reserved.

Lyrics used with permission kindly granted by Rare Blue Music, Inc., from "English Boys" by Deborah Harry and Chris Stein. Copyright © 1982 by Monster Island Music/Rare Blue Music, Inc. All rights controlled by Rare Blue Music, Inc. International copyright secured. All rights reserved.

Lyrics used with permission from "Johnny Soul'd Out" by Brian O'Neil. Copyright © 1980 WB Music Corp. and Maitre 'D Music. All rights administered by WB Music Corp. All rights reserved.

Lyrics used with permission from "Respect" by Kevin O'Neil. Copyright © 1980 WB Music Corp and Gracon Music. All rights administered by WB Music Corp. All rights reserved.

Lyrics used with permission from "No Guilt" by Chris Butler. Copyright © 1980 by Chris Butler.

Lyrics used with permission from "Ballad of a Thin Man" by Bob Dylan. Copyright © 1965 Warner Bros., Inc. All rights reserved.

Lyrics used with permission from "Twelve Thirty" ("Young Girls Are Coming to the Canyon"), words and music by John Phillips. Copyright © 1967 by MCA Music, a Division of MCA Inc. and Honest John Music, New York. All rights reserved.

Photograph of Elvis Presley used by permission of Elvis Presley Enterprises, Inc.

Photograph of Jim Morrison copyright Doors Music Company. Photo by David Sygal. Courtesy *The Doors: The Illustrated History*/W. Morrow, by Danny Sugerman.

Contents————————

Part 3: Revolution and Revelation ———129

Preface

A rather curious and not entirely unexpected paradox led to the creation of this book. In 1978, while teaching at George Mason University, I developed a special multidisciplinary course on rock music. It was going to emphasize its history, social impact, and meaning; my function was to make some philosophical observations. Everyone connected with the project was enthusiastic; all that was lacking was the normally pro forma assent of the appropriate university committee.

Unfortunately, the proposal was overwhelmingly defeated. Our pains to ensure its academic respectability were to no avail. Although I was disappointed, the rejection did serve to reaffirm my belief that rock music is still a living force. So my initial reaction was somewhat mixed. The committee's reasoning was specious, incredible, and decidedly angry, reminiscent of the original reception accorded rock and roll in the mid fifties. But in order for it still to engender such opposition, it had to be alive and well and living somewhere. Knowing this, my disappointment gave way to resolve—and the decision to do my part of the defunct course as a book.

The significance of rock music as a cultural phenomenon has long been recognized, even by its most ardent detractors. Thus the scholarly community has been unable to avoid its impact, and a few studies have mentioned it in passing. No one, however, has yet ventured to carry out a sustained, consistent, and holistic philosophical appraisal. Philosophers certainly consider the topic inappropriate for their scrutiny, beneath their dignity and perhaps their contempt. I also think that their reluctance stems in part from their unconscious fear of what the phenomenon might portend. For example, rock music might indicate that a truly revolutionary force is at work in our culture, providing a genuine threat to the traditional values whose existence is even now rather tenuous. Nevertheless, something is happening, and we don't know what it is (much like Dylan's Mr. Jones). And if ignorance exists only for the purpose of being overcome, we dare not let such a grand opportunity pass us by.

One final remark about the decision to write this book: if ever I had a modicum of doubt as to its importance, it was dispelled once and for all in December 1980 when the news of John Lennon's murder was announced. Even more than the death of Elvis Presley, Lennon's death was a classic instance of the tragic. There was the clear promise that much more could be expected from this man of forty—a promise that he may still partially realize in death. The enormous public reaction to this outrage has confirmed his symbolic importance and his status as one of the most creative individuals of our time. By extension, his death has also convincingly revealed the significance of the entire context in which he lived and for so long helped guide, the culture of rock music. Needless to say, this awareness has come at an incredibly high cost.

No book is written without the assistance and encouragement of family, friends, and associates. Among them are the following: Jan Pielke, whose editorial work, financial support, commitment to the project, and willingness to endure the various revolutions in our respective careers have provided all the necessary conditions for the manuscript's completion; Karen Pielke, who has kept me in touch with a generation to whom the torch has been passed; Debra Bergoffen-Lanman, without whom there would have been neither the courage nor the self-confidence to pursue my philosophical interests in popular culture in general and rock music in particular; Larry Houlgate and Dan Rothbart, whose collegiality has been both personally and professionally invaluable; the many students at George Mason University in Fairfax, Virginia, who accepted me as a fellow human being in the classroom, the cafeteria, and the Rathskeller; those folks I came to know in Shipping and Receiving at the Huntley Bookstore of the Claremont Colleges in California; Geri Thomson, whose typing of part one was not entirely in accordance with university policy; and copy editor David J. Deal, who also designed the book.

America's
Cultural Revolution
——————————— Introduction —

I hold it that a little rebellion,
now and then, is a good thing.

—Thomas Jefferson

You say you want a revolution
Well you know
We all want to change the world
You tell me that it's evolution
Well you know
We all want to change the world
But when you talk about destruction
Don't you know that you can count me out . . . in
Don't you know it's gonna be alright

—The Beatles

As I was passing as unconsciously as possible through one of humanity's most insidious institutions, junior high school, something dramatic yet subtle was taking place in my teenage consciousness. I didn't recognize it for what it was at the time. Nobody did. But it was happening to all of us, just the same. It didn't take long for the adult world to tell us what it was, however, and they weren't very happy. They called it primitive, African, the work of the devil, communistic, filthy, smutty, and obscene. We called it rock and roll. We were both right.

Today, with over thirty years of hindsight available, the whole thing seems relatively clear, and, if possible, even more provocative than at its inception. What I and my fellow sufferers were experiencing was the beginnings of America's first genuine cultural revolution. This statement may seem exaggerated for two somewhat contradictory reasons. First, we've always been taught that America's war of independence from England was a true revolution, something of an exaggeration in itself. Second, and more important, we're reluctant to give up the American myth of a slow and steady (but inevitable) progress toward an earthly perfection. Americans have always tolerated many more disagreements over the nature of their goals than over how they could be achieved. The process was expected to be rational, well-ordered, and continuous, though some small conflicts were probably inevitable. So even to suggest the possibility of a cultural revolution in America must appear not only factually absurd, but blasphemous as well. Revolution is as heretical a doctrine in America as abolishing the monarchy would be in England.

Nevertheless, despite the overwhelmingly conservative assumptions of most Americans, we are in fact in the throes of a genuine and dramatic revolution in our culture, and it behooves us to understand it before passing judgment. Others have tried, but, for one reason or another, have failed. Although still provocative, the optimistic retrospectives of Theodore Roszak and Charles Reich lacked the perspective to appreciate fully the magnitude of the period. Like all instant analyses, theirs found an equally instant oblivion as events overtook them. They were too anxious, too optimistic, too certain, and, without a doubt, too doctrinaire to make their case. Instead of providing an insightful and relatively unbiased overview, *The Making of a Counter Culture* and *The Greening of America* have themselves become artifacts of the period—interesting curiosities but not the kind of assessment from which we could learn something. Learning only takes place when it's possible to confront unpleasant as well as pleasant facts. Their impatience to celebrate a victory for the counterculture, I think, blinded them to the realities of historical change. Impatience rarely gets the job done.

More recent studies fail for different reasons, and Morris Dickstein's *Gates of Eden: American Culture in the Sixties* is a case in point. Although seemingly able to muster up an adequate historical perspective (published in 1977), he apparently has been seduced by the temptations of facile "decadization." In some of his more perceptive moments, he recognizes that history doesn't align its movements with the tens digit. Yet with no fully developed theory of historical change at his disposal (unlike Roszak and Reich, both of whom adopt a quasi-Hegelian-Marxian dialectic), he has produced little more than a documentation of the period. He thus lacks the capacity to see the sixties in their overall context. He does, however, employ a provocative methodological procedure—namely, the notion that history can be understood most profitably through its cultural manifestations. He opts for literature, but in so doing I think he is fundamentally mistaken. The most revealing cultural artifacts change as technology and human whims change, a fact of considerable significance which he seemingly ignores. It is not literature but music which opens up our recent past (and hence our present and future). His single chapter on contemporary music is so severely circumscribed in its time frame as to be worthless if not seriously misleading. Literature held sway during the first half of the twentieth century, but since the mid fifties it's been nothing less than rock and roll.

Harris Wofford's massive study *Of Kennedys and Kings: Making Sense of the Sixties* is similarly flawed, but even more so. He lacks Dickstein's cultural perspective, for one thing, preferring to see history through the actions of ''great men.'' Further, he too sees the sixties as a virtually isolated unit, as though chunks of time existed independently of our designating them as such. But most distressing is his omission of the music of this period. There is only one reference to the Beatles, for example, and this comes only in conjunction with references to Bob Dylan, Jimi Hendrix, and Janis Joplin.

A more accurate understanding of what's happening must take into account the phenomenon of rock music as a fundamental ingredient of contemporary American culture. And if the claim that we are in the throes of a cultural revolution is to make sense, we first have to examine the nature of such upheavals. Identifying their common features may be tricky, but it should help us to recognize a cultural revolution if one should happen to show up. In the summer of 1954, in a little recording studio in Memphis, Tennessee, one showed up—and America hasn't been the same since.

There are at least six characteristics shared by all cultural revolutions. It should become obvious how they are exemplified in contemporary American culture—and exemplified, more than anything else, by rock and roll. First, they embody a fundamental challenge to the prevailing values. I don't mean by this that all existing values are rejected. As far as I know, this has never happened nor is it likely to. I'm referring to the ultimate values on which all other values are based and from which they derive their justification. Just as important, the way these values are known and justified is also placed under attack. Revolutionaries not only put forward conflicting values, they also replace the epistemological scheme.

When Billy Ward and the Dominoes sang ''Sixty Minute Man,'' the established beliefs about race, sex, and the entire puritan work ethic were attacked. When Little Richard sang anything, we were introduced to an entirely new way of experiencing life. And when John Lennon sang ''Imagine,'' we were introduced to uncomfortable new ideas.

A second common feature, obvious but not usually recognized for its true significance, is the fact that cultural revolutions are never rapid. They take many years to develop, come to fruition, and have effect. Generally, their true beginnings are recognized as such only after several significant and highly visible events have occurred. In other words, cultural revolutions may be discernible *only* on the basis of hindsight. Be this as it may, they certainly involve considerable complexities, and their workings are obviously a central concern of this book. Remember how long it took before rock and roll was recognized as being more than a fad? (Judging from my own experiences, this recognition is still far from universal.)

Closely tied to this is a third feature, that cultural revolutions inevitably produce strong counterreactions. Often misunderstood as entirely new movements, they are actually revitalized, renewed, and strengthened manifestations of the established order. As such, they are an intrinsic part of the revolutionary process as a whole, and they provide the revolution with its greatest threat. With the election of Ronald Reagan as president in 1980, the counterreaction in America began.

A fourth feature is implicit, but it needs to be specified in order to correct a common misconception. Cultural revolutions are not merely political. Governmental institutions are altered to a greater or lesser extent, but only as a result of more fundamental changes. Thus a revolution that aims only at political changes (as did the one in eighteenth-century America) is not a cultural revolution. Only years after its inception did we see anything hinting at rock's political implications. Unlike the folk protest movement of the early 1960s, rock's target was more basic. As partial proof, we need only consider which of the two is still with us.

An even more serious misconception is the belief that revolutions are necessarily and/or inevitably violent. Hence, the fifth observation is simply that violence is not an intrinsic component of cultural revolutions. This is not to say that violence is lacking. Some violence is always present, of course, but so too is violence present in nonrevolutionary periods. As will become evident later, it was precisely the nonviolent element in rock that was most effective in purveying the new set of values.

The sixth and final characteristic is more substantive and certainly more controversial: Cultural revolutions, as such, always tend toward an expansion of individual freedom. How this idea is expressed will obviously differ, depending largely on the ways in which the status quo is understood to inhibit freedom. Yet no matter what its particular historical formulation, a revolutionary ideology will always express more confidence in the individual's capacity for self-regulation and governance than does the established order. This, in turn, is based on a conflict between two primal assumptions regarding humanity, one confident and the other pessimistic. The relatively pessimistic ideology of the established order is confronted by the relatively optimistic ideology of the revolutionaries, and this in turn is eventually confronted by a rejuvenated version of the pessimistic one. To put it another way, opposites are intrinsically related; in every affirmation there is an implicit negation. So a cultural revolution is necessarily predicated on that which it so fervently rejects.

In the fifties, rock and roll seemed clearly anarchistic to its detractors, a fact confirmed in the sixties and reconfirmed today. Advocates have never disputed this. Rather, disagreements have concerned the value of this degree of freedom. As a goal in progress, perhaps only to be approximated in reality, anarchy has always been an essential component of rock and of America's cultural revolution. But without the established order to begin with, this anarchistic ideal would have had no context in which to thrive. And without the resulting conflict, our two *Voyagers* would not now be carrying with them into the vast emptiness of the galaxy the voice of Chuck Berry singing, "Johnny B. Goode, Johnny B. Goode tonight."

This is the appropriate context for an understanding of that phenomenon we've come to call rock music. No wonder our parents flipped when we brought those first forty-fives into our respectable, middle-class homes. Although neither we nor the adult world knew it at the time, we were being incited to rebellion. It wouldn't be the last time, but in the future we'd know what was happening.

Music and Culture

Part 1

Our age does offer many horrible proofs of the
daemonic power with which music may lay hold
upon an individual, and this individual, in turn,
. . . may . . . grip and capture a multitude,
especially women . . . by means of the
all-disturbing power of voluptuousness.

—Sören Kierkegaard

Well bless my soul, what's wrong
with me?
I'm itchin' like a man on a
fuzzy tree.
My friends say I'm actin'
wild as a bug.
I'm in love—I'm all shook up.

—Elvis Presley

It is hardly necessary to argue for a relationship between music and culture, but the closeness of this relationship should be emphasized. John Blacking in his exceedingly provocative book *How Musical Is Man?* points out that "no musical style has 'its own terms': its terms are the terms of its society and culture, and of the bodies of the human beings who listen to it, and create and perform it." His is a musicological approach, but it's more than a mere study of music. For music is a "relatively spontaneous and unconscious process. It may represent the human mind working without interference, and therefore observation of musical structures may reveal some of the structural principles on which all human life is based."[1]

Susanne Langer, in *Philosophy in a New Key,* makes a similar claim. For her, "a work of art expresses a conception of life, emotion, inward reality. But it is neither a confessional nor a frozen tantrum; it is a developed metaphor, a non-discursive symbol that articulated what is verbally ineffable—the logic of consciousness itself." In particular, "music can reveal the nature of feelings with a detail and truth that language cannot approach."[2]

Of course the music I have in mind is not just any old music; it's rock and roll music. But the closeness of the relationship still holds. David Pichaske, in *A Generation in Motion,* notes the following:

A product of the new technology against which both the music and the sixties rebelled, which both it and the sixties took for granted, pop music is

3

the most accurate reflection of the generation in motion. Folk, country, soul, but most of all rock are not merely a record of the new age, they *were* the age in all its multiplicity.[3]

What this means, of course, is that a cultural analysis can be conducted by means of a musicological analysis. The key, I think, is in the fact that music is an immediate and unreflective expression of consciousness, totally unlike the deliberate, self-conscious creations of ideology. This truth holds for rock music as well as for all other kinds. So, an investigation into the nature of rock music will inevitably tell us something about the culture from which it has originated—ours.

Needless to say, I should say something about the nature of rock music and how it is related to American culture. Many people have done this in a variety of ways, but what follows, I think, is a unique attempt. It culminates in chapter 3's suggested typology, and while there is no category for the daemonic per se, it should adequately illustrate the extent to which many people have been all shaken up.

Rock Music and Contemporary American Culture

1

In order to defend my claims that America is in the midst of a cultural revolution, and that this is best apprehended through an appraisal of rock music, the many interrelationships among culture, the arts, music, and revolution have to be thoroughly explored. I'm convinced that music not only reflects cultural consciousness but also participates in creating, stabilizing, and changing it. If culture (and consequently cultural change) is the creation of our consciousness, then it's essential for us to know how this creative and re-creative process works. Only then will we be able to assess the peculiarities of present-day American culture and deal with the possibilities of a cultural revolution.

There are some things on which we can all agree. First, artistic expressions are manifestations of culture. We can also agree that by examining artistic expressions we should be able to determine whether or not a revolution is in progress and, if so, its ideological tendencies. Finally, we can agree that these indirect, nondiscursive expressions are more revealing than ideological writings and the like. In short, a cultural-artistic analysis is the best way to acquire this knowledge—it may even be the only way.

But why should we consider rock music to be more revealing about contemporary American culture than any other artistic expression? In answering this, we should keep in mind the following:

1. Arts and culture are dialectically related; the arts reveal the status of culture by expressing its fundamental values. Thus, artists can both reflect and re-create cultural consciousness—unpredictably and often unknowingly.

5

So it is with rock music, which reflects as well as brings into being a particular state of consciousness. More often than not, this occurs unintentionally. One of the most dramatic illustrations of this tendency is the creation of an "outlaw consciousness," which I'll discuss in chapter 4.

2. Technological innovations (invented means for accomplishing chosen ends) stem from what humans value; that is, their ultimate goals determine the selection or creation of means. Conversely, these various technological means can affect the kinds of values that people hold and how widely they might be disseminated.

The desire to maintain (or create) a stable and reasonably peaceful, albeit economically competitive, society has made the relative uniformity of ideological convictions among Americans essential. From this has followed the encouragement of improvements in mass communication. Without underestimating the role of the individual inventor, the impetus for developing certain kinds of technology has depended very much on positive social support. Conversely, numerous innovations, culminating in the radio, recording instruments, motion picture photography, television, and a variety of other electronic marvels, have had effects unforeseen by their original supporters. Aside from ensuring greater conformity, these new and highly influential media have informed the vast and complacent middle class about the existence of America's social outcasts. Not only was the extent of their plight revealed dramatically and forcefully to an extensive audience for the first time, but their basic values were shown to differ radically from those of the majority. Most important for our purposes, the enormous numbers of post–World War II adolescents had revealed to them the hitherto unknown consciousness of blacks and poor white southerners through their music. The result: an unavoidable internal conflict between tradition and experience, the values they had been taught and the values they were encountering. The tension, as everyone who grew up then can remember, was explosive.

3. All artistic expressions are at least partially explainable in terms of available technology (or technique). Innovations make new kinds of expressions possible, but only insofar as artists choose to adopt them. Unlike virtually every other kind of musical expression, rock music has developed around electronic innovations. Although not definable as simply the result of this technology, rock music has nevertheless made such effective use of it that it's hard to imagine nonelectric rock. Simon and Garfunkel's "Sounds of Silence" on their first album was acoustic; later, when electrified, it became a folk-rock classic.

4. The popularity of an artistic expression depends on its capability for reflecting or re-creating the consciousness (and thus the ideological

commitments) of a mass audience. Using all of the electronic media, rock music has had the unquestioned capacity to appeal to (or create) a mass audience from the very beginning. The radio and the newly developed 45 r.p.m. records, both comparatively inexpensive, were ideal means. Exploiting them to the fullest would come later, but the potential was obvious to everyone, including those whose only or main interest was personal profit. These varied devices for the creation of music and its propagation through modern mass communication were available for *all* musical expressions, yet only one chose, or perhaps could choose, to make successful use of them. Is rock music, therefore, no more than a media creation? In some way, it might be suggested that the nature of this music is intimately tied up with electric guitars, amplification, light shows and multimedia concerts. I agree, but this misses a more fundamental point: popular music must appeal to popular ideological convictions in order to be popular. It can't be created ex nihilo, relying only on modern technology in the service of greed (as was alleged during the payola scandals). With the conversion of white middle-class youths to a consciousness sympathetic to that of the social outcasts, a mass audience was brought into being that was responsive to rock music and only rock music. Obviously the media had an impact, but they would have availed nothing had there not been a receptive audience. Technology didn't create this audience; in a very real sense, the audience created the technology.

5. While all artistic expressions reveal something about the culture in which they exist, the most effective one in doing this at any particular time will be the most popular one. It would be superfluous to point out that rock and roll has by now inundated the very meaning of popular music. In 1954, only the Crewcuts' sanitized cover of the Chords' "Sh-Boom" in the top ten hinted at what was to come. By 1956, however, four of the ten were clearly rock and roll. And then, in 1959, despite the fact that many of the founding figures were tragically forced out of the game, you had to search down as far as number twenty-one before hitting a nonrock song. Needless to say, this trend continues, and in increasingly varied ways.

6. Popular art, when irreconcilably in conflict with the art preferred by those holding social and political power (that is, elitist art), represents a revolutionary set of values. Until the inevitable counterreaction, and the resulting conflict with an unpredictable outcome, this revolutionary art will necessarily be the most culturally revealing. (In its rejection of elitist values, it will—necessarily and paradoxically—express them at the same time.)

Though its meaning may be rigorously disputed, it simply cannot be ignored that rock and roll challenged and replaced a very different kind of music, relegating it to the status of total obsolescence in a matter of one or two years. Neither can the fact that, initially at least, a generational differentiation was involved. It is no accident that the term "generation gap" originated in the early 1950s. But this highly overstressed and underreasoned term pointed to a mere superficiality. What really happened was a clash of fundamental values, although few would have articulated it in this way. Things are much clearer now, and the term is used far less.

Because rock music was initially in the position of negating the prevailing values, it necessarily had to exhibit the very values it opposed. When pleasure and sex, for example, were put forward as positive values, deliberately intended to replace the established values, we can rather easily infer the tenor of the prevailing values. Moreover, sex and pleasure would never have assumed such significance had they already been morally acceptable. Hence, in a paradoxical way, the values of rock music are contingent on the very values they reject.

7. Art that expresses revolutionary values is always more optimistic about a self-regulated society than the established art it opposes. Its inherent tendency is toward anarchism. Suffice it to say that both proponents and detractors agree that rock music expresses anarchistic beliefs about the possibilities of a social life free from external authority. In all probability, this is the extent of their agreement. In chapter 9, this will be discussed in detail.

Should there be any lingering doubts that an understanding of rock music is essential for an understanding of contemporary American culture, they may be partially dispelled by a discussion of certain analogous situations in the history of popular music. Thus, if we were seeking to comprehend the consciousness of the seventeenth and early eighteenth centuries, we could hardly pass over the Baroque music of Purcell, Vivaldi, Handel, and J. S. Bach. Should we find a fascination with the eighteenth century, we would turn to Haydn, Mozart, the sons of Bach, and the early Beethoven for clues. If our interests were then to wander into the nineteenth century, we would never question the importance of looking at the Romantic music of Beethoven, Chopin, Brahms, and Tchaikovsky. And who would object to the serious consideration of the Impressionist music of Saint-Saëns, Ravel, Respighi, Stravinsky, and Copland in any appraisal of the late nineteenth and early twentieth centuries? All of these composers wrote the popular music for their own times, producing one monster hit after another. In so doing, they not only reflected but also helped create recognizably distinct states of consciousness, all of which had their own unique and identifiable cultural manifestations.

Since this is so obvious, I wonder why it should be so difficult for some to admit that an understanding of contemporary American culture beginning with the mid-fifties is contingent on an appraisal of Chuck Berry, Elvis Presley, Bob Dylan and the Beatles? Perhaps there is the lingering suspicion that granting rock music even this meager amount of respectability might seduce the unwary into a seditious frame of mind, dangerous to the prevailing ideology and scandalous to everything holy. However, if there is even a germ of truth in this fear, any attempt to impute respectability, great or meager, is bound to fail. The very essence of rock music would seem to be a *denial* of respectability. It would be like Pat Boone struggling to emulate the pre-born-again Little Richard: his attempt to make "Tutti Frutti" respectable was not only a failure, it was a travesty.

What Is Rock Music?

2

An entire book could be written about the many and varied attempts to derive and support such a definition, but it wouldn't be very helpful. Few of the definitions agree, and several are even contradictory. Selecting any one of them as authoritative could be nothing more than an arbitrary decision, since there's no possible basis for choosing other than on personal whims.

[A clear obstacle to defining rock music is that it actually has no unique musical quality (or combination of qualities) that allows us to distinguish it from nonrock. Peculiarities of rhythm, instrumentation, voice, volume, lyrics, etc. have all been suggested, yet every one of them can be found in other kinds of music as well.]Moreover, undeniable examples of rock exist that don't have any of these alleged peculiarities. So any standard definition would leave us with the absurdity of calling some things rock which clearly aren't and leaving others out which clearly are.

Given this problem, the closest we can probably come to the illusory ideal definition is to gather together a large and varied collection of "family resemblances," a device that only acknowledges the futility of the effort. Even specifying the clearest, most universally acceptable musical characteristics will not provide us with an accurate understanding of rock music.

As a cultural artifact, rock music participates in the process of historical change. It is conditioned by and, in turn, conditions its total environment, and it cannot be understood apart from its relationship to culture. Cultural creations are born, they live, and they die; but above all, they change and effect change. So, a permanent, unchanging definition of rock music is intrinsically impossible; it would amount to an abstraction from a particular part of its developmental process and would thus contradict itself: a part would claim to be the whole. In the following pages, I intend to show why this holistic approach is needed and why a purely musicological approach fails.

A Holistic Approach

Of the three major components of music (melody, harmony, and rhythm), a distinctive rhythmic styling has been cited most often as providing the key to its uniqueness. In 4/4 time, for example, with four beats to the measure (rarely are there three), rock music accentuates the second and fourth. Similarly, in 2/4 time or cut-time, the up-beat (or back-beat) is emphasized. To hear this, simply compare a rock classic such as Jerry Lee Lewis' "Whole Lotta Shakin' Goin' On" with the decidedly down-beat emphasis in any country-and-western standard, as with Loretta Lynn's "Coal Miner's Daughter." Another rhythmic feature is the rolling or boogie-woogie ("Yancy") bass, first prominently used in 1948 by such blues artists as Sonny Thompson in "Long Gone." Shortly thereafter, pianists like Fats Domino popularized the use of triplets as a rhythmic feature, usually in the treble clef. (Listen to Fats Domino's "Ain't That a Shame" for a reasonably good example.)

Instrumental configurations have also been cited as distinctively different. For example, no one who has ever heard rock music could ignore the importance of percussive instruments, especially the drums. While none of the components of the typical drum trap are entirely unknown outside of the rock genre, their centrality in providing a driving beat is a bit unusual. Almost as decisive is the virtually universal use of guitars, acoustic and electric, although the latter have clearly assumed the prominent role. (Interestingly enough, after their invention and introduction into popular music in 1937, electric stringed instruments quickly became differentiated according to genre: the slide guitar was preferred almost exclusively by country and western; blues stuck with the standard guitar to carry the lead; and rock added an electric bass.) Not quite as prevalent as they once were, but still very significant, are the saxophones: baritones, tenors, and altos. Played with gutsy insistence, often honking out the rhythm, they were virtually the epitome of early rhythm and blues. Finally, deriving primarily from honky-tonk, the technically percussive piano also has been an unquestioned presence in rock performances, more recently reincarnated as the electric keyboard, synthesizer, or mellotron.

Although the vocal characteristics of rock music have been far too diverse for anything distinctive to emerge as a defining feature, it has nevertheless given birth to at least one unique style—"doo-wop"—present in no other kind of music as far as I know. I mention it because of its obvious cultural significance. In the early fifties, black youths too poor to buy musical instruments began to emulate various instrumental sounds, providing background accompaniment for the lead singers. Because of the way this street-corner, a cappela music sounded, it came to be known as the doo-wop style. ("Get a Job" by the Silhouettes is doo-wop backed up instrumentally.) Other vocal styles were taken over and modified by rock: blues (Rolling Stones), gospel call-and-response (Isley Brothers), nasal country-and-western twang (Everly Brothers), operatic (Roy Orbison), and lush choral harmonies (Beach Boys). In other words, a distinctive rock vocal style does not exist.

Lyrically, one might at first find rock distinctive. In what other kind of music, after all, could you find something like "A Wop Bop Aloo Bop a Lop Bam Boom" (variously transcribed, from "Tutti Frutti") if not in rock music? Isn't unintelligibility a key feature of rock lyrics? Perhaps with some, but you also find Simon and Garfunkel's "Sounds of Silence," Dylan's "Blowin' in the Wind," and the Beatles' "Eleanor Rigby." Which type is more representative? Both, I think. Among detractors, however, the case is often made that rock lyrics do have certain distinctive themes, whether or not they are intelligibly expressed. Granted that sex, drugs, drinking, rebellion, and pleasure are emphasized, these themes are no more characteristic of rock than of blues and of C & W. So there's really not much to go on in terms of lyrics. Rock lyrics are certainly worth looking at for their own sake (within a holistic perspective, of course), but there is nothing definitional about them.

If rhythm, instrumentation, vocal qualities, and lyrics are, at best, only partially helpful in describing something as unquestionably rock, then maybe it is all of these things with the addition of excessive volume. Is loudness that little extra that can isolate rock music from other kinds? Certainly no one would ever claim that volume is *never* an attribute, but this doesn't say very much. As I recall, *The 1812 Overture* is also quite loud. Besides, there are such things as volume controls; we can make our music as loud or as soft as we like.

Now, even without citing borderline cases and exceptions (which would far outnumber the examples actually captured by the preceding musical characteristics), this approach must inevitably prove unsatisfactory. Consider the fact that rhythmically and instrumentally (the only two musical characteristics with any hope of providing a definition), the most unlikely music qualifies as rock: much of the commercial music on radio and TV, the theme music from numerous TV shows, "Disco Duck," and the material done by Donny and Marie! Something is obviously wrong.

What is wrong is that the musicological approach fails to consider the other components of rock music: the artists and what they intend with their music, the audiences and how they interpret what the artists intend, the media and how they affect and are affected by the message, and the entire cultural context in which all of this occurs. Rock music encompasses all of this, not just its own musical characteristics. "Rock and roll" is not musical terminology after all.

Referring back to the musical styles mentioned at the end of the previous chapter, Baroque, Romantic, and Impressionist, note that these too are not musicological characterizations. They connote instead something about what their respective artists and audiences intended, that is, the meaning the music had for them. The same is true with the modern stylings of blues, jazz, and C & W. Nothing in these terms denotes anything at all musical. On the contrary, they are clearly intended to portray the consciousness of the participants, the way the music is interpreted, its meaning, the intentionality of everyone involved. An attempt to define any of these genres would run into the same obstacles that we've encountered with rock: they are much more than their alleged musicological features would give us to understand.

The term "rock and roll" was not originally intended as a dance reference. Instead, as all of us were more or less vaguely aware, it had to do with sex—plain, raw, and undisguised. Its linkage with dancing was a thinly veiled attempt to make it more acceptable to white America in the mid fifties. But sex wasn't the whole story either. The meaning of rock was, and always has been, more than what the specific term might suggest at any given time. Billy Ward and the Dominoes' "Sixty Minute Man" (1951) and Hank Ballard's "Work with Me Annie" (1954) may have represented the intentions of its earliest participants, but rock and roll very soon came to mean much more than this. (Although Bob Seger's "Horizontal Bop" in 1980 illustrates the fact that its original intent hasn't been lost on succeeding generations.) Today, with the advantages of hindsight, we must approach rock music as a gestalt, as a whole larger than the sum of its individual parts, and certainly not something to be identified with one of its historically conditioned components.

—————————— A Revolutionary Art ——————————

If we now reflect on the characteristics of art per se, there's simply no possible conclusion other than to see rock music as revolutionary. Herbert Marcuse had quite a bit to say about art and its relationship to revolution. In his short collection of essays, entitled *Counter-Revolution and Revolt*, he saw the political potential of art in its ability to communicate two things: an "indictment of the established reality" and an encouragement to seek the "goals of liberation." Authentic art, in other words, communicates the general attitudes of both negation and affirmation. This duality is a necessary condition for art to be genuine. To communicate successfully, however, a nonconformist language (understood in the widest possible sense) is necessary. It can't be an invented language because this wouldn't speak to people in their own life setting. Language form can only be a subversion of traditional material. Only in this way can it reach "a population which has introjected the needs and values of their masters and managers and made them their own, thus reproducing the established system in their minds, their consciousness, their senses and instincts." To put it in other words, the established language must be "spoken," but in unforeseen and subversive ways. Notice that negation and affirmation are contingent on a subversive language—one that uses the common tongue but in ways which do not conform. Rock music is just such a language. Not only has it not conformed to musical convention, it has communicated a negation of the established reality and an affirmation of the goals of liberation.

All forms of art are intrinsically capable of this subversive activity, because they necessarily involve illusions about the reality they represent. Illusions always transform the prevailing order by showing the established reality in a far different and antagonistic way. As Marcuse put it, "words, sounds, images, from another dimension 'bracket' and invalidate the right of the established reality for the sake of a reconciliation still to come." What must emerge is a "new experience of reality, new values." Coming from this other dimension, artistic language is extraordinarily potent. "More effectively than its political goals and slogans, this 'existential' protest, hard to isolate and hard to punish, threatens the cohesion of the social system." The essence of art's revolutionary nature is thus its illusory character; whenever art "*wills* itself as illusion," it both preserves and transcends its cultural setting with the promise of liberation. For Marcuse, for example, the writings of Dickens, Ibsen, Defoe, Kafka, and Thomas Mann succeeded in this dual function. Today, we might cite Vonnegut, Mailer, J. D. Salinger, Doris Lessing, and Ray Bradbury. In every case the writer speaks to us in our own language, yet at the same time opens up a new world to us. Needless to say, this principle extends to art forms other than literature.

There is a danger, however, and much that passes for art succumbs to it: "where the world no longer sustains the dialectical unity of what is and what can (and ought to) be, art has lost its truth, has lost itself." Art can fail by leaning too much in either direction; both its immanence in the revolutionary process and its transcendence above it must be maintained if the creation of illusion is to have its revolutionary impact. Marcuse saw guerrilla (street) theater, the poetry of the "free press," and the music of Cage and Stockhausen as having lost touch with the people experiencing the revolution. Being so immersed in the revolutionary process, they lost their capacity for a transcendent critique of society.

On the other hand, most television and most popular novels fall prey to the opposite temptation. They have become too far removed from the revolutionary process, losing the quality of immanence.

Negation and affirmation are thus the two dimensions of one transforming (revolutionary) process—a process that must relate to and yet transcend the status quo. In the next chapter, this double dialectic will provide the basis for a decidedly different kind of typology of rock music.

Art performs its innately subversive role through its creation of illusions, but this necessarily means that art is a cognitive activity: it makes knowledge claims about what is and what ought to be. This latter claim, of course, is always threatening to the prevailing order. But it is especially so since this knowledge claim is never rational. In fact, the less rational it is the more threatening it becomes. According to Marcuse,

> Art is recollection: it appeals to a preconceptual experience and understanding which reemerge in and against the context of social functioning of experience and understanding—against instrumentalist reason and sensibility.
>
> When it attains this primary level—the terminal point of the intellectual effort—art violates taboos: it lends voice and sight and ear to things which are normally repressed: dreams, memories, longings—ultimate states of sensibility. . . . These extreme qualities, the supreme points of art, seem to be the perogative of music.[1]

For some incredible reason, which Marcuse never disclosed, he found rock music to be a one-dimensional form of art. He saw it as being far too preoccupied with bourgeois culture—its loss of immanence in the revolution dooming it to almost total ineffectiveness. At best, it was an imitation of genuine revolutionary art—rock music had not yet developed the capacity for transcendence. But Marcuse ignored the obvious. For example, he was seemingly oblivious to what was said about the transforming role of rock music by the very people in whom he placed most of his hopes for change—youth, students, the New Left, and blacks. Didn't he know what music they listened to? Didn't he trust or understand what they were saying about it? Why also was he unaware of the genuine ambivalence within rock culture itself about revolution? Even the most strident calls for action were coupled with fears for what might follow, e.g., in "Won't Get Fooled Again," when the Who sang "Meet the new boss/ Same as the old boss." And why wasn't he at all sensitive to rock music's almost total preoccupation with alienated human existence, expressed as a universal truth as well as in numerous examples? Could he, perhaps, have overlooked the Beatles' "Eleanor Rigby," Simon and Garfunkel's "Sounds of Silence," the Beach Boys' "In My Room" and Chuck Berry's "No Particular Place to Go"? In all of these songs, the alienation expressed is total, including the self-alienation of rock culture itself.

Despite his failure to understand the true import of rock music, Marcuse's discussion of art's (and music's) revolutionary potential is invaluable. His belief that "a subversive potential is the very nature of art" cannot be overestimated. For, at the very least, this potential must operate as an ever-present critique of the revolution itself. It can't cease its negating/affirming posture in any sense without ceasing to be art. Thus rock music must stand with (immanent in), and yet above (transcendent to), the revolution, estranged from the very transforming situation it seeks to invoke.

The Implications of Revolutionary Art

Before leaving Marcuse, we should pause for a moment to reflect on what is implied by the subversive nature of art. Since he believed that "revolution is in the substance of art," we can at the very least infer that genuine art is necessarily revolutionary. There is more that can be said, however. First, because "art can and will draw its inspiration, and its very form, from the then-prevailing revolutionary movement," a mere revival of past expressions cannot ever be genuine, authentic. Art, in other words, is historically conditioned; to be true to itself it must emerge from or reflect its situation in life. This is the imminent dimension of art, and successful communication is contingent on satisfying its demands. Genuine art must speak the language of the people who are engaged in the revolutionary process, whatever form their "language" may take. Today the popular form of music is rock—in any one of its many forms.

Second, a genuine art must at the same time transcend the revolution it expresses. It cannot be so submerged in the movement that it forfeits its essentially subversive role. The revolution itself must be subjected to constant critical review; hence, the canons of authenticity include a fundamental estrangement of art from its cultural setting. Nothing can kill the revolutionary potential of rock more than crass commercialization. Needless to say, rock music has more than occasionally succumbed to this temptation.

The dialectic between immanence and transcendence must always be maintained. The loss of either one would necessarily condemn an artistic expression to the status of nonart. The loss of immanence would obviously involve a failure to communicate, for it would lack a true involvement with the revolutionary process. It could neither negate nor affirm as a result. Ultimately, music like this would be characterized by "selling out"—being co-opted or exploited by the established order. Its revolutionary substance would be removed and replaced by a substance antagonistic to change. It would have to use a language so far removed from the movement toward liberation that its speech would necessarily be that of the counterrevolutionaries. My prime examples of this failure are the four "Bobbys" (Darin, Rydell, Vee, and Vinton).

On the other hand, the loss of the transcendent dimension would result in almost total ineffectiveness; art would be relegated to a purely masturbatory enterprise, satisfying only to its proponents. Lacking the capacity to engage its own revolutionary movement from a critical perspective, it would as a consequence lose its capacity to engage the establishment as well. This in effect would be another way for art to "sell out," to be co-opted or exploited, but in this case it would occur by its having *too much* of a revolutionary consciousness. Art would become mere propaganda. By "selling out" to a particular historical embodiment of the revolution, it would cease to be genuinely revolutionary (and so the establishment encourages such moves). True art must not sell itself out to either side if its subversive character is to be maintained. (Keep in mind that the loss of one facet is not compensated for by increasing the other. Such an increase does not take up the slack but only magnifies the loss.) As an example, the first Lennon/Ono album, *Two Virgins*, filled as it was with various electronic noises, had little to say to anyone. It came to be regarded as a joke—exactly what the establishment wanted.

Third, as one facet of both immanence and transcendence, authentic art will negate the established order, focusing on its fundamental values and the ways they may be institutionalized. (This includes the negation of how these values are allegedly known.) Of course, the negation must also involve a critical perspective on the historically conditioned embodiment of the revolution itself. The negation of art is total, all-encompassing. By far the best example of this is the ambiguous ''Revolution'' by the Beatles.

Fourth, another facet of authentically immanent and transcendent art is affirmation. Positive values must be proposed as replacements for what is being rejected (along with an alternate way of knowing). As I've mentioned many times before, this would not involve a wholesale substitution; only the basic values are at issue. But again, this must never be an affirmation of a specific, momentary part of the process. Affirmation is always from ''beyond.'' Elvis Costello's ''(What's So Funny 'bout) Peace, Love, and Understanding'' epitomizes this aspect of rock music.

Obviously nothing is ever negated without something being affirmed. Conversely, nothing is ever affirmed without something being negated. A less obvious truth is that negation should not be regarded as automatically ''bad'' and affirmation ''good.'' This depends on what values are at issue. Attacking the accepted beliefs about race shows the role of negation in rock and roll at its best.

Finally, there is no necessary correlation between negation and anger or hate on the one hand and between affirmation and joy or love on the other. Negation and affirmation can be, and are, expressed with a variety of moods and feelings, often confounding our expectations and disturbing our sensibilities. The negation embodied in Frank Zappa's work is pure joy, while the affirmation in the Waitresses' ''No Guilt'' is one of the saddest in contemporary music.

My own beliefs about how these four implications relate to rock music ought to be pretty obvious. Essentially I maintain, à la Marcuse, that rock music should be understood as the artistic expression of America's cultural revolution. Hence, contemporary American culture provides the substance of rock music. The two are intrinsically related.

Since the mid fifties, the revolutionary language of America has been the language of rock and roll, and it has spoken at times with great effectiveness. At other times, however, it has lost either its immanence or its transcendence, winding up as a counterrevolutionary tool in either case. Musically, these losses have not always been apparent; musical characteristics can easily be duplicated and can thus disguise an exploitive use of the art. So we have to pay attention to the entire culture of rock to see what's really been happening.

The same is true of the second dialectical pair, of course. The negative and affirmative facets of rock music are revealed only when we look at the whole, rarely (if ever) by the music alone. Moreover, when a holistic perspective is taken, a decidedly existential flavor becomes clearly evident. In the contemporary classic *Irrational Man*, William Barrett finds modern art to be a revealing testimony of modern consciousness.[2] And without altering one jot or tittle of his remarks, they might just as well be referring to rock and roll.

"Art," he says, "is the collective dream of a period, a dream in which, if we have eyes to see, we can trace the physiognomy of the time most clearly." Hence, rock music "touches a sore spot, or several sore spots, in the ordinary citizen of which he is totally unaware." Joined by "the learned and sensitive traditionalist," they all object to its content: it is "too negative or nihilistic, too shocking or scandalous; it dishes out unpalatable truths." It voices the impoverishment of traditional ideals, sometimes violently and aggressively, and it pictures "a world where man [kind] is a stranger." In such a world, there is no "final intelligibility"; human existence "is no longer transparent and understandable by reason." Reality is portrayed "as opaque, dense, concrete, and in the end inexplicable," and "at the limits of reason one comes face to face with the meaningless." In its earliest manifestations rock and roll was castigated for the unintelligibility of its lyrics—as if intelligibility would have redeemed it. And to many, it was beneath contempt no matter what it "said." Further, in its stress on living for now, rock implies that there is no final goal, no purpose, no meaning. This is pretty unpalatable for those stuck in the traditional order.

Barrett then claims that "this break with the Western tradition imbues both philosophy and art with the sense that everything is questionable, problematic." Hence, the themes that obsess him are alienation, finitude, and the encounter with nothingness. Not religion, nor reason, nor science can offer us any security, for the traditional certainty that there are timeless truths to guide and protect us is no more. We are on our own, the sole source of whatever meaning there is. Despite the enormous power we have developed, none of it is to any avail. On the contrary, it provides us with a frightening symbol for the "dreadful and total contingency of human existence: existentialism is the philosophy of the atomic age." Total annihilation is with us always as a permanent potential. One song, "Red Car" by the Trees, is such a stark portrayal of the specter of nuclear devastation that it voids all hope in powers political or religious.

From its beginnings, rock music has challenged the basic values of the culture in which it emerged, not all at once, not always self-consciously, certainly not programatically, but surely and steadily nevertheless. First came challenges to the accepted beliefs about sex, race, and work; then, nationalism, war, and economics came under attack. By implication, of course, the entire conception of reality which supported these values was negated. Essentially, what was being rejected was a Protestantized incarnation of the Judeo-Christian tradition, with its firm convictions about destiny, inevitable progress, absolutist morality, fixed social positions, and eternal punishments and rewards. Max Weber and R. H. Tawney long ago explored the Protestant work ethic and its relationship to capitalism. More recently, manifestations of this religiosity have been studied by theologians and sociologists everywhere. Rock and roll, however, didn't propose to study this value scheme; rock and roll proposed to abolish it.

A Suggested Typology

3

By tying together several of the important strands of the discussion so far, we should now be able to create a typological scheme that may enable us to interpret the phenomenon of rock music accurately, that is, within its cultural context. In order to do this, the close correlation between contemporary American culture and its music obviously needs to be more specifically illustrated. I also need to pinpoint the crucial symbolic events within what I'm claiming to be a revolutionary process. Precisely where and when, for example, were the received values negated and the new ones affirmed? And what of the alleged counterreaction?; can it be identified? We need a collective look over our shoulders.

American Culture and Rock Music

A consideration of contemporary American culture starts no later than August 6, 1945 (the atomic bombing of Hiroshima), but earlier events must be kept in mind. These include the first widespread commercial uses of radio (1920 for AM, 1939 for FM), film (1900s) and audio recordings (1900s). Also vital is a rough indication of the beginnings of jazz (1900s), blues (1910s), country music (1920s) and swing (1930s). But there is a lot more: FDR's incumbency and the New Deal (1932–45); Pearl Harbor (December 7, 1941); World War II (1941–45); the Great Depression (1929–World War II); the rise of the modern Ku Klux Klan (1920s); the labor movement (1920s–1930s); the first major black protest march on Washington, D.C., led by A. Phillip Randolph (1941); the

Harlem and Detroit race riots (1943); and perhaps the heyday of Hollywood (1920s through the early 1950s).

1945

Culture. Prior to 1945, the American consciousness was almost universally preoccupied with the war. One of the problems with our society
today is that most people holding political power still view events in these
terms, a perspective that ceased to have much validity after Hiroshima
and Nagasaki. Together with the death of FDR and the ending of the war,
the atomic bomb dragged America out of the one era and into another.

Music. Aside from the established music of the period (big bands, show
tunes, crooners and the like), songs like ''The Honeydripper'' by Joe
Liggins were beginning to hint at a new set of sexual values. But explicit
references like this to the pure joy of sex were at this time confined to the
''race'' market. Many unconventional ideas about race, sex, and work,
kept in check by a unified concentration on the war effort, would now be
released, to the chagrin of many.

1946

Culture. The Cold War began in earnest despite the hopeful founding of
the United Nations. Bad feelings about the Yalta Conference would release the hatred and fear of Soviet communism held back by the wartime
anti-Nazi alliance. Dr. Benjamin Spock published *Baby and Child Care,*
a book that would have an enormous impact on postwar babies, the generation that would begin reaching adolescence in the mid fifties. Spock
sowed the dangerous seeds of a free consciousness by encouraging parents to allow a child a decisive role in its own development. The ''baby
boom'' was, as a consequence, inherently subversive. Television programming also began, a development that would eventually end the dominance of the film industry in popular entertainment and cause the radio
industry to emphasize music in order to survive.

Music. Black blues music, still called ''race music,'' recovered nicely
from its temporary eclipse. (The Great Depression hit its audience harder
than anyone else.) And black migrations into northern urban areas began
giving this music a different character: rawer, gutsier, and angrier.

Much of it sounded a lot like what we later called rock and roll, but at this point it was just "urban blues."

1947

Culture. Electioneering dominated this year, with no one expecting Harry Truman to beat Thomas E. Dewey. Americans couldn't adjust to the fact that FDR wasn't around any longer. Loved or hated for almost thirteen years, Roosevelt was the primary symbol for American hegemony. Truman simply couldn't compete with his predecessor's image. Nevertheless, his scrappiness and earthiness appealed to more people than Dewey's elitist diffidence. Ominously, however, the Democratic party was split when Truman pushed his beliefs in civil rights at the convention. The "Dixiecrats" walked out and ran Strom Thurmond as their candidate, and he picked up not a few electoral votes. Henry Wallace's Progressives did pretty well also. Meanwhile, Jackie Robinson became the first black to play major league baseball, winning Rookie of the Year honors.

Music. The thinly disguised sexuality of rhythm and blues was becoming more and more open. Black Americans were asserting themselves more clearly in their music than perhaps anywhere else. Both "Shake Your Boogie" (Sonny Boy Williamson) and "We're Gonna Rock, We're Gonna Roll" (Wild Bill Moore) were released; the latter included the first clear reference to "rocking and rolling." A dance reference this was not, unless it is remembered that "dancing" was a euphemism for sex.

1948

Culture. Truman kept himself busy. He desegregated the armed forces by executive order and responded to the Soviets' blockade of Berlin with a massive airlift. The United Nations created the modern state of Israel, ending the first stage of recovery from the Holocaust. Alfred Kinsey published his first sex report (on males), and "The Ed Sullivan Show" aired for the first time.

Music. Continuing the trend toward sexual explicitness, "Good Rockin' Tonite" by Wynonie Harris was released (later covered by Elvis in 1954). Specific music developments included the characteristic rolling, boogie-woogie bass (originally introduced by a person named Jimmy

Yancy, a groundskeeper for the Chicago White Sox); it achieved prominence in Sonny Thompson's "Long Gone." Technologically, the 33 r.p.m. long-playing record was placed in the market, but it was reserved almost exclusively for classical music.

1949

Culture. Feeding the fires of an already virulent anticommunism, the Chinese Communists pushed the Nationalists off the mainland onto Taiwan. And the mutual recriminations began as to who was responsible for "losing" China to Mao and his Communist hoards. Meanwhile, flying saucers were sighted, Gorgeous George's wrestling shows competed with roller derbies for the new TV audience, and Levittowns were being built. The Soviet Union made its own atomic bomb, and nuclear testing was underway with all deliberate speed. Some people were getting worried.

Music. While "Chicken Shack Boogie" (Amos Milburn) and "Boogie at Midnight" (Roy Brown) represented the growing openness about sexuality unsullied by romance and love, "Drinkin' Wine, Spo-De-O-Dee" (Stick McGhee) represented a new avenue of dissent; now, outrageous drinking and uninhibited language were aggressively proclaimed with unashamed abandon. (The nonsense lyric "Spo-De-O-Dee" replaced a scurrilous phrase having to do with the sexual proclivities of some unspecified "mother.") A couple of other happenings were important as well: the term "rhythm and blues" began to replace "race music," and the 45 r.p.m. was introduced.

1950

Culture. The Cold War turned hot: the Korean police action began along with McCarthyism and the Internal Security Act. Not only was the Communist Party of the United States of America harassed, but anything or anyone with even the faintest leftist leanings was suspect and officially blacklisted. To many, America had now become the land of the repressed and the home of the cowardly. Few were willing to voice an objection, especially those without power and influence.

Music. Fats Domino's career began about this time, establishing him as one of the earliest, major figures of the rock era. Meanwhile, something was happening in white music that would produce significant waves later: the top song of the year was the innocuous "Goodnight Irene," recorded by the Weavers, one member of which, Pete Seeger, was to be blacklisted for his outspoken socialist sympathies. A revolutionary had achieved cultural prominence—through popular music. It would not be the last time for such an occurrence.

1951

Culture. Again a war consciousness prevailed, but this time the war was ambiguous. Not only was General Douglas MacArthur relieved of command in Korea, no clear threat to U.S. security was perceived and no symbolic affront to America's dignity had set off the war (as had been the case in so many earlier wars—Pearl Harbor, the sinking of the *Maine* and *Lusitania,* the Alamo, etc., all of which Americans were encouraged to remember). Americans, however, were losing their moorings; the "lost generation" was emerging, that is, American youths were increasingly perceived as having no guiding orientation in their lives; and J. D. Salinger published *Catcher in the Rye,* which expressed this development perfectly.

Music. Something curious was happening. After the FCC lifted its freeze on new TV licenses, radio began its inevitable shift to music programming. Alan Freed began his "Moondog Show," using the term "rock 'n' roll" on the airwaves for the first time. He played such songs as "Sixty Minute Man" (Billy Ward and the Dominoes) and "Rocket 88" (Jackie Brenston), the latter covered immediately by Bill Haley and the Saddlemen. Haley also covered Jimmy Preston's 1949 R & B hit "Rock This Joint," beginning a process that was to reach its apogee from 1954 to 1957. Alan Freed and Bill Haley were picking up on something significant. White adolescents were finding in this music a kind of freedom not available to them anywhere else in American society. An underground, barely discernible, halting fascination with black culture was in its infant stages—and rock and roll had presided at the birth.

1952

Culture. With the election of President Dwight D. Eisenhower, America revealed its continuing attachment to the clear, World War II distinctions between good and evil; the unquestioned truths of duty, honor, country; the simplicity of a nondenominational, civil religion; and the stability afforded by a moral code that kept all the passions in check. In short, Americans wanted security. More than anything, they feared upsetting questions and unsettling problems; things like that had to be kept out of sight. The only cloud on Ike's horizon was the disclosure of a slush fund kept by his vice-presidential candidate, Richard M. Nixon. But after Nixon's confessional "Checkers" speech in the midst of the campaign, Adlai Stevenson didn't stand a chance; he was overwhelmed. Security had a price, however, for a new cloud appeared on the horizon: the hydrogen bomb.

Music. While sexual themes were becoming more explicit ("Rock Me All Night Long," "5-10-15 Hours," "Lawdy Miss Clawdy," "No More Doggin'," "Have Mercy Baby," and "Middle of the Night"), rock and roll was acquiring a wider meaning, threatening to negate still other traditionally accepted values. Amos Milburn's "Thinkin' and Drinkin' " juxtaposed two activities usually regarded as contradictory. Elsewhere, Pete Seeger and the Weavers were suppressed by the House Un-American Activities Committee; a concert in Cleveland's Arena, organized by Alan Freed and attracting far more than the hall could possibly hold, developed into America's first rock-and-roll riot; and "Bandstand" had its TV debut in Philadelphia.

1953

Culture. Josef Stalin died, and the Korean War ended, giving rise to some speculation that these two events were related. An uprising in East Germany certainly did serve to point out that the Soviet Union's "steel" grip had been severely shaken. Kinsey released his second sex report (on females), showing as before that something disconcerting was lurking beneath the surface of social calm. Three-D movies had their brief life span, suggesting that technological innovations succeed only when they're really wanted.

Music. More food for controversy was provided by the increasing popularity of rhythm and blues with white middle-class youths. They were listening to songs such as "Crying in the Chapel" by the Orioles, "Good Lovin' " by the Clovers, and "Money Honey" by Clyde McPhatter.

Bill Haley continued to pick up on this trend with his first hit, "Crazy Man Crazy." He knew what he was doing; the year before he had renamed his group the Comets, leaving behind his C & W image forever.

1954

Culture. If ever there was a big year, this was it—it was the very voice-in-the-wilderness of years, baptizing all those who had ears to hear and eyes to see. The established order was mortally wounded by a series of events with far-reaching implications. The French were decisively defeated at Dien Bien Phu in the then little-known region of Indochina; the resulting treaty divided the northern and southern parts of the newly created Vietnam into Communist and non-Communist segments, ending Western influence in the area for a brief moment. More apparent to the typical American was the crushing of Sen. Joseph McCarthy in the televised Army-McCarthy hearings, a spectacle that dominated American consciousness and gave the United States its first TV phenomenon. Furthermore, the Supreme Court's decision in *Brown* v. *Board of Education* called for an end to segregation in public education with "all deliberate speed," a legal and moral watershed. Not so obvious, but just as influential, the drug-oriented *Doors of Perception* by Aldous Huxley was published—giving a positive perspective to chemical epistemology as well as providing the name for one of California's and rock's most important groups. Adding to this, the exceedingly controversial movie *The Wild One* was released. Starring Marlon Brando as the leader of an amoral motorcycle gang that pillaged a small town, the film portrayed no just retribution. Accordingly, having no redeeming quality in the eyes of the established order, it was banned in England (having only one showing) and in many other places as well. Something was afoot.

Music. In order to capture the allowances and part-time earnings of the vast and growing audience of white middle-class youths, white performers began quite consciously to cover black music as soon as it came out (in the process, smoothing it out and cleaning it up to make it more palatable and thus more salable). An unintended side effect would be to popularize the originals far more than would have been possible otherwise. As with country music, black music was produced by small regional labels with no capabilities for mass distribution. The cover artists performed on national labels that did have this capability; so those who hadn't yet heard the news soon did. Most notorious was "Sh-Boom" by the Chords (Cat), covered by the Crew Cuts (Mercury); "Tweedle Dee" by LaVern Baker (Atlantic), covered by Georgia Gibbs (Mercury); and "Sincerely" by the Moonglows (Chess), covered by the McGuire Sisters (Coral).

But crossovers began to kill the cover business almost immediately. (It had about two more years to go.) The original black versions began to outsell the covers and to appear on ("cross over" to) the pop (white) charts as well as the R & B (black) charts. What the Supreme Court had just proclaimed as a desired future goal—integration—was already a reality in rock and roll. Whites were now listening to blacks, unmediated. The songs mentioned above illustrate both the covering process and the crossover reaction (produced, in good dialectical fashion, by the cover itself). White America still wasn't ready for Hank Ballard's sexually obvious "Work with Me Annie" in any form, but it wouldn't be long. (Too blatant even to be sanitized effectively, it was later recorded by Etta James in a revised version as "Dance with Me Henry," instantly covered by Georgia Gibbs.) A technological transition occurred, with enormous implications: the wholesale conversion of the popular music business to 45 r.p.m. records from 78s. LPs were still being reserved for classical music. And in the summer, a part-time truck driver walked into Sam Philips's Sun Studios in Memphis to record a few of his country favorites in a style he had picked up from listening to black music and gospel. His name was Elvis Aaron Presley when he walked in, but he walked out as the "King of Rock and Roll." His early recordings were only regional hits, but to perceptive executives at RCA they told the story of the future. Elvis wasn't about to remain a regional phenomenon much longer.

1955

NOTE: My conviction is that the demarcation of decades is an interpretive act, with dates and events playing a symbolic, not a literal, role. Hence, 1955 is when I see the "fifties" beginning. Symbolically, then, 1955 can now be seen as the beginning of America's cultural revolution and, as such, a key turning point in American history.

Culture. Internationally, America began its intervention in Vietnam as an effort to halt the election agreed on by treaty, which was clearly going to be won by Ho Chi Minh, the Communist candidate. Secretary of State John Foster Dulles was largely responsible for this turn of events. Ike's heart attack forced the nation to consider the possibility of a Nixon presidency, but the Davy Crockett craze diverted its attention.

Meanwhile, in Montgomery, Alabama, Rosa Parks refused to move to the back of a segregated bus, and the bus boycott under the leadership of Martin Luther King, Jr., was underway. The boycott captured the imagination of all those people who had developed a fascination with black culture—through its music. On the fringes of American society, a small group of disaffected "hipsters" was reading Allen Ginsberg's newly released book of poetry, *Howl.* And in backyards everywhere, bomb shelters were being built and made ready for what everyone knew was the inevitable outcome of the arms race and continued nuclear testing.

All the ingredients for revolution were now set; America's consciousness was divided and in conflict. A youth culture had developed antagonistic to the traditional culture of the adult world. Blacks had finally made their organized move against white repression. The established order, with its quasi-religious ideology, had removed all legitimate avenues for the expression of alternate views within the system. Technological innovations, however, had brought into being new media and had altered the character of the older media, providing different means for the expression of countertraditional ideas. Underlying all of this was the fact that a conflicting set of fundamental values had emerged in opposition to the traditional ones, and these new values were shared by a very large and diverse group of people. Racism was questioned; sex was seen as good in itself; and the work ethic was considered irrelevant. Granted that these antitraditional beliefs were often semiconscious, voiced for the most part negatively and not carefully reasoned out, they were nevertheless real and potentially explosive. All that was needed was a catalyst.

Music. Then it happened, suddenly, unexpectedly, and coming from a most unlikely source: "Rock around the Clock." As the theme for the film *Blackboard Jungle,* it became "the *Marseillaise* of the teenage revolution," according to rock historian Lillian Roxon in her *Rock Encyclopedia.* Bill Haley was not the stereotypical revolutionary by any stretch of the imagination, and he was hardly young (thirty in 1955). Moreover, the song had already been out for a year and was a cover besides. Despite all of this, "Rock around the Clock" became a genuine revolutionary phenomenon. Whether or not they were aware of it, when teenagers bought this 45, they were taking a stand against the established order. Even today, the song has considerable symbolic power. Whenever *Blackboard Jungle* played, rioting was likely, and teenagers often attended just to join in. Slashing seats in the theater was common. Of course, riots didn't *always* happen, which came as a disappointment to at least one young Ted attending its Liverpool showing. Nevertheless, he found it inspirational enough to form his own band, comprised of classmates from Quarrybank High School. Two other significant films were released, *Rebel without a Cause* and *East of Eden,* both starring James Dean. The complementarity they provided for *Blackboard Jungle* was enormous. Together they overshadowed the emergence of Chuck Berry, Ray Charles, and Bo Diddley.

1956

Culture. On the international scene, de-Stalinization was getting underway in the Soviet Union, with its effects being felt in the Hungarian revolt and in Polish anti-Soviet elections. In the non-Communist world, England and Israel jointly invaded Egypt and temporarily occupied the Suez Canal. At home, the "I Like Ike" supporters overwhelmed Stevenson for a second time. America wanted the peaceful, stable, secure and ordered, mythic past more than ever. But C. Wright Mills was exposing the undemocratic workings of America in *The Power Elite,* and Jack Kerouac was expressing the will to be free in *On the Road,* suggesting the revolutionary dialectic of negation and affirmation. It became increasingly prudent to keep abreast of current events, which threatened daily to break open the established and repressive social order. Hence, "The Huntley-Brinkley Report" came into being (sending the Camel News Caravan into retirement and John Cameron Swayze to do Timex commercials).

Music. The Elvis phenomenon had now begun, initiated symbolically by his appearances on "The Ed Sullivan Show." The facts about these appearances somewhat belie the mythic tales about his being shown only from the waist up; nevertheless, it was something not to be equaled in intensity by anything in American culture for another seven years. Even at this moment, "skiffle" groups were forming in England in the wake of "Rock around the Clock." Based on a newly awakened interest in the American blues tradition, Elvis, Bill Haley, and rockabilly in general, these amateurish jug bands were causing all sorts of musical havoc along the Mersey and the Thames. One skiffle group formed in Liverpool called themselves the Quarrymen. Seven years later, they too would appear on "The Ed Sullivan Show," finally succeeding where Lord Cornwallis had failed so long ago.

As black artists were becoming increasingly recognized as the originators of much of the music white middle-class youth were listening to, "covering" for commercial purposes came to an end. This was the year of Little Richard, Fats Domino, Carl Perkins, and Chuck Berry. But it was also the year that an ominous note was sounded: Gene Vincent ("Be Bop A-Lula") was in a near-fatal car wreck, portending that rock and rollers did indeed live in the fast lane. Movies of consequence included *Rock around the Clock* and *The Girl Can't Help It.* The former had more to do with musical performance than with plot. The latter, however, was a wonderful satire of the music business, that nevertheless included some fantastic footage of Little Richard and Gene Vincent, among others.

1957

Culture. Tension was everywhere. Eisenhower sent federal troops to Little Rock, Arkansas, in order to ensure the integration of public schools, and he somewhat reluctantly signed the Voting Rights Act. The Soviets launched *Sputnik,* stunning Americans and shifting educational emphases to science and mathematics. Short shrift was given to the humanities and the arts. Soon afterward, America's first attempt exploded on takeoff at Cape Canaveral. People were reading Paul Goodman's anarchistic book *Growing Up Absurd* and were beginning to believe it.

Music. "American Bandstand" premiered on national television, playing daily with Dick Clark as host. Alan Freed held his first rock-and-roll show in New York and appeared in the film *Don't Knock the Rock.* Elvis made *Jailhouse Rock,* one of his best films. Rockabilly added Buddy Holly, Jerry Lee Lewis, the Everly Brothers, and Ricky Nelson to its ranks; R & B added Sam Cooke. But the first skirmishes of the cultural revolution were about to come to an end.

1958

Culture. As if to counteract the threatening noises of America's troops landing on the coast of Lebanon to shore up a friendly government, Ban the Bomb parades began in both America and England. SANE (Committee for a Sane Nuclear Policy) was born, beginning a very diverse movement that continues to this day. Nuclear testing, however, went on unabated, unimpressed with the increasing opposition provided by the likes of Bertrand Russell. The John Birch Society was also founded this year,

and Nixon was pelted with stones in Caracas, Venezuela. But millions of
Americans had something else on their minds: the Hula Hoop.

Music. In response to the growing political awareness, an older style of
music was resurrected that seemed better able to express ideological sentiments: folk music, which had been highly successful advancing the
cause of labor. Now, however, it was increasingly wedded to a pop style,
and thus came into being such groups as the Kingston Trio. Distinguishing folk from the developing rock tradition was the fact that it was almost
always recorded on the new stereo LPs; rock was still recorded on 45s.

The established order was now fighting back in earnest; the values put
under attack by rock were being reasserted with a heavy hand. Work, not
sex, was again proclaimed as an end in itself, and anything hinting at racial mixing was quashed. Alan Freed's concert in Boston turned into another riot, and Freed was accused of inciting it. Elvis was drafted and
went willingly, thus ending his role as a revolutionary negation. Symbolically, however, he would always retain this meaning. Jerry Lee Lewis's
marriage to his fourteen- (or thirteen-) year-old cousin led to his prema-
ture retirement from rock. And anti-rock-and-roll demonstrations were
held throughout the country. Rock and roll was on the defensive.

1959

Culture. Fidel Castro came to power in Cuba, overthrowing the unpopular,
American-supported Batista regime. When his Communist sympathies became clear, the CIA began plans to remove him. Nixon and Khrushchev
exchanged visits, each with enormous TV exposure. Also exposed was
Charles Van Doren, who finally confessed to being "prompted" on TV's
"$64,000 Question." We soon learned he wasn't alone.

Music. A two-year series of congressional hearings on "payola" in the
music industry began, focusing on rock and roll. Somehow its popularity
had to be explained, and the prevailing theory was that disc jockeys were
being paid to play it. Why else would American kids listen to such trash?
It was the only music available. Rock and roll was being forced on them,
and teenagers simply weren't strong enough to resist it. Chuck Berry was
arrested for technically violating the Mann Act. Buddy Holly was tragically killed in an airplane crash along with Richie Valens and J. P. Rich-
ardson, the "Big Bopper." And Little Richard converted to Christianity
after a near accident aboard an airplane, becoming the first "born again"

rock and roller. Still part of the reaction, the music industry began its attempt to co-opt the form of rock music without adopting its substance, killing its revolutionary potential. Hence, there emerged the tame, bland "schlock rock" favored by "American Bandstand" and the established order. Some of the premier examples were Fabian's "Tiger," Connie Francis's "Lipstick on Your Collar," Paul Anka's "Put Your Head on My Shoulder," Frankie Avalon's "Venus," and Dodie Stevens's "Pink Shoelaces." But the folk trend was continuing: the first Newport Folk Festival was held, giving Joan Baez national recognition.

1960

Culture. The narrowness of John F. Kennedy's presidential victory indicated a fundamental uncertainty in America, but his New Frontier symbolized something other than Nixon's clear identification with the old order. No matter that Kennedy himself was far different than the image he projected. The image was the important thing and even the marginal preference sent America in a new, as yet unspecified direction. He represented innovation, change, the hope for a better future, and a way out of America's domestic and foreign travails. Yet the travails followed him into office. Sit-ins gave the black liberation movement a new and effective tactic and good publicity besides. Caryl Chessman was executed over the growing opposition to the death penalty. The production and sale of birth-control pills introduced a new factor into the struggle for sexual liberation. And hopes for peace were dampened when Francis Gary Powers' U-2 was shot down on a spy mission over the Soviet Union.

Music. Elvis was discharged from the service but never regained his revolutionary stature. Much of his later material was schlock or worse. Broadway's *Bye Bye Birdie* (based on Elvis's induction) reflected his almost total co-optation by the established order. Eddie Cochran, a minor rockabilly rebel, died in a London taxi accident. And the "payola" hearings continued, absolving Dick Clark and castigating Alan Freed.

1961

Culture. Not a good year for realizing much of the Kennedy promise. He watched the Berlin Wall being built (making a lot of political hay out of it), permitted the CIA's debacle at the Bay of Pigs, and sent America's first combat troops ("advisors") into Vietnam. Meanwhile, back in the United States, the race revolution was taking an even more aggressive turn; freedom rides into the South pushed Kennedy farther than he was willing to go. Books published included Updike's *Rabbit Run*, Heller's *Catch-22* and Heinlein's *Stranger in a Strange Land;* they portrayed anomie, negation, and affirmation, respectively.

Music. Both schlock rock and folk continued, but the latter picked up one Robert Zimmerman from Hibbing, Minnesota. America would hear more from him. The revolution, suppressed in one of its forms (rock) was emerging in another (folk). Neither was to remain static, however. The pressures of social change wouldn't allow it: schlock was counterrevolutionary, and pure folk was outdated.

1962

Culture. Kennedy emerged a hero after the Cuban missile crisis, but this would prove to be the last popularly approved Cold War act in America. He would be more favorably remembered as one who boosted America's space program, with John Glenn's orbit of the earth. Another very traditional value came under attack when the Supreme Court struck down school prayer, and new values were introduced with Rachel Carson's *Silent Spring,* a warning about the abuse of the environment with modern technology. Yet James Meredith could still only register at the University of Mississippi with military force. As a preview of coming attractions, the Students for a Democratic Society was organized around the idealistic principles of their founding charter, the Port Huron Statement. And when Marilyn Monroe died under suspicious circumstances, the sad event seemed to symbolize the end of an era.

Music. As in American culture as a whole, new things were happening in music. Schlock and folk both died a quiet death, and in their place came folk rock (Peter, Paul and Mary), contemporary protest music (Dylan, Joan Baez, Tom Paxton, Phil Ochs, and another Newport Folk Festival), surfing music (Beach Boys), the Phil Spector wall of sound and the twist phenomenon. LPs were now becoming the preferred medium, connoting a new degree of seriousness for the values being affirmed through the music.

1963

NOTE: The fifties had by this time come to an end, their function being primarily to negate the established order. Since the election of Kennedy, however, something amorphously new was being affirmed. More than anything else, this is what the sixties were about: the affirmation and clarification of a new set of fundamental values, such as radical individuality, pleasure, pacifism, nonnationalism, and a nonreligious spirituality. The period lacked only a symbolic beginning, but 1963 was to provide one.

Culture. The sixties began on a Friday in Dallas, at 12:30 P.M. (local time) on November 22, with the assassination of John F. Kennedy, tragically ending a year of high promise and grim foreboding. The values of the established order and those of the revolution were about to clash. The optimistic symbol of peaceful, cooperative, and nationally unified change was gone. But the promises arising earlier in the year were not: the civil-rights march on Washington capped with Martin Luther King, Jr.'s "I have a dream" speech; the Nuclear Test Ban Treaty; Vatican II; and the resurgence of feminism with the publication of Betty Friedan's *The Feminine Mystique.* Unfortunately, the forebodings remained: the assassination of civil rights leader Medgar Evers; the murder of four black children attending Sunday school in Birmingham; the televised police-led attack on civil-rights marchers in Birmingham; the death of Pope John XXIII; the CIA assassination of South Vietnamese President Diem, and the firing of Timothy Leary from his teaching position at Harvard for advocating the use of LSD. Burdick and Wheeler's *Fail Safe,* Knebel and Bailey's *Seven Days in May,* and James Baldwin's *The Fire Next Time* were published. To report it all, network TV news expanded its daily coverage from fifteen minutes to thirty.

Music. The conflict was already a reality in the folk-rock scene, the third Newport Folk Festival providing a veritable tour de force of revolutionary expressions ("Blowin' in the Wind" and "The Times They Are a-Changin' " not the least of them). Protest music had now reached its peak. Motown was on the rise despite Sam Cooke's shooting death, and Diana Ross was to become the first openly acknowledged black sex fantasy for white males. The R & B charts were abolished, illustrating that integration had been accomplished in music at least. Very shortly the naiveté of this ideal would also become evident, again a fact to be revealed first in music. The big story, however, was somewhere in England—Liverpool to be exact.

1964

Culture. Despite his innate contradictions and enormous ego, Lyndon Johnson won the presidency as the peace candidate and brought us war. He led a tough Civil Rights Act through Congress, proclaiming "we shall overcome" on prime-time TV. But he also forced through the Gulf of Tonkin Resolution, placing America firmly in the Vietnam war. Aside from the continuation of civil-rights murders in the South and the Berkeley free speech movement, however, it appeared that Johnson had things pretty much under control. Yet, this was also the year that Cassius Clay became Muhammad Ali, "That Was the Week That Was" appeared on TV, and *Dr. Strangelove* was released. Obviously, some people weren't quite so happy with LBJ and his Great Society.

Music. We met the Beatles! Beginning with their appearance on "The Ed Sullivan Show" early in February, their first tour of the United States overwhelmed everyone, including the Beatles themselves. With the first five singles on the charts ("Can't Buy Me Love," "Twist and Shout," "She Loves You," "I Want to Hold Your Hand," and "Please Please Me"), they completely dominated popular music. But Beatlemania was far more than a mere phenomenon of music; it was charged with quasi-religious significance. The musicians became demigods. They thumbed their noses at authorities of all kinds; they were joyous, free, and witty; they took nothing seriously, least of all themselves; and they gave us hope. Soon, even the establishment fell in love with them, thus conceding to them the most effective role possible: symbol stature. The Quarrymen had come a long way.

1965

Culture. Antiwar demonstrations began in earnest, right along with the continued and progressively larger military escalation. Somewhat lost in the shuffle was the American invasion of the Dominican Republic. A Quaker's self-immolation at the Pentagon dramatically illustrated a growing popular reaction. Even with another strong Civil Rights Act and Bill Cosby being featured in TV's "I Spy," black discontent was still on the rise: thus the Selma marches, the Watts riots, and the assassination of Malcolm X (followed immediately by his *Autobiography*). Seemingly the only hopeful events were urban peace during the New York City blackout and the beginning of Frank Herbert's *Dune* trilogy (now a longer series).

Music. The Beatles, Dylan, Simon and Garfunkel, the Byrds, soul (featuring James Brown, Otis Redding and, consequently, the reinstatement of the R & B charts), and psychedelia dominated the year. Protests against the war and racism were increasingly the messages, and their media were becoming TV and films, as well as radio and records. Dylan changed his musical style to rock with *Bringing It All Back Home,* to the consternation of the fans of pure folk music, and Alan Freed died. It was a year of gradually developing bitterness.

1966

Culture. The Black Power movement competed for attention with more and more war protests, and "death of God" theologies began calling traditional religion into question more publicly than ever before. Christian and Jewish atheism became fashionable, but a spiritual dimension was curiously still affirmed. Sex and drugs were in the news too: Masters and Johnson's report was released and the use of LSD was placed under government regulation. Bad news was aplenty: the Richard Speck murders in Chicago; riots in Chicago, Brooklyn, and Baltimore; Lenny Bruce's tragic death by heroin overdose; and the shooting of James Meredith in Mississippi. Curiosities too: hippies were flowering; "Star Trek" was on TV; and the Red Guards' idealism, based on the *Quotations of Chairman Mao,* shook almost everyone's naive understanding about China.

Music. The Beatles (who, with the existentially oriented *Revolver,* entered a much more serious stage), the Rolling Stones, Dylan (and his near fatal motorcycle accident), soul ("Say It Loud—I'm Black and I'm Proud" by James Brown), the Fugs (who united fifties beatdom with sixties hippiedom), and the arrival of FM rock were all clearly responding to a time of turmoil but giving it direction at the same time. The Beatles' performed their last live concert in San Francisco, and Lennon made his infamous "We're bigger than Jesus" statement. On the lighter side, but just as controversial, the Monkees were appearing on TV. To their credit, they eventually did learn to play their instruments and their songs.

Finally, the only prowar song to come out during Vietnam hit the top of the charts: Barry Sadler's "Ballad of the Green Berets."

1967

Culture. Opposition to the war and racism continued as cultural nega-tion, while alternative life-styles were affirmed as part of the positive side of the revolution. Communes of every conceivable type were set up, and modifications of the traditional marriage relationship in greater or lesser degrees were tried. The year included a march on the Pentagon (countered by a prowar march in New York), "The Smothers Brothers Comedy Hour" on TV, *MacBird* on the stage, Mohammed Ali's de-thronement as heavyweight boxing champion (because he didn't have anything against "them Viet Congs"), and the massive Newark riot. San Francisco's Human Be-In and Tom Wolfe's *Electric Kool-Aid Acid Test* pointed to "the summer of love," despite the "Hippie Funeral" and chartered tours through the Haight-Asbury ("Hashbury") district. Else-where, Che Guevara was killed while trying to incite another Cuban-style Communist revolution in Bolivia, and the Israelis defeated the Ar-abs in the Six Day War.

Music. The Beatles' *Sgt. Pepper's Lonely Hearts Club Band* outdid everything, including *Hair,* Monterey Pop, the Jefferson Airplane, the Doors, the Grateful Dead, Country Joe and the Fish, Jimi Hendrix, Sly and the Family Stone, and underground radio. Sly and the Family Stone deserve a special mention. Being comprised of blacks and whites, males and females, they presented a rare sight in 1967 and a pretty rare one today as well. Some unfortunate deaths: folk singer Woody Guthrie, soul singer Otis Redding, and Beatles' manager Brian Epstein—all losses of the first magnitude.

1968

Culture. There is no way a mere list of events can convey how it felt to live through this year: both Robert Kennedy and Martin Luther King, Jr., assassinated; the police riots at the Chicago Democratic National Con-vention; the Tet offensive; the My Lai massacre; the Berrigan brothers' war protests; the "National Mobilization" against the war, created by a coalition of many antiwar organizations; "Resurrection City," the massive tent-in on the Mall in Washington, D.C., to protest poverty; the Paris student protests; the Czech uprising; campus demonstrations too numerous to identify; Black Power; the seizure of the *Pueblo;* the retirement of LBJ; and the election of Nixon as president. "Laugh In" emerged on TV, *2001* on the movie screen, and Eldridge Cleaver's *Soul on Ice,* Norman Mailer's *Armies of the Night* and Kurt Vonnegut's *Slaughterhouse Five* on the bookselves.

Music. Always the Beatles (the "White Album"), Dylan, the Who, the Rolling Stones, hard rock (Led Zeppelin), country rock (the Band), a blues revival (Janis Joplin) and, in general, the search for something new in something old. Elvis's return, with a spectacular pre-Christmas TV special, showed us the past wasn't dead. It was hardly a Christmas show, however; instead, it was designed by his manager, Colonel Tom Parker, to demonstrate that Elvis hadn't lost anything in the past ten years. And he hadn't—he could still do it all.

1969

Culture. The disruptions of the previous year continued, both negative and affirmative: violent antiwar demonstrations in Washington, D.C., and elsewhere; the Weathermen; police raids on the Black Panthers; the soldiers' strike in Vietnam; the Chicago Eight trial; Senator Frank Church's antiwar bill; cancellation of the "Smothers Brothers"; UCLA's firing of Angela Davis; the seizure of Alcatraz by Native Americans; the Charles Manson murders; the death of Ho Chi Minh; Chappaquiddick; the Apollo XI moon landing; *The Graduate;* Charles Reich's *The Greening of America;* and more. There was no end in sight.

Music. Woodstock and its negation, Altamont, headed the list, but the Beatles were a close second (with Paul McCartney's alleged death, their internal legal battles, and their last album, *Abbey Road*). Country rock continued (Creedence Clearwater Revival; Crosby, Stills, Nash and Young), and a rock-and-roll revival was in full swing. Meanwhile, *Easy Rider,* starring Jack Nicholson, Peter Fonda, and Dennis Hopper on a drug-laced motorcycle trip across America, surprised the film industry with its low cost and high quality. With an extraordinary sound track (the Band, the Byrds, Jimi Hendrix, and Steppenwolf), it demonstrated the culture-music linkage as few films have ever done.

1970

Culture. Still the trauma continued and, if possible, intensified with the killings at Kent State and Jackson State; the invasion of Cambodia; nearly universal campus demonstrations and even a few bombings; the repeal of the Gulf of Tonkin Resolution; and the election of Socialist party leader Salvador Allende Gossens in Chile. The mood of the country had now shifted almost entirely to an antiwar posture, and the linkage between the peace movement and the struggle against racism was no longer questioned. *M*A*S*H* premiered, and universities began recruiting minorities for the first time.

Music. Tragedy here too: the deaths of Janis Joplin and Jimi Hendrix and the dissolution of the Beatles. Simon and Garfunkel's last album, *Bridge over Troubled Water,* was the top album of the year, and a fitting commentary it was.

1971

Culture. It seemed endless: the Attica prison riots; the unsanctioned publication of the Pentagon Papers; the invasion of Laos and the resulting massive antiwar march on Washington, D.C., with thousands of illegal arrests. Meanwhile, "All in the Family" began a new TV era with its portrayal of fundamental values in conflict.

Music. The deaths this year included Jim Morrison and Duane Allman, but hope was expressed in ways that would develop in years to come: *Jesus Christ Superstar,* George Harrison's *Concert for Bangladesh,* and John Lennon's *Imagine.* Led Zeppelin replaced the Beatles as England's most popular group; an era was winding down.

1972

Culture. During the sharply divided presidential campaign, the shooting of George Wallace in Maryland ended his candidacy but not his life; in the following months, Nixon overwhelmed George McGovern to win a second term. Nixon then visited China and the Soviet Union but began his own downfall by overseeing, and helping to cover up, the Watergate break-in. And the war continued: massive saturation bombings of North

Vietnam preceded a United States–initiated cease-fire. Otherwise, the death penalty was temporarily halted, and "M*A*S*H" began as a TV series.

Music. Country rock continued and diversified, and the Rolling Stones toured the United States. But another Britisher, Elton John, was the big news. His fourth album, *Honky Chateau,* is perhaps his best. Although it attacked an old enemy, racism, it also expressed an underlying fear that the revolution had begun to stall (in "I Think I'm Going to Kill Myself").

1973

Culture. The climax of the sixties: the Paris Peace Accords were signed, ending direct American military intervention in Vietnam; Spiro Agnew resigned the vice-presidency in disgrace; Congress passed the Equal Rights Amendment; the Supreme Court legalized abortion; and the Watergate hearings got under way.

Music. Already looking to the future, reggae (for example, in the film, *The Harder They Come* with Jimmy Cliff) and disco emerged with contradictory messages. Jimmy Cliff was warning that liberation would require a renewal of the struggle with "You Can Get It If You Really Want It," as was Johnny Nash with "Stir It Up." But the Spinners, with "One of a Kind (Love Affair)," the Stylistics, in "Rock 'n' Roll Baby," and Manu Dibango's "Soul Makossa" were advising us to dance our troubles away. As if to keep Woodstock alive, 600,000 rock fans came to Watkins Glen, New York, for another peaceful concert. Bruce Springsteen was looked to as the new Dylan or Elvis, and fifties nostalgia erupted with the highly mythic *American Graffiti,* an interpretive portrayal of the period.

1974

NOTE: Another symbolic year, bringing an end to the sixties but not the cultural revolution. The fact that the revolutionary values were not institutionalized is not important. What mattered above all else was the fact that they had been voiced in a coherent way; they achieved legitimacy. The denouement was to last for the next several years.

Culture. Nixon's resignation, after the indictment to impeach him, was the symbolic event that closed the tumultuous era. Neither the bad feelings created by Gerald Ford's pardon of Nixon nor the diversion provided by the Patty Hearst kidnapping could spoil the relief. But the relief was hardly joyous; it was just relief.

Music. Nothing really new or eventful was happening. Elton John's popularity continued, but the incipient reggae and disco trends were more significant. Stevie Wonder's "Boogie on Reggae Woman" and Eric Clapton's cover of Bob Marley's "I Shot the Sheriff" illustrated the former, while MFSB's "TSOP (The Sound of Philadelphia)," Betty Wright's "Where Is the Love," and George McCrae's "Rock Your Baby" illustrated the latter.

1975

Culture. There were only aftershocks now; as Cambodia and South Vietnam were overrun, the remaining Americans were unceremoniously snatched from the top of the U.S. embassy in Saigon. Nixon's cohorts were convicted for assisting him in covering up the Watergate break-in. And future U.S. international problems were presaged in the Cambodian seizure of the U.S. merchant ship *Mayagüez*.

Music. Something genuinely new, "Saturday Night Live," one of the most remarkable shows ever to appear on TV, made its debut. It featured classic and soon-to-be classic rock performers (such as Randy Newman in 1975, Jimmy Cliff in 1976, Joan Armatrading and Elvis Costello in 1977, Devo in 1978, and the Talking Heads in 1979), introduced new variations in music (such as the Lockers, Toni Basil, the Roches, the B-52's, Leon Redbone, Brick and Kate Bush), spawned a series of clones, and invited the Beatles to reunite on the show—for $3,000. (Lennon and McCartney, watching the broadcast together in Lennon's New York apartment in the Dakota, almost drove over on a lark.)

1976

Culture. Aside from Jimmy Carter's presidential election, nothing much happened. The country was preoccupied with the bicentennial and the repression of the Vietnam experience. A space feat helped to do the job as well; two Vikings landed on Mars and sent back spectacular photographs.

Music. McCartney was back, illustrating through his world tour that the Beatles and what they symbolized was far from dead—dormant, perhaps, but not dead. Despite their personal desires, the Beatles legend lived on in each one of the four. Otherwise, Fleetwood Mac was becoming a phenomenon; Elvis's *Sun Sessions* was released; Parliament/Funkadelic, the film *Car Wash,* and *Dr. Buzzard's Original "Savannah" Band* signaled the rise of funk; and the *Outlaws* album pointed to a new trend in C & W.

1977

Culture. Carter's major action was to pardon Vietnam draft evaders, inflation increased, John Irving's *The World According to Garp* was *the* book to read, the "Roots" sensation on TV illustrated an almost universal awareness of the black American's historic plight, and with Gary Gilmore's execution, capital punishment was reinstituted for the first time in ten years.

Music. Reggae developed into a cult phenomenon; but with the punk rock group, Sex Pistols, a renewed revolutionary awareness was also growing. Disco was at its peak with *Saturday Night Fever,* which starred John Travolta as Tony Manero, a Brooklyn youth seeking recognition and self-fulfillment in a discotheque. The movie illustrated, as so many times before, that the intricacies of dance are directly proportional to social divisiveness. Whereas, earlier the dances were simple and unsophisticated enough for everyone to participate, now they required lessons. Punk rockers countered with the ultra-unsophisticated pogo (jumping up and down). The death this year was a big one: on the eighth anniversary of Woodstock, Elvis was found dead at Graceland, burned out as his music had been for years. The negation he symbolized, however, would endure. The music was getting interesting: Elvis Costello, the Ramones, Steely Dan, David Bowie, Talking Heads, Randy Newman, and Little Feat all released critically acclaimed and thought-provoking albums. The only official live Beatles album was also released, *The Beatles at the Hollywood Bowl.*

1978

Culture. Billy Carter was beginning to embarrass his brother, Jimmy, as was the uncontrollable inflation. But Jimmy Carter had spectacular success in bringing Israeli Prime Minister Menachem Begin and Egyptian President Anwar Sadat together, setting in motion the peace process between their two countries. The international horror created by the Vietnamese "boat people" refugees, however, presented Carter with insoluble problems. The Supreme Court set back affirmative action programs with the Bakke decision. And an ugly travesty occurred with the mass suicide of Jim Jones and his People's Temple followers in Guyana.

Music. Dormancy and waiting. With no clear embodiment of the established order, there could be no catalyst, no enemy to spark the stalled revolution. The old order had been banished in luxury to San Clemente, and the new order had no direction. The death of rock and roll was both lamented and celebrated, but as with Mark Twain's, its death was highly exaggerated. Blondie's *Parallel Lines,* Bruce Springsteen's *Darkness on the Edge of Town,* Warren Zevon's *Excitable Boy,* Funkadelic's *One Nation under a Groove,* Patti Smith's *Easter,* Elvis Costello's *Armed Forces* and Teddy Pendergrass's *Life Is a Song Worth Singing* are a few notable counter examples.

1979

Culture. The Iranian takeover of the U.S. embassy in Teheran dominated American consciousness, providing an illusory unity. The civil war in El Salvador, the Sandinista takeover in Nicaragua, and the Three Mile Island nuclear accident, however, showed the cracks beneath the surface. Sixty-five thousand people protested against nuclear power in Washington, D.C., and Jerry Falwell's "Moral Majority" was making some really ugly noises about defining those holding nontraditional values as both non-Christian and un-American. His antiabortion, antigay, anti-ERA and anti–nuclear freeze positions almost made him a parody of the revolution's opposition.

Music. The antiwar movement now took shape in the emerging no-nukes sentiment. The *No-Nukes* concert and album helped keep the movement alive. Present were Bruce Springsteen; Crosby, Stills, and Nash; Tom Petty and the Heartbreakers; Chaka Khan; Bonnie Raitt; the Doobie

Brothers; Jackson Browne; and Gil Scott-Heron among others. Also, Dire Straits' *Dire Straits*, Pink Floyd's *The Wall*, and Prince's *Prince* were pointed reminders that the revolution was far from dead.

1980

NOTE: Again a symbolic event, indicating this time the beginnings of the counterreaction—a revived, renewed, and reconstituted version of the old established order delivered an enormous counterpunch. Having learned its weaknesses and profited from its mistakes, it would be a formidable opponent for the stalled revolution.

Culture. With Reagan's election, the counterreaction had begun, embodied in someone almost always underestimated. He would not provide an easy target as had LBJ and Nixon. The bitter memories of Iran's holding American hostages, the strikes in Poland, and the Soviet Union's invasion of Afghanistan (along with Carter's boycott of the Olympics in Moscow) would provide convenient, external foci for American attention, and Reagan would make wise use of them. His domestic program ended the last vestiges of FDR's welfare liberalism and brought back into the limelight classical liberalism supported by a healthy dose of Social Darwinism. And, to top this off, he revived the puritan ethic as well. Meanwhile, the revolutionary values of liberation were not being adequately expressed, headed off at the pass by Reagan and his wealthy and security-conscious supporters. "Reaganomics" was on the horizon. But problems were developing: three American nuns were murdered by government troops in El Salvador; Ku Klux Klan and American Nazi party members were acquitted of murdering Communist demonstrators in North Carolina; and Miami experienced race riots.

Music. There was only one event, coming late in the year in New York, on December 8: Lennon's murder. The public reaction showed, as the McCartney tour had shown already, that what the Beatles symbolized was living still and maybe not quite as dormant as it had been. Lennon, after all, was immersed in the movement more than all of the other Beatles combined (as his solo albums more than adequately demonstrate). The reunion rumors were finally put to rest. Many thought Lennon *was* the Beatles; so without him, there would be no second coming. A few albums, however, do deserve mention for helping to preserve the revolutionary consciousness: the Clash's *London Calling*, Lennon/Ono's *Double Fantasy*, Rockpile's *Seconds of Pleasure*, the Police's *Zenyatta Mondatta*, Stevie Wonder's *Hotter Than July*, Bob Marley and the Wailers' *Uprising*, Adam and the Ants' *Kings of the Wild Frontier*, the Bus Boys' *Minimum Wage Rock and Roll*, and the Ramones' *End of the Century*.

1981

Culture. Although the big story was Reagan's program of massive government deregulation, his support for the MX missile and El Salvador's government with money and advisors was even more significant. Solidarity Day in Washington, D.C., attracted over a quarter of a million protestors. But attention was diverted by the assassination of Anwar Sadat and the woundings of Pope John Paul II and Reagan himself. On TV we were watching "Hill Street Blues." And we were getting to know our first woman Supreme Court justice, Sandra Day O'Connor.

Music. Kim Carnes's "Bette Davis Eyes" was the song of the year, but Prince's *Controversy* (which included "Ronnie, Talk to Russia Before It's Too Late") would be remembered far longer. Less explicit, but equally effective albums of negation were *The Blasters* and *Was (Not Was)*, the former updating the past and the latter manifesting the present. Two documentary films performed the same function: *This Is Elvis* and *The Decline of Western Civilization* (about the Los Angeles punk scene).

1982

Culture. The beginnings of an economic recovery disguised the emergence of several serious and long-term conflicts: the CIA's support for the anti-Sandinista "Contras" in Nicaragua, right-wing victories in El Salvador, a proposed constitutional amendment permitting public-school prayer, the official defeat of the ERA, the EPA scandal caused by zealous deregulators, and the MX missile—all of which had Reagan's support. The dedication of the memorial to Vietnam veterans in Washington, D.C., reopened old wounds. But we were distracted by the war in the Falkland Islands, the Tylenol poisoning scare, another race riot in Miami, and the death of John Belushi.

Music. Antiwar sentiment was undergoing a revival with a no-nukes concert in New York's Central Park; Billy Joel's "Goodnight Saigon" on his *Nylon Curtain;* the Clash's *Combat Rock;* Crosby, Stills and Nash's "Wasted on the Way"; and the film *Atomic Cafe.* There was an appeal to the old (in albums by Marshall Crenshaw and George Thorogood) and to the new (in albums by the Waitresses, Juluka, X, and Elvis Costello). We danced (to Michael Jackson's *Thriller*), we brooded (to Bruce Springsteen's *Nebraska*), we laughed (to the Go Go's *Vacation*) and we cried (to Paul McCartney's *Tug of War* with his farewell to John Lennon in "Here Today"). Technologically, cassette discs and players were introduced, providing the clearest reproduction of sound to date.

1983

Culture. The renewal of the conflict was now well under way. Reagan's policies in Central America were seeming more and more like those of Vietnam. (There were even posters available with the names of one area superimposed on the map of the other.) In numerous cities throughout Europe, over two million people gathered for a day of protest against Reagan's military policies. Catholic bishops in the United States voted overwhelmingly to oppose Reagan's reliance on nuclear weapons. Over two hundred American soldiers were killed by a terrorist's bomb in Lebanon. We had a "splendid little war" in Grenada. The government was forced to buy the entire town of Times Beach, Missouri, because of the uncontrolled toxic wastes. The Reagan administration was also forced to accept January 15 as a federal holiday commemorating the birth of Martin Luther King, Jr. Over a quarter of a million gathered at the Washington Monument to remember the 1963 civil-rights march at which King gave his "I have a dream" speech. Numerous other events acknowledged the symbolic significance of John Kennedy's assassination and the Beatles' first American tour. Meanwhile, there were other serious developments: the outbreak of AIDS, the Soviet's downing of Korean Air Lines 007 and a steadily improving economy (which many felt did not include the poor).

Music. There were some more pointed blasts from the past (Dylan's *Infidels,* Paul Simon's *Hearts and Bones,* Pink Floyd's *The Final Cut,* and Randy Newman's *Trouble in Paradise*), all having antiwar messages. There were also previews of coming attractions: neoprotest (Peter Schilling, the Blasters, and the Talking Heads), neopsychedelia/paisley underground (the Bangles, Dream Syndicate, Rain Parade, and the Three

O'Clock), country-punk (Jason and the Scorchers, Rank and File, the Long Ryders, Lone Justice, and Blood on the Saddle), Latino rock (Tierra, Los Illegals, the Plugz, Los Lobos, and the Brat), to say nothing of hard-core punk (Suicidal Tendencies) and African rock (King Sunny Adé). As Huey Lewis and the News sang, "The Heart of Rock and Roll (Is Still Beating)." With the increasing conflicts in society at large, rock was entering one of its most active and creative periods. Music videos were coming into their own to capture all of this visually (Randy Newman's "I Love L.A." and Michael Jackson's "Billie Jean" being two superlative examples). And *The Big Chill* maintained ties with the sixties by dealing with the apparent loss of ideals—its soundtrack being comprised of some of Motown's finest.

1984

Culture. There was no lessening of conflict. For the first time, a black American (Jesse Jackson) was a serious contender for the presidential nomination, and a woman (Geraldine Ferraro) was nominated for vice-president on the Democratic ticket. The Democratic party, because of its opposition to Reagan, also came to embody the more explicitly political aspects of the cultural revolution. Carly Simon's "Here Comes the Turning of the Tide" was adopted as the party's official theme song. But a still-improving economy made a Democratic victory impossible, especially since the Democrats had been unable to separate Reagan's personal popularity from his increasingly unpopular policies. A travesty of a trial was held in El Salvador to convict some underlings for the murder of three American nuns, and a demented gunman slaughtered over twenty people in a McDonald's near San Diego. Tragic deaths included Marvin Gaye and Dennis Wilson.

Music. The resurgence of the revolutionary conflict over fundamental values was evident in the film *Footloose.* Its theme was a contemporary conflict between an irrational and repressive establishment and liberated youth, and the music was an essential component of the plot. The past recharged the present in Bruce Springsteen's *Born in the U.S.A.,* Lou Reed's *New Sensations,* and the Rolling Stones' *Undercover.* Newer artists, of course, were even more active: UB-40, Prince, Cyndi Lauper, X, Grandmaster Flash, Elvis Costello, the Alarm, Billy Idol, Culture Club, Laurie Anderson, and Kate Bush. Prince and Culture Club's Boy George deserve special attention. Together they illustrate the intrinsic connection between negation and affirmation—people either loved them or hated them. The torch was being passed.

1985

Culture. Reagan's "teflon coating" began to wear a little thin, with attacks being mounted against his policies on the budget, tax reform, trade, the Strategic Defense Initiative ("Star Wars") and his "constructive engagement" approach toward South Africa. Opposition to South Africa's Apartheid system became increasingly vociferous, with campus demonstrations and protest marches dredging up memories of the sixties. Some of the most active participants were quite familiar, albeit a little older. When Rock Hudson's battle against AIDS became public knowledge, it suddenly became respectable to voice concern and sympathy for AIDS victims. The plight of drought-ridden and starving Africans also caught wide-spread attention.

Music. Collaborative charity efforts manifested a ground swell of concern throughout the year, beginning with the British Band Aid project, continuing with the American U.S.A. for Africa performers, and climaxing with the gigantic, world-wide Live Aid concert, and its offshoot, the Farm Aid concert. Some of the most popular albums provided a mix of old and new artists and diverse themes and styles: Bruce Springsteen's *Born in the U.S.A.*, Tina Turner's *Private Dancer*, John Fogerty's *Centerfield*, Huey Lewis and the News's *Sports*, Madonna's *Like a Virgin*, Prince's *Around the World in a Day*, and Bryan Adams's *Reckless*. Springsteen's "No Surrender" exhibited an antiwar theme as did Turner's "We Don't Need Another Hero," from the apocalyptic movie *Mad Max beyond Thunderdome*. The fifties and sixties were revived with Fogerty's "Big Train from Memphis," Adams's "Summer of '69," Huey Lewis and the News's "The Heart of Rock and Roll (Is Still Beating),"and Springsteen's "My Hometown." And Sgt. Pepper was resurrected with Prince's album. More specifically, anti-Vietnam songs became more prevalent: "19" by Paul Hardcastle, "Killed in Action" by the Dead Kennedys, "The Wall" by Bernie Higgins, "Clean Cut Kid" by Bob Dylan, and "Born in the U.S.A.," by Springsteen, a song often misunderstood as merely a patriotic anthem. Madonna and some heavy metal groups came under attack by the PMRC (Parents' Music Resource Center) for their allegedly obscene, blasphemous, violent, occult and degrading music and videos. The PMRC's ostensible purpose was to encourage placing "warning labels" on albums. Much of this is symptomatic of the renewal of the revolutionary struggle, and more like it should be expected.

A Typology of Rock Music as Revolutionary Art

		The Fifties (1955–63)	The Sixties (1963–74)
REVOLUTIONARY	**NEGATION**	Elvis Presley, Chuck Berry, Little Richard, Bill Haley, Penguins, "Race" music, R & B, Doo-Wop, Rockabilly / Bo Diddley, Jerry Lee Lewis, Coasters, Midnighters, Billy Ward	Rolling Stones, Doors, John Prine, Bruce Springsteen, Alice Cooper, David Bowie, Frank Zappa, Blues-rock, Heavy metal / Folk–Protest, Randy Newman, Jimi Hendrix, Janis Joplin, Jefferson Airplane, Santana, Velvet Underground, Led Zeppelin
	AFFIRMATION	Ricky Nelson, Ray Charles, Buddy Holly, Drifters, Roy Orbison, Alan Freed, Beach Music	Beatles, Moody Blues, Beach Boys, Mamas & Papas, Harry Chapin, Stevie Wonder, Bob Dylan, Byrds, Grateful Dead, Joni Mitchell, Simon & Garfunkel, Folk–Rock, Jazz-Rock, Motown, Soul, Acid–Rock, Art–Rock, *Hair* / Monkees, Sly & the Family Stone, John Denver, Carly Simon, Love, Joan Baez, Kinks, James Brown, Supremes, CSNY, CCR
COOPTED	**LOSS OF THE IMMANENT**	Pat Boone, Bobby Darin–Rydell–Vinton–Vee, Annette Funicello, Paul Anka, Frankie Avalon, Connie Francis, "Covers," Schlock rock, Dick Clark	Insignificant or Nonexistent
	LOSS OF THE TRANSCENDENT	Insignificant or Nonexistent	Fugs, MC5, Lennon/Ono, Velvet Underground, Georgie Fame, Art–Rock, *Jesus Christ Superstar*

	The Interim (1974–80)		The Counterreaction (1980–___)	
REVOLUTIONARY NEGATION	Steely Dan B-52's Patti Smith Blondie Heart Clash Pink Floyd Devo Punk, Southern 　Boogie 　Outlaw-Country	Lou Reed Warren Zevon ZZ Top Kiss Rolling Stones Sex Pistols Billy Joel Tubes	B-52's Blondie Clash Billy Joel Robert Gordon Rockpile Adam & the Ants Stray Cats Devo Rick James Dead Kennedys Prince Crass Blasters Alarm Quiet Riot Neorockabilly 　Punk, Funk	Public Image 　Limited X Violent Femmes UB-40 Pink Floyd Bruce Springsteen Heavy Metal Punk–Country Neoprotest Bangles Randy Newman Rank & File Billy Idol Grandmaster Flash Rolling Stones
REVOLUTIONARY AFFIRMATION	Elton John Jimmy Buffett Al Stewart Rufus ELP John Lennon Paul McCartney War New Wave, Funk, 　Country-Rock, 　Reggae	Fleetwood Mac Supertramp The Band ABBA Bob Marley Kool & the Gang Eagles Santana	Elvis Costello Talking Heads John Lennon Paul McCartney The English Beat Human League Juluka Police Culture Club Peter Tosh Manhattan Transfer Pointer Sisters Reggae, New Wave, 　Female Rockers, 　African Rock	Waitresses Go-Go's Joan Jett U-2 Michael Jackson Big Country Bus Boys Los Illegals Cyndi Lauper Bob Dylan Neopsychedelia Latino Rock
CO-OPTED LOSS OF THE IMMANENT	Chicago Knack Carpenters Bee Gees Shawn Cassidy Village People Neil Diamond Jefferson Starship Bubblegum–Rock Disco, ''Soul Train''		Rick Springfield Rush Journey AC/DC Foreigner REO Speedwagon Linda Ronstadt Sheena Easton Pop–Rock, Top 40 Radio	
CO-OPTED LOSS OF THE TRANSCENDENT	Bob Dylan Holly Near Tom Waits Brian Eno Religious Rock, Feminist Folk–Rock, 　Art–Rock		Orchestral Manoeuvres in the Dark The Teardrop Explodes Japan Suicidal Tendencies Cabaret Voltaire Killing Joke Hard Core Punk, Avant-Garde, 　Electro-techno Rock	

The future is unpredictable, but I wouldn't be surprised to see the continued resurgence of revolutionary values and, consequently, an intensification of the conflict between the revolutionaries and the reawakened counterreaction. Just as the reaction is not merely a clone of the earlier established order, but something new and stronger, the resurgent revolutionaries cannot be the same as their past embodiment either. They too must prove stronger and renewed—or die.

In the previous pages I've made references to the media and the messages they have conveyed. Unlike many people, I feel that the revolutionary message subverted the media as often as the reverse. The second part of this book will explore this idea in some detail. At this point I only want to propose this notion.

The dialectic between music and culture really deserves a complete analysis of its own; nevertheless, the mutual influence should now be unmistakable. I do, however, plan to deal with selected episodes in the third part: The inception of the revolution in the fifties, the Beatles and Elvis Presley as its symbols, the sixties focus on liberation, California as a paradigm of cultural change, the soul/black power dynamic, and the resurgence of the revolution represented by new music phenomena such as punk, new wave, reggae, neorockabilly, and Third World rock.

The Typological Scheme

Recalling some of the ideas from the previous chapter is essential at this point. So here's a quick review: an authentic communication of a revolutionary message through art entails both *negation* and *affirmation*—inseparable facets of the dialectic between art and culture. However, the popularity of some artistic expressions (in this case rock music) has made them ripe targets for *co-optation* and exploitation by the established order, and not a few artists have been seduced or have "sold out." (The inducements to do so are not inconsequential.) The inevitable result is art that is either completely out of touch with the revolutionary movement of culture (*loss of immanence*) or completely submerged in the cultural dynamics with no overall critical perspective (*loss of transcendence*). In both cases, the effective communication of revolutionary values is rendered impossible, and the capability for negation and affirmation is not exercised as a result. Nevertheless, I still regard such lapses as authentic rock music; schlock, for example, didn't cease being rock; it just ceased being effective.

———————————— Other American Music ————————————

Obviously, not everyone has been listening to rock music during this period, a fact which can be very informative. Since people tend to identify with the kind of music that best portrays their values, the music they listen to can reveal the existence and character of the divergent groups in society. Although it is not possible to explore fully how these other musical expressions relate to America's cultural revolution, I do need to suggest how such an exploration might proceed.

Using the same categories developed for the typological scheme, I'll discuss in turn classical, jazz, blues, country and western, and pop. The first thing to notice about all of them is that despite the numbers of people who listen to and identify with them, the styles all originated prior to the mid fifties. They reflect the culture of an earlier time, in other words, not the time of cultural turmoil in which we now live. Hence, though they might have originated in a different period of cultural change, they cannot possibly communicate negation and affirmation today. As Marcuse so correctly observed, past traditions cannot be revived as revolutionary art. The only real effect they can have is to represent and support the established order to one degree or another. Put simply, they're all counterrevolutionary.

Classical music is the most difficult to deal with, involving as it does so much diversity, so many cultural groups, and such a long stretch of time. What interests me, however, is the classical music which has grown out of the American experience, the music of Copland, Piston, Ives, Rogers, and Gershwin for example. Perhaps the most striking feature about this music is its almost total transcendence. Using the ingredients of a past language and tradition, it attempts to relate to a present with which it has no real connection. Its contemporaneity notwithstanding, its representatives are atavisms, their language incapable of revolutionary (subversive) communication. In its extreme form, it even loses its connections with the past, becoming virtually pure transcendence in the process (as with the formless and spontaneous sounds and nonsounds of John Cage).

Much the same is true of jazz. Its dialect, so to speak, is outdated, even though it may have been authentically revolutionary at one time. As a matter of fact, it spoke quite effectively to the Beat Generation of the late forties and early fifties. Unfortunately, the Beats were far too small in number to bring off the revolutionary changes they all-too-cautiously and metaphorically suggested. Besides, the fundamental value orientation revealed by jazz is not as clearly contrary to the established order as that of rock music. In any case, like American classical music, it too no longer has any genuine dimension of immanence; it remains outside the actual movement of history.

Blues and C & W are similarly disabled, but their failure to communicate stems from the opposite flaw: they are too fully immanent to negate or affirm anything. Both, when expressed authentically, exhibit an acquiescence to the trials and miseries of life and a resignation that nothing can really be changed. Drinking, carousing, fighting, cheating, traveling, and the like, themes common to both of them, are merely efforts to suppress the pain and hurt of an unfriendly world. Despite the similarities with many themes in rock, these two styles lack the anger necessary for genuine negation and the enjoyment necessary for genuine affirmation. Insofar as they function as an expiation or catharsis, they drain off any revolutionary energy that might be present and thus play into the hands of the established order. Actually, C & W quite often reflects and recreates traditional values directly and seemingly offers the established order positive support. (But this may be so only to the extent that it is influenced by pop music.)

Of the styles noted so far, pop is the only one intrinsically inauthentic. It reflects no one's present experiences and so has no immanence whatsoever. Nor does it convey with any conviction any particular set of values, so it is totally devoid of transcendence as well. Pop music is best described as early rock and roll once was, namely, music consciously contrived to make money by appealing to the widest possible audience. Whatever is currently popular is imitated and marketed, and as such, it is form without substance, mere empty calories. All styles of music have fallen prey to "pop-ularizations"—classical, jazz, blues, C & W, and even rock; nothing is sacred. Muzak and the material played by the numerous "EZ" radio stations across the nation are only the most blatant examples. Others are revivals of earlier styles with no attachment to their experiential bases. In rock, Sha Na Na is the paradigm par excellence, although top-40 radio is hardly immune to the disease. In all cases, however, *imitation* (not making money) is pop's key distinguishing feature, no matter how difficult it might be accurately to diagnose its presence.

To summarize, except for pop music, all musical expressions are authentic. Rock, however, is the sole revolutionary styling. Blues and C & W are too immanent to be subversive, while classical and jazz are too transcendent. All of these latter, then, can only function as counterrevolutionary, despite the fact that rock has made enormous use of them (and owes them a considerable debt as a result).

Medium and Message
Part 2

Everybody experiences far more than he
understands. Yet it is experience, rather than
understanding, that influences behavior,
especially in collective matters of media and
technology, where the individual is almost
inevitably unaware of their effect upon him.

—Marshall McLuhan

Well I'm a-writin' this letter,
Gonna mail it to my local DJ.
Yes, it's the jumpin'est record I
    want my jockey to play.
Roll over Beethoven.
I got to hear it again today.

You know my temperature's risin',
The juke box blowin' a fuse.
My heart beatin' rhythm,
And my soul keep's a-singin' the blues.
Roll over Beethoven.
Tell Tchaikovsky the news.

—Chuck Berry

Once the darling of academic sophisticates, media observer Marshall McLuhan is now no more than a scholarly version of the Hula Hoop. (His sin was having become too popular, the kiss of death in the academic world.) But, dead though he may be, Marshall McLuhan cannot be ignored. Granted, he was pretentious, opaque, absurd, and frequently given to contradictions. But, at the same time, he was insightful, provocative, original, and, more often than not, right on the mark. He clearly saw America in the midst of a cultural revolution; he regarded the artist as partly a reflection and partly a shaper of the future; and he looked forward to the harmony of all in a new, more perfect world. This is my McLuhan.

The overall theme of McLuhan's *Understanding Media: The Extensions of Man* (1964) is precisely the prediction that the new electronic media have "wholeness, empathy and depth of awareness" as their "natural adjunct." McLuhan was confident that, no matter how long it took, a new world was in the process of being born. It couldn't be stopped short of returning to a pre-electronic age, and he was well aware of how that might occur.[1]

With the invention of the printing press, Western thought and culture assumed the logical structure we've come to accept uncritically as the nature of rationality itself. The revolution it brought about he called the Gutenberg Galaxy, and in a book of the same name he added the subtitle, "The Making of Typographic Man." Typographic people, from that time until the present, have attached the highest value to such things as uniformity, continuity, discreteness, specialization, and, perhaps above all, detachment. Among the many blessings of the Gutenberg technology has been the creation of nationalization, warfare, and selfish individualism. Literacy in the West, based on the incredibly flexible phonetic alphabet and made endlessly repeatable with typography, has held these rather disconcerting messages for us (along with their more positive results).

All of this, however, is slowly and inexorably coming to an end. With the introduction of electronics, another revolution has occurred. The possibility of instantaneous communications has expanded our perceptions and has thus made the world a very much smaller place. The term ''global village'' is McLuhanesque in origin, and it foreshadows a higher level of civilization in which the harmony of the tribe will be returned. Yet this harmony will recognize and even encourage individuality and diversity. (No wonder he was such a hot item during the sixties.) Unfortunately, as with all radical transformations, the process is bound to be painful at times and maddeningly slow; it takes cultures quite a while to catch up with new technologies and their concomitant values. The fact that these changes have come about far more slowly than he anticipated, imperceptibly some would say, should not lead us to conclude that he was wrong about everything. Cultural revolutionaries are notoriously impatient, and McLuhan was no exception.

Perhaps if he had paid more attention to what he himself was saying, he would have been able to discern more accurately the character of radical change, namely, that it does proceed imperceptibly and, for the most part, subliminally. Few are aware of what's happening until later, and some not even then. Only the ''arts'' have within them the capacity to know, in advance, which way the wind is blowing. On this, I think McLuhan was right on the mark; however, as he admits, this is not really a startling revelation: ''The power of the arts to anticipate future social and technological developments, by a generation or more, has long been recognized. . . . This concept of the arts as prophetic, contrasts with the popular idea of them as mere self-expression.'' But there's more than prophecy in McLuhan's notion of the artist's role: ''It is the artist's job to try to dislocate older media into postures that permit attention to the new . . . even though the majority of his audience may prefer to remain fixed in their old perceptual attitudes.'' Artists, in other words, are nothing less than the vanguard of the revolution.

They perform this function most effectively, however, when their work is manifested in commercial entertainment, and again I think he was right on target. Far from rendering the media universally inoffensive and neutral, entertainment ensures that program content will receive maximum exposure, pervading every aspect of our psychic and social lives. And even more pointedly, "entertainment pushed to an extreme becomes the main form of business and politics." (All of a sudden, entertainer-politicians become almost comprehensible.) Yet too much recognition and acclaim, as is the wont of those in the entertainment business, can be counterproductive. "To reward and to make celebrities of artists can . . . be a way of ignoring their prophetic work, and preventing its timely use for survival." Although McLuhan never expanded on this idea, in all probability he meant that a narrow fascination with personalities will inevitably blind us to the meaning of what artists create.

In what is perhaps the most suggestive (and confusing) slogan associated with him, "the medium is the message," McLuhan attempted to capture the essence of his complex and often unfathomable thought. Unquestionably, according to any reasonable measure, he failed. For the phrase remains almost as cryptic today as it was when he first introduced it. It always seems to require further clarification.

McLuhan intended to equate all media with technologies, and technologies with extensions of our bodies, senses or mind. Put a bit differently, but still in his own terms, media translate the human presence into other forms, thus linking the individual and society in an organic way. Technological innovations accomplish the translation with increasing speed and to a greater extent; hence, new media expand our social awareness and bring the world closer to us. Just about anything can qualify as a technology, like clothing as an extension of our skin, the telegraph as an extension of our hormonal system, and the credit card as an extension of our grasp. So the message of media *per se* is the extension of ourselves into time and space.

New technologies force a readjustment of all existing patterns of human relationships, and they cause all existing media to change so as to accommodate the new. In short, technological innovations are disruptive, accompanied by greater or lesser degrees of stress and strain. Since society is in effect the organic extension of humanity, social stress and individual stress are essentially undifferentiated.

Media, as extensions, also provide us with perceptual apparatus, so that new media introduce new perceptual tools. They alter our perceptions and thus our very consciousness. The meaning conveyed by this (its message) is nothing short of the creation of a new world. What we "see" is what we get.

The ostensible "content" of any medium is simply another medium. Speech for example is the content of writing, writing the content of print, and print the content of telegraphy. Hence, it should be obvious that there can be no such thing as the study of "content," for there is no such animal! There are only media, with their varied specific messages. Every medium has something particular to "say"; so media study should focus above all on the characteristics of the form in question.

When you put all these interpretive comments together, they add up to the fact that media are never neutral, with the capability of being used in many and various ways. Rather, the media themselves are value laden, communicating and often "imposing [their] assumptions on the unwary," irrespective of "what" is being communicated. The medium, as it were, is indeed the message.

McLuhan distinguished between "hot" and "cool" (or "cold") media. Usually, hot media involve the extension of but one sense; yet the really key feature is their intensity. They convey a lot of well organized, highly structured information. As a result, there is little need for audience participation to "fill in the blanks." Generally, the Gutenberg (or print) technology is hot. Cold media, on the other hand, are not nearly so well organized and structured. An example is electronic technology. Unlike its warmer kin, it has no fixed "point of view," no thematic perspective to be foisted already developed on the audience. Cold media are more like mosaics, necessitating a high degree of involvement and participation. What they present must be actively created and grasped; organization and structure are imposed, not passively received. But only under these conditions can genuine learning take place; coolness is an indispensable condition for the assimilation of any kind of data. (Seminars are, accordingly, far better than lectures as pedagogical techniques.)

The temperatures of the included media can apparently vary. For example, sometimes McLuhan saw radio as hot; at other times he described it in cool terms. In these latter instances, he seemingly had in mind the features that differentiate radio from some form of the print media, like newspapers. Newspapers, however, he often characterized as fundamentally mosaic! But he did so when referring to books and film, both having a decidedly fixed point of view.

Mixed media make the interpretation of McLuhan exceedingly complicated, with the results being unpredictable at best. In the most general sense, he felt that electronic media have now begun to mix with the mechanized, print media; and the message being sent by the hybrid forms is charged with energy. His analogy for the entire process was nuclear fusion (as opposed to fission); so he clearly anticipated a dramatic impact. "The hybrid or meeting of two media is a moment of truth and revelation from which new form is born . . . a moment of freedom and release.'' Apparently, out of the conflict something new is born, as when film emerged from the marriage of mechanical and electronic technologies, and the phonograph from the telegraph and telephone. But the electronic invasion of our overheated American culture has yet to fully and completely transform our thinking. In one of his most interesting series of observations, McLuhan said that, ''we have confused reason with literacy, and rationalism with a single technology. Thus in the electronic age, man seems to the conventional West to become irrational.'' IQ testing was a particularly good example of this tendency: ''Unaware of our typographic cultural bias, our testers assume that uniform and continuous habits are a sign of intelligence. . . .'' The West isn't prepared for the transformation of thought that it is presently undergoing.

Music, of course, is a medium, and it functions both as a ''content'' for other media (radio, records, film, etc.) and as a medium with ''contents'' of its own (language, sound, dance, etc.). Needless to say, music as medium and message is the concern of this second part of the book, and McLuhan will be popping up in various places throughout.

Though he never acknowledged rock music, he was nevertheless aware of the contrasts between the (hot) specialization and fragmentation of the symphonic idiom beginning in the sixteenth century and the (cool) participatory and unifying mosaic of jazz. He also stressed that the highly intense and ordered music of the symphony found embodiment in the waltz, while jazz dancing (and the twist) exemplified involvement and improvisation.

In any case, McLuhan was convinced that the impact of electronics would eventually bring about the revolution. Maybe McLuhan was right after all.

In the second part of the book, I've chosen to re-create my own experiences of the media and how I came to know and identify with rock culture through them. As will become quite evident, there has been a common element throughout all of my encounters with rock music; however, it's only become apparent to me after years of listening to and reflecting on the music and its attendant culture. I have in mind the almost always unexpected results of the dialectic between media and culture, especially when rock music is involved. This suggests the revolutionary power of this kind of music, which, when you really think about it, is merely another medium.

Radio:
The Creation of a
New Community

4

As with virtually every historical and personal turning point, this one, too, happened quite unintentionally. The specific events leading up to such changes can never be planned in advance, and the results of these changes are most certainly unforseeable. Turning points, especially the most important ones, are like this. Even conscious and deliberate efforts to control the flow of events are destined to be disappointing, perhaps all the more so for having been attempted. For all such attempts tend to be fundamentally mistaken: they center their efforts on the highly visible events thought to be ''causes,'' when in fact the genuine causes are likely to seem so insignificant as to be invisible. Concentrating on the pseudo-causes is inevitably self-defeating. Of course, all of this is only evident in retrospect, and even then I'm not so sure we can really know why things happen.

In any case, as I continue to look back over my shoulder, here is what seemingly happened to me and millions of others. No doubt the specific, invisible events differed in every case, but the eventual consequence was pretty much the same for all of us. For a variety of reasons, we had all reached a turning point in our lives; we had coalesced into a new, revolutionary community, despite all the efforts made to prevent it.

In the fifties, while most of my preteen peers in Baltimore had recently abandoned their radios for the newest toy on the market, television, I still enjoyed listening to the radio, especially at night. I was hardly immune to the seductive glow of the tube, but television pretty much went off the air in the early evening (''prime time'' was then somewhere around 6:00

P.M. to 8:00 P.M.), rendering our brand-new, twenty-inch Muntz totally useless at bedtime. I would go to sleep listening to the likes of "Fibber McGee and Molly," "Burns and Allen," "The Great Gildersleeve," "The Jack Benny Show" and, my only musical selection, "American Patrol." Every once in a while, I'd pick up a late-night talk show with some exotic guest who had just returned from Venus with proof that death was the most effective means of space travel. "Long John" from New York tended to emphasize or perhaps encourage the unusual (and sometimes dangerous) denizens of the night. (Rumor has it that early in the sixties one of his guests was none other than Lee Harvey Oswald, proclaiming something about aid for Cuba.) I realized that my interests were somewhat outside the norm, but I did pursue them in private at least. What I didn't realize was that I was listening to the dying gasps of radio as America had come to know it.

The decisive event for me seemed innocuous enough—troublesome, but hardly the kind of thing that could possibly alter the course of my life. Somehow, perhaps because my radio was cheap as well as ancient, the little station indicator broke off of the turning knob, rendering the search for the desired station something of an acquired skill—a skill I never completely mastered. I had to twist the knob until I heard something familiar and proceed from that point. And that's how it happened.

It was during one of my evening searches for the proper station that this seemingly insignificant event had its effect. It was the same effect that numerous other invisible events were having all across the country: random occurrences without a doubt, but no less momentous for their being no part of a master plan. As the direct consequence of my having to search for my desired station, I had chanced upon some music the likes of which I had never heard before, music I knew for certain I shouldn't be listening to.

I was familiar with the songs on the Hit Parade, of course. Everyone knew them: Perry Como's "Don't Let the Stars Get in Your Eyes," Patti Page's "(How Much is That) Doggie in the Window?," Les Paul and Mary Ford doing "Vaya Con Dios," Eddie Fisher's "Oh My Papa," and the latest, "Sh-Boom" by the Crew Cuts (or so I thought). All these ditties were harmless enough. But the music I had happened upon was different, incredibly different. All at once it was raw, sexy, exciting, gutsy, angry, scary, and unquestionably dangerous. I loved it.

As luck would have it, I had happened upon one of Baltimore's few black radio stations. And they were playing such songs as "Lawdy Miss

Clawdy'' by Lloyd Price, the Chords' (original) version of "Sh-Boom," and, unbelievably, the Dominoes' "Sixty Minute Man." With a swiftness unparalleled by anything other than a teenager's change of moods, I knew with absolute certainty that my parents wouldn't exactly appreciate this discovery with the same degree of ardor. Their reactions would have been nothing short of apoplectic, disclosing instantaneously (and perhaps even helping to create) a gap of understanding between us that would never be fully bridged again. Within days, for the first time in my life, I felt a comradery with my peers that I had never believed possible. I had never really liked very many of my fellow preteens, but at least most of them were now listening to same kind of music as I was—and we were doing it in secret, needless to say, a fact that further bonded us together.

We all knew, without ever having it spelled out for us, that this "nigger music" would be regarded by our parents as an imminent threat to our white, middle-class well-being. They were right, of course, although this was hardly something we were capable of admitting to ourselves, much less to them. In any case, even if we had been conscious of this threat, it wouldn't have made any difference in our behavior. To us at the time, all we were doing was listening to music, nothing more. Such is the extent of adolescent naiveté. Had we realized what was happening to us, I'm not sure we would have continued, not all of us, that is. I'd like to think that I would have been one of the few, but the traditions of centuries are not so easily overcome. In a very real sense, our naiveté was our salvation.

It became the "in" thing to do, listening surreptitiously to black radio stations and cluing in our friends. Not that we were by any means alone. The practice had become quite extensive, completely apart from anyone's intending it so. But with millions of teens and preteens tuning into and turning onto black music, it was not about to remain an underground phenomenon for very long.

As early as 1951, Alan Freed was on the air on WJW in Cleveland, with his "Moondog Show," an R & B ("race music") program oriented to whites. And as the decade moved on, more and more disc jockeys followed suit, which in a sense validated our vaguely disconcerting behavior (at least to ourselves). We could now listen to black music on white stations. Nevertheless, to even the most casual observer, something was afoot, and to the overwhelming majority of American society, it was something insidious. For if nothing else, blacks were communicating with whites through the language of music, and radio was largely responsible.

—————————————— Black Fascination ——————————————

Alan Freed wasn't alone for very long; he had tapped into something he himself probably never understood, something momentous; and others were exceedingly quick to pick up on it. Almost every major city had at least one station devoted to playing black music for whites, and they were usually placed at the ends of the AM dial. In Baltimore, I remember two black stations (WSID and WEBB) and two white imitators (WCAO and WITH), but I don't want to create the impression that these latter were exact duplicates. Far from it! Only some black music was acceptable to our parents, and a radio station would have been crazy to ignore the unspoken guidelines.

Much of the music played by these white stations was imitation as well. For some time, perceptive white artists had begun to "cover" black originals, usually cleansing them in the process. "Sh-Boom" is the paradigm par excellence, but the examples of this practice are plenteous. Other white musicians tried to duplicate the sound and sense of black music without explicitly covering anything. For example, LaVern Baker's "Tweedle Dee" was covered by Georgia Gibbs; Fats Domino's "Ain't That a Shame" by Pat Boone; Smiley Lewis's "I Hear You Knocking" by Gale Storm; and Gene and Eunice's "Ko Ko Mo" by Perry Como. (It goes without saying which versions made the most money, a situation which on reflection seems to have verged on larceny.) The white airwaves were filled with this kind of material. Not that all of it was bad, of course; it was, however, derivative and sanitized where necessary. Black music had to be judged "safe" before it could be played. From the perspective afforded by the passage of more than a few years, it might justifiably be wondered why such imitation stations were necessary to begin with. Why didn't we just listen to the black stations and be done with it? In reply, it must be remembered that this was still before Orval Faubus departed the governorship of Arkansas. Times were not yet changing.

Radio, contrary to portions of McLuhan, is a unifying medium; in no way does it isolate us from one another. Even while listening alone we are aware of others doing the same, even if this awareness isn't always conscious. The medium itself overcomes the physical separation and is, in a sense, its fundamental message. It retribalizes our diversified and alienated culture, creating empathy among listeners where none existed, bonding people together who would otherwise remain alienated. Therein lay radio's revolutionary import: whites were becoming involved and unified with blacks.

In Baltimore, as elsewhere, rock-and-roll radio attracted an intensely loyal following. Though defections most assuredly took place, a fickle listener would never be so foolish as to admit to such dissolute behavior. We proclaimed our allegiance while reviling all other stations not so fortunate as to have earned our favor. (The more contemporary practice of affixing bumper stickers is merely a continuation of the less formal protestations of allegiance.) A typical activity after a dance or movie was for aficionados of a particular station to co-opt one section of the local drive-in, open all the windows, and turn up the volume so high as to render the all-pervasive steak subs and french fries into cinders.

If any of us made a habit of listening to black radio, we most assuredly wouldn't admit it publicly. Very few of us would admit it privately. Most of us hadn't even met a black person outside of a service occupation. Our schools and (of course) our communities were rigidly segregated, and while many of us had mixed feelings about this, we weren't about to open ourselves to the accursed invective "nigger-lover." Listen to black radio? It would have been tantamount to inviting ostracism if not worse—especially since their songs included the Midnighters' "Work with Me Annie" and the Drifters' "Money Honey," pretty rough stuff for the early fifties. Prior to the late sixties, to identify in any way with blacks was not only a social abomination, it was positively dangerous and potentially life threatening. Contrary to what might have been intended, the white imitators kept us in contact with genuine black music.

I wonder to this day how many of us were aware of the subtle contradiction involved in our attitude. We mirrored our parents' racial prejudices while at the same time we became devoted to black music and indirectly to black culture. Imagine, if you will, a typical high school dance in the fifties, in a typical middle-class neighborhood: a sea of white faces writhing to the strains of decidedly black music. A consciousness thus divided is inherently unstable. Sooner or later such contradictions are bound to bring about changes, and we were teetering on the precipice of a dramatic conversion. We didn't think very much about it at the time, but the taste of black culture we were getting via the radio was addictive. It offered us something we couldn't get anywhere else.

McLuhan wrote that "radio affects most people intimately, person-to-person, offering a world of unspoken communication between writer-speaker and the listener. That is the immediate aspect of radio. A private experience. The subliminal depths of radio are charged with the resonating echoes of tribal horns and antique drums.'' And even more to the point, ''the message of radio is one of violent, unified implosion and resonance.'' It can and does create community where none before existed. Hence, ''our teenagers in the 1950s began to manifest many of the tribal stigmata. . . . To the teenager, radio gives privacy, and at the same time it provides the tight tribal bond of the world of the common market, of song, and of resonance.'' McLuhan even noticed that this ''independent isolation of the young makes them remote and inaccessible.'' But this inaccessibility was *not* from one another, as these words might suggest. Far from it. The inaccessibility he had in mind was from the adult world. He mentioned also in this connection that radio created the disc jockey and, not long thereafter, the disc jockey cult: ''The natural bias of radio to a close tie-in with diversified community groups is best manifested in the disc jockey cults,'' a fact that served to magnify and reinforce this isolation and inaccessibility.[1]

The unavoidable consequence of radio in the fifties was the creation of a new community, a community beginning to be fascinated with the black experience in America, regardless of whether or not its members were fully aware of what was happening to them. And most assuredly, they weren't.

Something had to give, and soon. The internal contradictions were becoming increasingly intolerable and had to be resolved one way or another. But no matter what the outcome, it had to have been something entirely different, something new. And most assuredly, it was.

The Backlash

Considering the values intrinsic to the kind of music that white middle-class youths were listening to, there was no way a reaction could have been avoided. And it wasn't long in coming, in the form of the payola hearings of 1959 and their assorted clones throughout the country. Everywhere it seemed that somebody was castigating and banning ''that nigger music.'' In what is perhaps the only genuine instance of Soviet-American agreement, rock and roll was found by both to be responsible for almost every lamentable social condition. If civilization were to crumble into dust, the blame would no doubt rest entirely on this new music of the young, so they proclaimed. Curiously enough, however, each side accused the other of instigating this insidious sound.

Accordingly, moves were made to destroy rock and roll or, at the very least, keep it under strict controls. By 1959, their efforts had suddenly become much easier. With Elvis willingly submitting to the draft, Chuck Berry jailed for a Mann Act violation, Jerry Lee Lewis disgraced by his marriage to his young cousin, Little Richard converted to the ministry, and Buddy Holly dead in an airplane crash, the way was clear for a major attempt to co-opt the heart and soul of rock and roll. Soon we began hearing something strangely different on our radios. Not that all of it was bad; it wasn't. It was, however, cleaned up and less raunchy. It was more about love and less about sex. And from what we were hearing, drinking had apparently come to an abrupt end in American life. But perhaps more significant than anything else, it wasn't angry anymore.

Among rock historians and authorities, it has become a commonplace, if not a divinely revealed truth, that nothing of any consequence was produced during this period before the Beatles. Fortunately, Dave Marsh and Kevin Stein help to discredit this idea in their *Book of Rock Lists*. Citing some of the Number One hits from this period makes their point quite well: Lloyd Price's ''Stagger Lee,'' Wilbert Harrison's ''Kansas City,'' the Drifters' ''Save the Last Dance for Me,'' Del Shannon's ''Runaway,'' Ernie K. Doe's ''Mother-in-Law,'' Dion's ''Runaround Sue,'' Little Eva's ''The Loco-Motion,'' the Crystals' ''He's a Rebel,'' and Stevie Wonder's ''Fingertips—Pt. 2.'' There is certainly enough in this list alone to shatter the myth.

On the other hand, beliefs of this kind (no matter how literally unsupportable they may be) originated and still have currency for some reason. In other words, there are more than a few grains of truth to the allegations made about this period. It wouldn't take too much effort to construct an even longer list of sanitized rock—music acceptable to those who intuitively understood the revolutionary meaning of genuine rock, and who just as intuitively feared it. Such a list would no doubt include David Seville's ''The Chipmunk Song,'' Frankie Avalon's ''Venus,'' Percy Faith's ''Theme from a Summer Place,'' Connie Francis's ''Everybody's Somebody's Fool,'' Pat Boone's ''Moody River,'' Bobby Vee's ''Take Care of My Baby,'' Shelley Fabares's ''Johnny Angel,'' Bobby Vinton's ''Roses Are Red,'' Little Peggy March's ''I Will Follow Him,'' and, rounding out the year 1963, giving credence to the charge as perhaps no other song could possibly do,

"Dominique," by the Singing Nun. To be sure, there's certainly nothing dangerous in this crowd.

Actually, a survey of the hits for any year would in all probability yield a comparable division: some gold, some trash. Needless to say, sincere minds are likely to differ on precisely where to locate the dividing line, but this dispute is not nearly as significant as the fact that this period was and still is perceived as being productive primarily of trash. This perception is what is crucial.

Although the period from 1959 through 1963 has been interpreted as stiflingly inauthentic and repressive, and although this is generally thought to be responsible for the poor quality of the music, this conviction has only become clear in retrospect. To be sure, there was a vague uncertainty gnawing away at our consciousness (which has also become apparent in retrospect). We were all perfectly aware of the tragedies, defections, and attacks with which this period began; we just didn't reflect on them very deeply, if at all. Not surprisingly, given our merest of overtures toward maturity, we weren't exactly perspicacious about any potential threats to our freedom. We sang to, danced to, hung out with, and necked to the schlock just as we did the good stuff. All we had to do if we didn't like a particular song was to switch to a different station. (As I recall, no one was in the least reluctant to voice an opinion about musical preferences, and such opinions were usually very strong.) Schlocky tune? No sweat. Just punch in something different. Yes, we were ignorant; yet our ignorance hardly mitigated the reality of the times. They *were* repressive, and all the more so for our blindness.

The effort to inhibit the growth of rock and roll or make use of it for nonrevolutionary purposes—in short, to defang and declaw it—is beyond dispute. The payola hearings epitomize the effort, yet they were merely the most visible sympton. The effort was widespread and thorough. Concerts were banned, disc jockeys smashed records on the air, and ministers of the gospel preached against it as the work of the devil. The white middle-class establishment was frightened; its actions were confused, uncoordinated, and generally ineffectual. Yet they were not without some impact. As far as radio is concerned, one of the most significant actions was the creation of top-40 programming, which took the choice of what was to be played out of the hands of individual disc jockeys. Executives, who were (and still are) much more amenable to the influence of the established order, now made up the playlists, and security and profits guided them in their selections as much as ideology. Together, these values led to the creation of an ironclad list of "safe" hits, the continual playing of which reinforced their sales, of course, making it doubly difficult for anything "dangerous" to succeed.

Despite the pervasiveness of this practice, however, radio had helped produce an audience on which it now depended for its very existence. No matter how offensive rock music seemed to be, its audience would have to be served. (The seventies TV program "WKRP in Cincinnati" was this reality incarnate.) And therein lay the seeds of self-contradiction, followed by conflict and change.

—————————— Switching Stations ——————————

Listeners to rock-and-roll radio are intensely loyal to the point of chauvinism, but not always to only one station, and not by any means forever. It is a little like remaining faithful to one spouse at a time. Actually, radio listening habits aren't nearly so restrictive; loyalty to more than one station at a time is acceptable without the accusation of being indiscriminate, so long as the stations are musically compatible.

What interests me is the process whereby loyalties are changed, the process of conversion. How is it that devoted fans abandon one station and commit themselves to another? Even more interesting, and perhaps more significant as well, is how they convert from one *type* of station to another, that is, from one type of music to another.

One thing I'm sure of, and that is that disc jockeys have very little, if anything, to do with it. Loyalty is given to the music that's played, not to the personality that plays it. I don't mean to suggest that disc jockeys do not become cult objects (as McLuhan suggested they were). On the contrary, on occasion they have been as popular as some of the musicians they broadcast. All I mean is that their popularity is derivative. Allegiance is given first to a kind of music, and only then to the jockeys who play it—*because* they play it. Where would Alan Freed have been without R & B? Who would have mythologized Wolfman Jack if he hadn't been playing rock? And needless to say, if it hadn't been for Liverpool's major contribution to the civilized world, very few would recognize the name of Murray the K.

My explanation for this process presupposes certain technological innovations and legislative reactions, but alone these are not sufficient. Some other factor is necessary if we are to grasp how and why such conversions take place. To illustrate, it is undeniably true that the rise of television destroyed the kind of radio programming that had existed so successfully from its inception: between 1949 and 1951, radio, practically en masse, converted to a music and deejay format. Also beyond dispute is the impact of the payola controversies in elevating the program director to a position of almost absolute authority in selecting which records would be played (if not their exact order). The restrictive playlists and top-40 programming that resulted were no doubt a prime cause of album oriented rock and underground radio, which came into being in the sixties. No less certain is the questionable role of market research in designing very limited programming for audiences defined with increasing specificity (thereby contributing to a resegregation of rock listeners). None of these developments, however, singly or in combination, can account for why any given listener might switch stations or alter listening habits.

Actually, the very success of AM radio (along with massive commercialization) and the invention of the push button radio (especially since such radios are almost exclusively located in the family car, which has always provided a place of refuge away from the adult world) go deeper in helping to explain the conversion process. Push buttons make it totally unnecessary to submit to the interference of commercials; more desirable songs can be sought out with a mere touch of the finger. Yet neither the push button nor commercialization can explain why a different *kind* of station might be punched into the radio, why someone might buy an FM tuner to avoid the AM dial, and why such intense loyalty is at the same time fickle.

The clue is contained in the counterproductive strategy of the radio networks and independents in the wake of the payola scandal. By this time, radio was fully and completely dependent on a vast teenage audience for its continued existence, so there was no question that their needs would be met. Yet at the same time, the traditional values of the established order had to be protected, for the radio stations were legally dependent on the political establishment for their existence as well. So radio found itself in the midst of two contradictory forces: On the one side were the vast hordes of American adolescents with a barely suppressed fascination with black culture, the values of which were anathema to the white middle-class establishment. On the other side were the "powers that be," manifested in the FCC—the agency that grants licenses to broadcasters—and, of course, their own personal sympathies.

The solution to these conflicting pressures, unbeknownst to all parties, was to result in strengthening the fledgling community of adolescents far beyond what any intentional effort to do so might have accomplished. Schlock rock and playlists were supposed to be the means for controlling the influence of undesirable music and what it represented; they were supposed to produce nothing more than "entertainment" and hence be completely inconsequential and most certainly harmless. McLuhan had some interesting observations about just such a tactic:

> The commercial interests who think to render media universally acceptable, invariably settle for "entertainment" as a strategy of neutrality. A more spectacular mode of the ostrich-in-sand could not be devised, for it ensures maximal pervasiveness for any medium whatever. . . . The commercial entertainment strategy automatically ensures maximal speed and force of impact for any medium, on psychic and social life equally. It thus becomes a comic strategy of unwitting self-liquidation, conducted by those who are dedicated to permanence, rather than to change.[2]

To put it a bit differently, schlock and top-40 were destined to produce their own downfall. They were programmed to self-destruct, much to the consternation of their most fervent advocates.

Radio for McLuhan was "the tribal drum" because it inevitably caused unification to occur. In the American environment of the fifties, this unification was disturbing to many. Radio, he felt, "provides the tight tribal bond of the common market, of song, and of resonance. . . . Our teenagers in the 1950s began to manifest many of the tribal stigmata." And by stigmata, he meant the indications of the unified group; among them are isolation from others, a self-identity, and the instinct of self-preservation. The first thing that comes to mind regarding these characteristics might be the teenage gang phenomenon of the fifties, but this is to miss the essential point, namely, that teenagers themselves, as an entire category, were unified into a definable group. Prior to the fifties, the term *teenager* simply didn't exist, for there was nothing to which it could refer.

Why people convert from one kind of music to another (from one station to another) has to do with the self-consciousness that radio has helped create. Given group identity and the instinct for self-preservation, it seems only natural for stations to be selected with these criteria in mind. When a particular station no longer offers support, another will be found (or brought into being by radio executives interested in their own self-preservation). Obviously not every adolescent is self-consciously a member of the same group; it's hard to conceive of any contention more ridiculous. But they can and do see themselves as members of the same *kinds* of groups, since they, for the most part, have the same kind of consciousness. This is what radio has helped bring about: a similarity of consciousness, a consciousness defined by its opposition to the established order.

—————— An Outlaw Consciousness ——————

No one knows better what can and cannot be broadcast over the air than the musicians themselves. I sincerely doubt that the MC5 expected the full, live version of their "Kick Out the Jams" to be played on any radio station. (They used the word "fuck.") Similarly, the Rolling Stones are hardly kept awake at night waiting to hear "Sweet Virginia." (The forbidden word "shit" this time.) And how many times has the Velvet Underground's "Heroin" been on any station's playlist? Or anything from Prince's *Controversy* album?

This is hardly surprising. In each of these cases (and the list of unplayable music could be expanded to become a book of its own), the offense against "community standards" is egregious. The wonder is that they were recorded in the first place. Some musicians are content to be heard only in a live performance; others, however, want as much exposure as possible, for a variety of reasons. Money and fans are obvious goals, and few artists of any kind are immune to such seductions. When these become the sole reasons for desiring mass exposure, it is not unreasonable to allege that a sellout has occurred (especially since such artists are likely to take great pains not to offend anyone who might possibly contribute to their care and feeding). In any case, there are many others who want the exposure for reasons in addition to these flagrantly materialistic blandishments, reasons having to do with the propagation of values. Now it is probably obvious, but it is worth pointing out anyway: whenever people see the need to propagate their cause, it is because their cause is not presently receiving much support. Hence, their music will almost inevitably be counter to the prevailing values and offensive as a consequence. So, like the establishment in the radio industry, this latter group of musicians found themselves in an apparently impossible position—trying to satisfy demands from two different directions: the values of the established order (as reflected in the radio industry) and those of their audience (which they shared).

An uneasy alliance was created by this coincidence of dilemmas. Radio executives and rock musicians both sought a way to play over the airwaves a kind of music that was threatening to the prevailing ethos. And, as mentioned above, the solution was to strengthen the community that radio had inadvertently brought into being.

This kind of jointly faced dilemma wasn't always the case, however. Not only was there a rigid segregation of music programming by race (with a relaxed standard for what could be broadcast by black stations), but until the midfifties there was also no mass adolescent audience on which most stations depended for their existence. Prior to the inception of America's cultural revolution, radio audiences simply mirrored the values of those in charge of broadcasting, to say nothing of their racial characteristics. The color lines were rigid and, for all practical purposes, teenagers didn't yet exist.

The solution to the mutually felt dilemma was no doubt obvious to everyone: tone down the expressions of antagonistic values without exactly denying them. To carry through with this solution, however, was another matter, requiring considerable skill and talent. For what was needed was an indirect method of communication, a way of saying it all without quite saying it all. Perhaps another way of putting it is that the form of the music needed to be softened so that the content could pass more easily. I don't mean to suggest that anything conspiratorial took place; much of what happened was probably unconscious. Indirect communication is simply a way of using the language (understood in the broadest possible sense) that suggests its meaning through a variety of literary, dramatic, auditory, and visual devices. Symbols, puns, double entendres, euphemisms, innuendos, ironies, surrealistic imagery, and the like have all been employed in the cause. Further, the sound of the music, the style of the performers, the context of the performance and even their costumery all "say" something, and they "say" it indirectly, and often unconsciously.

The effect of all this indirect communication, unintended, unanticipated and no doubt barely recognized by anyone, was nothing less than the creation of an outlaw consciousness, the often vague but nevertheless real awareness of oneself as being in some way illegitimate. In "I Dig Rock and Roll Music," Peter, Paul and Mary sang, "But if I really say it/The radio won't play it/Unless I lay it between the lines." They were only making explicit something everybody already knew, for laying it between the lines had by then become no less than the tribal language. The term "rock and roll" itself originated as a sexual reference, while "dancing" functioned as a more general sexual euphemism. So when Elvis sang "Good Rockin' Tonight" and Bobby Freeman "Do You Want to Dance?" there was little doubt as to what was being communicated. The Coasters, however, warned us about the consequences of indiscriminate sex with "Poison Ivy," a veiled reference to VD. Sexual aberrations have provided some interesting themes too: "Lola" by the Kinks and "Walk on the Wild Side" by Lou Reed are both rather celebratory of transsexuality and homosexuality. The proverbial generation gap is exacerbated by the Coasters' "Yakety Yak" and the Silhouettes' "Get a Job," while the Who did the same with "My Generation" and Chuck Berry with "Almost Grown." Although this content is pretty obvious, these latter songs also attacked more subtly the puritan notion of work and its alleged direct correlation with rewards. The Drifters despaired of the same correlation with "Money Honey." Naturally, political change was emphasized, especially as the sixties came into full swing, but with a particular slant: "Revolution" on the Beatles' "White Album" was ambiguous about the desirability of revolution; "A Hard Rain's A-Gonna Fall" by Bob Dylan has a specific meaning only if the listener attributes one to it; "Thank You Falettinme Be Mice Elf Again" is Sly and Family Stone's double-edged commentary about personal suppression, for the song appeared also in a very dark version as "Thank You for Talkin' to Me Africa." And the Who's "Won't Get Fooled Again" has those wonderful lines about "Meet the new boss/Same as the old boss." These are hardly naive sentiments, but neither are they obvious to the casual or alien listener. Also attacked is religion: "With God on Our Side" by Dylan (and sung by Joan Baez and Manfred Mann, among others) questions the basis of Western religion; groups such as Black Sabbath openly portray devil worship (probably to confound fundamentalists and to affect the guise of outrageousness); and numerous others have slyly advocated obeisance to Satan as a way of rejecting the received traditions, as with "Friend of the Devil" by the Grateful Dead and "Sympathy for the Devil" by the Rolling Stones. But as with "Revolution," only a careful listening will reveal that it's not spirituality but the Judeo-Christian spirituality that's being denounced. Again, not exactly a naive distinction. Finally, the attitude toward drugs is not nearly as simplistic as detractors are likely to think, for here, too, sophisticated distinctions are drawn: "The Pusher" by Steppenwolf and "Sam Stone" by John Prine are decidedly against drugs, while "Coming into Los Angeles" by Arlo Guthrie and "Let's Go Get Stoned" by Ray Charles are pro. More ambiguous songs include "Cracklin' Rose" by Neil Diamond, "Witchy Woman" by the Eagles, "Eight Miles High" by the Byrds, and numerous others.

Perhaps it's a bit too neat, but the antidrug songs are mostly about hard drugs, prodrug songs are about marijuana, and the ambiguous songs are about alcohol, cocaine, and hallucinogens, respectively. And this is only a small, sketchy sample.

Sometimes, of course, the lyrics and every other element of indirect communication are profoundly unintelligible, a fact that serves to illustrate an important point about this tribal language (and any language for that matter): namely, it is not so much what's said but how it's interpreted that counts. "Louie, Louie" by the Kingsmen is an excellent illustration. No one to my knowledge has ever been able to make sense out of what the Kingsmen are singing (assistance provided by other versions doesn't count). But this terminal uncertainty didn't halt the flow of reputedly "real" lyrics from circulating on college campuses across the country, few of which agreed; nor did it prevent radio stations from banning the record for a long time. All this when no one knew what was being sung! In essence, the true meaning of the song was its interpretation, regardless of what the Kingsmen might have actually sung. And without question the song was interpreted as clearly counter to the prevailing values. The film *Animal House* used it as its de facto anthem, and to this day it still evokes the feeling of genuine revolution.

This is precisely the process by which an alternate, underground consciousness arose. It came into being as a peculiar way of receiving or interpreting the sometimes cryptic musical messages. Whether the music caused the consciousness or the consciousness was there to begin with, having arisen from other causes, is probably impossible to recover. Probably they were mutually influential. In any case, it makes no real difference whether or not "Lucy in the Sky with Diamonds" is a reference to LSD; what matters is how it is interpreted by its listeners, and on this there is little doubt.

The consequence of all of this was, and continues to be, a reinforcement of a particular sense of self as outsider or outlaw. Of course the music of today is much more explicit than it was in the fifties, and censorship over what can and cannot be played has been relaxed, but the damage, so to speak, has already been done. This outlaw consciousness no longer depends on musical obscurities to reinforce its existence. On the contrary, the reverse is probably more the case for today. Berlin's "Sex," Prince's "Controversy," and Cyndi Lauper's "Girls Just Want to Have Fun," for example, leave little to the imagination. The various expressions of alternative values (both direct and indirect) result now from a sense of already being outside the mainstream of American culture; yet it remains true that the music still serves to strengthen this consciousness. The effect is still reciprocal.

It is worth remembering that our conception of reality is largely determined by our consciousness. Outlaws, being what they are, must inevitably see themselves in conflict with the established order, antagonistic to the status quo. And, in turn, the established order will inevitably see itself as threatened, and it will necessarily respond with hostility. In this kind of atmosphere, is there any wonder why a cultural revolution has come about?

Commercialization

A perennial critique of claims such as this concerns the allegedly overpowering lure of money. Supposedly, the pursuit of wealth is too strong for any revolutionary movement to withstand, especially in America where materialism is magnified to monstrous proportions. It is no doubt true that many revolutionaries do "sell out," but this reasoning alone misses the point. Cultural revolutions are more complex, more enduring, and more subtle than we are led to believe by equating them with political struggles. They have a life and power of their own, completely apart from any of their participants (proponents and opponents). Once set in motion, change is inevitable; nothing ever remains the same. To paraphrase Heraclitus and Bob Dylan, we can never watch the same river flow.

So, no matter how much money is used to reestablish the status quo ante, the effort can never work out as intended. It is not that the revolutionaries prevent it from happening, or that the allure of money is not as strong as feared, or that the establishment is weaker than hoped for. The fact is that the movement of history is in no one's control; the future is not a mere product of deliberate manipulation—anyone's.

Consider the various attempts to seduce and co-opt genuine rock and roll with covers and imitations. Such attempts, along with restrictive playlists, led not to a diminution of its impact but rather to the relocation of creative programming to FM, the hitherto forgotten child of radio. Thus an outlet was provided for the increasingly sociopolitical commentary of the music that began to characterize the midsixties. Covering in particular had the effect of publicizing the relatively unknown black originals, and it wasn't long before this practice ceased to exist.

But history continues to move, often contrary to our wishes, and certainly without giving us any advance warning. With the enormous increase in FM's popularity, commercial interests again entered the scene and brought with them the formulas that worked so well on AM: playlists and a top-40 format. With the exception of its being broadcast in stereo (which is even now changing), FM became little different than AM. This trend pretty much characterized radio during the interim period.

Now, however, just as the revolution seems to be confronted with a newly reinvigorated and more potent opposition (and as a consequence is being forced to make itself viable again), radio, too, is undergoing another change. Stations devoting some of their air time to what is increasingly being called "new music," including new wave, punk, techno-rock, avant-garde, neorockabilly and the like, have found a sudden and unexpected surge in their popularity. From 1979 to 1981, for example, the *Rolling Stone* readers poll conducted found Cleveland's WMMS, which has a new-music format, to be the nation's top station. In 1982, WMMS was joined by KLOL in Houston, WNEW in New York, WMMR in Philadelphia, and KROQ in Los Angeles, all of which play a variety of new music.

Consider also how commercialization has affected our perceptions about race relations. As radio in the fifties more or less capitulated to rock and roll, segregated programming was ended for all practical purposes—only on rock radio, of course. Integration had occurred in music and on the radio, if not in society. Now, by means of an exceedingly complex process, the attempt to exploit the popularity of this kind of racially indistinguishable music led to the semblance of resegregation. Although it was a genuine meeting of the races, this early achievement of integration was accomplished by whites allowing blacks to enter white society: white radio was the active agent, black music was passive. The commercial support for rock-and-roll radio then acted as an encouragement for blacks to develop apart from the now-unnecessary white support. Hence, in the sixties, along with the rise of black power and black pride movements, came Motown and soul. When this trend continued into funk and disco, radio stations were again exhibiting racial distinctiveness, but this time the separation was largely the result of black initiative. As this development, too, became popular, commercial interests stressed the creation of narrowly defined radio stations so as to cater to these "separatist" demands, further strengthening and encouraging black consciousness.

With the resurgence of a revitalized establishment, the revolutionary opposition has been forced to respond with a revitalization of its own, and this has meant a reformulation of the old coalition of outcasts. This time, however, blacks have joined on more equal terms, and most definitely with a stronger sense of self. The resulting merger has been, as it was in the fifties, a source of renewed creativity and energy, giving new life to the revolutionary values. This mutual rediscovery is a part of the new programming just now beginning to emerge, but it has a significance all its own. For during their period of separation, blacks and whites developed their musical traditions independent of one another, a situation that served to produce an enormous dynamism when again they met. Today, whites are listening to black music and blacks are listening to white music (McCartney's "Say, Say, Say," for example), and as before the primary medium of communication has been the radio. The resulting experience is remarkably similar to the excitement of the fifties, and we can thank commercial pressures for allowing us to recapture this revolutionary impetus. Soon blacks will recognize and appreciate Elvis Costello, the Jam, and the Clash; while whites have already come to know the likes of Prince, the Pointer Sisters, Rick James, and Patti Austin and will soon appreciate the Gap Band, Skyy, the Sugar Hill Gang, Angela Bofill, and Maze. Already a genuine breakthrough has happened with Michael Jackson's *Thriller* album; its top singles, "Billie Jean" and "Beat It," have topped both black *and* white charts, as has the album. The Jacksons' 1984 "Victory Tour," as well as their *Victory* album, was as popular with whites as with blacks. Perhaps even more significant, Michael's sex appeal is unselfconsciously biracial. Prince has had the same kind of biracial appeal, but with a harder and sharper edge. Michael Jackson is cute, but Prince is dangerous. Another significant breakthrough concerns Hall and Oates, a white duo with a large black following, evident in their performing and recording with Eddie Kendricks and David Ruffin of the original Temptations. A portent, I think.

So, the allegedly deadening hand of commercialization has not had the kind of effect so often attributed to it. It has neither stifled the creativity of rock nor corrupted the basic values of the cultural revolution. On the contrary, a good case could be made for the opposite. It seems that whenever pressure is applied at one location, another path is found or created to release the suppressed energy. Hence the temptation to observe, the greater the repression, the more creative the eventual response.

Records:
The Newest Testament

─────────────────── 5 ───────────────

The message of radio is records: it plays them, sells them, overexposes them, and eventually disposes of them. Along the way, the essential meaning of the electronic media is reinforced. It makes little difference which records are played or even what kind of music is on them. What is important is that they are records.

Every age has had its method for communicating the important news of the day. In the long period before the invention of movable type, oral communication was the dominant means. The ancient Greeks favored the allegory, and Jesus used the parable. Later, with stringed accompaniment, the troubadours of the eleventh through the thirteenth centuries entertained and passed along the latest news. With the introduction of the printing press, however, society became far more hierarchical and closely organized, and as a consequence, the masses became decidedly more passive. An increasing differentiation and isolation of one society from another also occurred. Such was the impact of a common culture spread through the medium of print. So said McLuhan.

The electronic media have changed all of this, not instantaneously of course. Nevertheless, a steady, revolutionary transformation has occurred since the inception of this new technology (this, too, according to McLuhan). All these changes have been in the direction of decentralization, unification, and retribalization—tendencies that McLuhan regarded as inevitable. The term he used to describe this movement was *implosion*, a rather graphic term. As the very opposite of the overheated explosive media of print, implosion suggests the contraction brought along by cooling.

If we understand implosiveness in terms of the values implicit in rock music, it is bound to include such stances as opposition to nationalism, religions, the military, authoritarianism, racism, sexism, and ignorance. Correspondingly, the values affirmed include freedom, individuality, happiness, mutuality, and harmony. All the electronic media tend in this direction; some, of course, more so than others, depending largely on how purely electronic they are (or how mixed they are with mechanical media). Also, specific media perhaps necessarily emphasize certain values over others. Not all implosive values are equally expressed, in other words. So it is important to keep in mind which electronic medium is under discussion—in this case, audio recordings.

Unfortunately, McLuhan himself wasn't very helpful when it came to a consideration of records. He did offer a few tantalizing suggestions regarding the phonograph, but he seemingly ignored his own notion that, as a medium, the message of the phonograph was necessarily another medium—records. I certainly don't wish to disparage what he said about record players, but I'm convinced that it is more important to concentrate on what they are designed to play. Nevertheless, there are some points to keep in mind about the equipment, namely, the progressive improvements in sound quality. From the earliest mechanical devices, through the perfection of tape (as the means for making records), to hi-fi and stereo, the enhancement of sound has contributed enormously to our developing revolutionary consciousness. McLuhan termed this "sound in depth," the multiplicity of sensory factors in one unified experience: "When a medium becomes a means of depth experience the old categories of 'classical' and 'popular' or of 'highbrow' and 'lowbrow' no longer obtain." He went on to add that anything approached or acquired "in depth" inevitably has the quality of seriousness about it, regardless of what it is. Total involvement makes this possible, so the development of stereo (and continuing improvements) cannot be overlooked.[1]

One of the maddening things about McLuhan was his refusal to offer sufficient evidence for some of his more provocative claims, and this idea about an in-depth experience was no exception. Yet, if we reflect on the time when stereo was introduced, there is an amazing coincidence between this and a new attitude toward rock music. Of course, it is equally possible that the new sound potential inspired rock musicians to new heights in artistry, but even if this were the case, it would only serve to provide an explanation for McLuhan's idea, it wouldn't call it into question. But in any case, my interest is in the recordings themselves and how they aided the implosive process in its creation and propagation of revolutionary values.

Having gone through adolescence in the fifties affords a unique perspective on this development and can provide as much confirmation of the impact of records as is perhaps possible. I can still recall, for example, buying my first few 45s almost as if it were earlier this afternoon. What really mattered was having my own personal record collection, something different than my parents', something that would establish my linkage with others of my own age and experiences. (Since what few records my parents owned were all 78s, this wasn't hard to accomplish; just owning those few 45s was quite sufficient.) Thinking back to the records I actually bought, the selection gives enormous credence to the medium's truly being the message. Since it was 1955, I bought a copy of "Rock around the Clock," but that was it as far as rock and roll was concerned. (Elvis wouldn't make it nationally until the following year.) The others included "Lisbon Antiqua" (Nelson Riddle), "The Yellow Rose of Texas" (Mitch Miller), "Cherry Pink and Apple Blossom White" (Perez Prado) and something taken from a Disney TV show called "The White Buffalo" by persons long since faded from my memory. I did have *some* discretion, of course; I didn't pick these at random. They represented what I was hearing on the radio. Yet, while I was secretly listening to the new and dangerous black music, to actually purchase one of these recordings was out of the question, no matter how much I liked it. There were limits to how far you could go with this new music, and no one had to tell me what they were. Besides, having my own collection was the significant thing, not so much what was in the collection. Only later would I begin to realize the effect that owning records had had on me, and by then the content of my collection would matter very much.

The War of the Revolution and the
—— Dissemination of Revolutionary Values ——

Today, few people remember the "Battle of the Speeds" in 1948. Very shortly after tape recordings made vast improvements in sound quality possible, CBS (Columbia) introduced the 33 1/3 rpm disc, mainly in order to produce symphonic music more cheaply and thus make it more attractive to consumers. At about the same time, RCA introduced its own highly improved disc, the 45 rpm. The spectacular increase in fidelity evident in both rendered the 78 rpm recording obsolete almost immediately, and by 1957, the record industry ceased making these fragile relics entirely.

The record-buying public was now confronted with a rather curious dilemma because of this rather sudden transformation in the technology: all existing equipment had to be replaced, or at the very least potential consumers had to contemplate which kind of equipment to buy. Initially, neither disc was compatible with the other's equipment. Unfamiliarity with the rapid succession of technology was yet another cause for hesitancy. (When my parents bought me my first LPs, all classical, we initially played—or rather tried to play—them on my grandparents' 78 rpm machine, which had a tone arm as heavy as a brick and a stone needle that mercilessly plowed through the grooves. We simply didn't know any different.) But, to the rescue came the ever-popular law of supply and demand. Both CBS and RCA soon offered their new equipment practically at cost, and Capitol began pressing *both* sizes, thus setting the trend for the future. From that time on, the newest equipment was designed to play all three speeds.

Sales took off. Jerry Hopkins, in *The Rock Story*, traces a steady, sharp rise from about 1954 on—precisely the year when rock music entered the American consciousness. (From 1921 to 1948 the growth in sales had increased but hardly at a rate likely to attract much attention.) The only significant exception to this meteoric rise (until the recession in the 1970s) occurred in 1959, when sales plummeted 25 percent, coinciding with the tragedies, defections, and scandals of the immediate period in rock music. Nevertheless, the new technology made possible the dissemination of this new form of music, which just happened to make its entrance onto the American scene at about this time.

Certainly Columbia didn't intend for popular music to be the prime beneficiary of this new technology, let alone music largely influenced by black culture and other assorted outcasts. Peter Goldmark, the president of CBS Labs, hoped that the LP would make classical music more appealing. It took about five 78s, for example, to record an entire symphony, something that could be accomplished on a single LP. Apparently, Goldmark and others like him thought that this and poor sound quality presented prohibitive difficulties for the enjoyment of classical music; however, while this is not untrue, it is only a small part of the explanation. Times were a-changing.

At first, classical music occupied most LPs. "Pop" sounds were relegated to the 45, with a resulting three minute or so time limit for any given song. In fact, the "song" itself was just about the only musical structure available for popular music. Significantly, ever since, the LP has retained this connotation of importance, while the 45 still seems to be the epitome of superficiality. Relating this to radio, "serious" rock music since the sixties has been associated with FM, which has always favored the LP and thus has helped to define a new genre of broadcasting: album-oriented rock. And still today, top-40 stations are almost exclusively limited to playing 45s. These acquired qualities should be kept in mind when considering the kind of message being conveyed by a given medium, for in many ways album rock has inherited the mantle of significance from the classics.

But history never pauses, and the technological changes just keep coming. Two new developments promise to have especially important impacts on values. One is the twelve-inch single, and the other is the new cassette laser disc and player.

The former really doesn't involve any new technology; it is more or less an elaboration of the single. Since it plays longer than the typical 45, its AM airplay might be somewhat limited, but the twelve-inch disc is very popular in dance clubs. Its real importance, however, concerns its impact on race relationships, and I'll comment on this in the next section.

Compact discs are another matter entirely; they are a genuine advance in technology and as such carry a decidedly new message. Although McLuhan never offered any observations about records per se, his theory about sound is helpful at this point. Referring to the introduction of high fidelity, or hi-fi, he maintained that "realistic sound" merged the senses of hearing and touch, with the result that the distance between performer and audience is largely overcome: "For the sensation of having the performing instruments 'right in the room with you' is a striving toward the union of the audile and tactile in a finesse of fiddles that is in large degree the sculptural experience. To be in the presence of performing musicians is to experience their touch and handling of instruments as tactile and kinetic, not just as resonant." Thus he characterized the "in depth" experience mentioned earlier.

With still greater improvements in sound quality, it stands to reason that the sensory involvement will become correspondingly greater. According to every audiophile and rock fan whose hearing is reasonably intact, the compact disc provides a quantum leap in this direction. As such, once the price for the equipment drops, it has the potential for creating an even more complete merger between performer and audience. Those familiar with it say that it quite literally sounds like the musicians are not three feet from your skull: you not only hear them you can almost see, feel, smell, and even taste them. Finally, it needs to be kept in mind that the more perfect the merger, the more complete the identification of

ideas and feelings. Such improvements as these tend to give the performers an enormous degree of influence over their audiences.

———————— Race and the Little Labels ————————

Being excluded has its curious advantages—one hopes to the chagrin and
consternation of those doing the exclusion. For those living on the outside, the prevailing norms weigh less heavily, and sometimes they can be
successfully ignored altogether. Outsiders have a certain freedom that
those on the inside can never possess; after all, social pariahs have no
power to threaten the established order, so they aren't considered dangerous. Their comparative freedom costs society little. (Of course they
receive no social benefits either.) Prior to the advent of the cultural revolution marked by the rise of rock music, this was precisely the situation
with record companies that were producing black music (at that time
called "race" or "sepia" and later "cat" music). They were outsiders,
excluded, barely existing in the enormous shadows of the then big three
(Decca, Columbia, and RCA Victor, with Capitol trailing as a poor
fourth). They were such labels as Aladdin, Argo, Aristocrat, Atlantic,
Chance, Chess, Cobra, Dot, Duke, Dunhill, Federal, Gee, Herald, Im-
perial, Jubilee, King, Rama, Savoy, Specialty, Stax/Volt, Sun, Vee-Jay,
and many others that have long since faded from memory. Much of their
output was devoted to black music, and it isn't hard to imagine the extent
of their distribution capabilities—just about nil. If you wanted to buy
something they produced, you pretty much had to go to where they
recorded—if you could even know what they produced.

Because of its relatively high degree of freedom from the prevailing
cultural norms, black consciousness was permitted to express itself in an
almost undiluted form. Music has always provided this kind of outlet,
from the time of slavery up to and including the present. In fact, music
has been one of the few means of black expression available to whites.
This is the kind of material that disc jockeys like Alan Freed began playing for white adolescents in the early fifties.

The rapidly increasing popularity of this music caught the attention of
the majors and forced them to revise their practices in order to compete.
The competitive struggle that ensued was obviously unequal, and many
of the small companies were bought out or otherwise put out of business
(for example, Jubilee, Herald/Ember and Savoy). Only a few survived,

and fewer still went on to become majors in their own right (for example, Atlantic, Roulette, and Dot).

Despite the fact that financial success did not follow the popularity of the music they recorded, there was nevertheless success of another kind. A different and conflicting set of fundamental values was introduced into American culture, acquainting white adolescents with the black side of America in the process. But more important than even this was the fact of communication itself: the years of slavery and segregation had made it virtually impossible for the races to communicate honestly face to face. Now, for the first time in American history, whites were authentically hearing what blacks were saying. (Blacks were always capable of knowing what whites were saying and thinking, for it was never risky for whites to reveal themselves to blacks, much as servants are often privy to knowledge about their employers that even the employers' families never know. The powerless need not be feared.) To be more accurate, it was principally white youth who were doing the listening; white parents were mainly becoming apoplectic because of what their children were hearing.

Prejudice, ignorance, superstition, hatred, and fear can only exist in the absence of genuine communication. With the invention of cheap 45s, authentic communication between the races began to take place. I don't mean to give the impression that white adolescents, en masse, bought into black culture. Hardly. This no doubt would have been quite dramatic, but not altogether significant. What was really significant was the fact that they were truly listening. It shouldn't seem so strange, then, that it was precisely this generation that found itself uncomfortable with the whole ideology of racism and all its attendant beliefs. Not that racism immediately came to an end with the listening to black music. Far from it. But white youth could no longer feel secure with the attitudes bequeathed to them; they now knew too much. One incredibly naive belief shared by most whites throughout American history was the notion that blacks were either happy with their lot in life (no doubt since they realized their innate inferiority and were grateful for whatever blessings were bestowed on them) or too stupid to know any different. Listening to virtually *any* black recording would dispel that belief almost instantaneously. Well, maybe you'd need to listen to several. Certainly any recording by Grandmaster Flash, the Bus Boys, or Run–D.M.C. should do the trick. Anyway, the nagging suspicion gradually, but inevitably, arose that other beliefs about blacks were equally absurd. No, racism didn't magically die with a few records, but at least for the adolescents of the fifties, racist ideology could never again provide one of the unquestioned building blocks of American society.

Today, interracial communication is just as vital, and as before, it tends to occur through music. Partly as a result of blacks' withdrawing from mainstream (white) society for reasons of pride and integrity, isolation of a different kind developed. Since the mid sixties, rock music has reflected and has served to reinforce this separation. In this case, the separation was not all bad; the reestablishment of self-esteem was its major accomplishment. Yet something new is afoot, and as before it has to do with technology. A few artists are now being recorded on twelve-inch discs (33⅓ and 45) as well as on the standard LP and single. Although this may seem to be nothing more than a clever marketing device (since it gives them exposure to the dance floor in preference to the other two), note well what rock critic Robert Hilburn has to say about them (*Los Angeles Times*, February 13, 1983):

> The lure of the 12-inch single is partly functional. The large discs generally allow better sound because the discs utilize wider grooves. In most cases, they also provide a longer and even punchier rendition of the song. . . .
>
> The 12-inch revolution also is tied to a musical style: a disco/new wave merger that may turn out to be the biggest commercial and creative force in pop over the next few years.
>
> Besides providing many of today's most exciting and adventurous records, this "dance" or "modern" music hybrid could also be enormously helpful in breaking down much of the racial and cultural isolation that has plagued pop music since the early '70s.
>
> The best of the new music combines the sensual urgency of the peppy, R&B-affiliated sound that first found favor in disco with the wry sensibility of punk and new wave rock.
>
> Once outspoken enemies, disco fans and the electro-pop new wave followers have now discovered a common meeting ground in the hot pulse of 12-inch dance records. . . .
>
> Indeed, the 12-inch single could be as integral a part of pop in the '80s as 45-rpm singles were in the '50s and long-play albums were in the '60s.[2]

Hilburn's optimism might be considered excessive, since there really hasn't been enough time to assess the impact of the twelve-inch disc. Nevertheless, there is again communication across racial lines, and this does give some basis for hope. Also worth noting is the possibility of genuine communication between "straights" and "gays." One of the unspoken reasons for the widespread antipathy against disco was its association with homosexual dance clubs, and with this new musical merger, some of the ignorance about sexual preference might be dispelled as well.

———————— Sex and the 45 ————————

One of Hilburn's points is undeniably correct: the 45 was indeed an integral part of the fifties, and probably to a greater extent than he had in mind. For its impact, in good McLuhanesque fashion, had as much to do with its form as with its content.

It is hard to image what the fifties would have been like without this doughnut-shaped seven-inch disc. Quite simply, the fifties, as we've come to know them, would never have existed were it not for the 45. Consider for a moment the challenge it presented to the puritan notion of sexuality and the traditional conception of the family. These were among the most important pillars of prefifties American culture, and the Samsonian task of pulling them down was accomplished to a large extent by this seemingly innocuous novelty.

With regard to its impact on sexual morality, the ends-and-means relationship was simply reversed. The preponderant attitude toward sexuality in the Western religious tradition has always been one of barely suppressed suspicion, especially in Christianity. Although the dualism between flesh and spirit had long ago been declared heretical, and despite the fact that sex was regarded as part of the goodness of God's creation, it was, and continues to be, good only as a *means*. Roman Catholics have traditionally viewed sex solely as the means for the propagation of children; more recently, however, the Catholic church has begun to interpret this goal more broadly. Protestants and Jews have almost always acknowledged a wider role. Nevertheless, for them, too, sex is properly a means and only a means. Propagation is only one facet of its intended end; the enhancement of marriage and the strengthening of family life in general are its other goals. In *no* case has sex been regarded by Western religious thought as valuable in and of itself. This notion, however, is precisely what emerged as a result of the 45 r.p.m. record.

The typical teenage party is a case in point. In the fifties, and no doubt still today, a necessary prerequisite for any *valid* party was music, and this may actually have been sufficient as well. In any case, a "stack of platters" on that little RCA record player would permit uninterrupted dancing for quite a while. No one but the most prodigious, of course, could maintain such a pace for very long, and besides, there were other things to do—necking to be specific. Once the parents frequented the downstairs rec room less often (or wherever else the party was held), the real party could begin. Couples would take turns being stationed by the door to warn of the parents' impending return; then the lights would be lowered or simply turned off. The key deception was provided by those easily handled 45s, since from upstairs it would still sound like dancing was going on. The "stack of platters" would now provide uninterrupted cover for necking and even some heavy petting; the giant holes in the records and the configuration of the player made turning them over in the dark "no sweat."

To modify a proverb, opportunity may be the mother of invention; in this case the opportunity allowed for the invention of sex as something desirable (valuable) in and of itself. The party was merely one of the means to accomplish this end, and parties were rated as to how effective they were. Sex had become the sole measure of success.

"Record hops" (or "sock hops" when held in the school gym, since leather shoes and the wood floor were deemed incompatible) became yet another way to approximate the goal. The measure of success or effectiveness in this case, however, was partly in terms of whether a party date could be arranged. Another measure concerned what could be arranged for *after* the dance, at the local "passion pit." The record hop has always been hormone city, everyone restlessly maneuvering for position (literally and figuratively). Take the "slow dance" for example: the slower and closer the dancing, the greater likelihood that things bode well for afterwards. ("Need a ride home?") The adult authorities, of course, didn't stand idly by, allowing this to go on unimpeded. There were rules! One was that dancing must always include perceptible movement (presumably to prevent pure, uninhibited embracing on the dance floor; the semblance of a dance had to be retained after all). Often a yardstick or a plumb was used to assess the degree of compliance, and just as often it became a joke to see who could comply with the *least* amount of motion. Another rule prohibited the so-called "dirty boogie," the jitterbug with suggestive pelvic gestures—a portrayal of copulation. The "dirty boogie" would always attract an appreciative audience which would circle around the offending couple and thus provide them with a temporary, protective screen. The fact that this practice no longer occurs to any appreciable extent merely illustrates how threatening any open display of sexuality was in the fifties.

So, you ask, what has this to do with the 45 rpm record? They weren't called "record hops" for nothing! Their very *raison d'etre* was to play and dance to the latest recordings. Often, local disc jockeys would be hired as a special attraction, but their appearances were incidental. Sex was the goal, and the records provided the means.

The family was affected just as much, although the impact was more indirect. Prior to the advent of the infamous record hop, the whole boy-meets-girl courtship ritual was carried out under the auspices of the family. I don't mean to suggest by this that parental control was either complete or even very effective. If this were *ever* true, it was characteristic of an age long before the emergence of the automobile. What I mean is that courtship was at one time legitimated by being carried out under the guidance and patronage of the family; the effectiveness of this guidance and patronage is another issue entirely.

Prior to the record hop, dances were major events requiring planning, organization, and cooperation. For dancing to take place, the group needed a live band, which has always given such occasions a decidedly different flavor. Parents necessarily had (and still have) a greater role: they gave permission to use the car (or they drove the couple), provided the funds, met the date, took the pictures for posterity, and waited up late hoping for the couple's safe return. Record hops were something entirely different. Their casualness and informality obviated the parental role almost completely. Many were held immediately after school or after a sporting event, ruling out any possibility of formality. Others were sponsored by the local department of recreation ("recs" or "teen centers") and were held every weekend, eliminating their uniqueness. Rarely was dating practiced (no "stag or drag" pricing), so meeting parents and having them take pictures became irrelevant. Since the events were held early and/or regularly, parental worrying was minimized. Sometimes parents didn't even know their children had gone to a record hop: it didn't seem important enough to be concerned about; so parents didn't ask and their children didn't say. But what neither clearly recognized was the fact that the accepted pattern of courtship was being flagrantly violated: the parents were unaware because the interactions were all happening out of their sight, and their children because they didn't know any different.

When this challenge to the family's authority is added to the value reversal regarding sex, there is considerable evidence for the impact of the 45—quite apart from the songs recorded thereon.

—————————————— Politics and the LP ——————————————

Without the LP, rock would have remained essentially apolitical and would have provided no real threat to the established order. The LP has always connoted an element of seriousness, so when rock music was first recorded on LPs in about 1960, it was inevitably regarded differently. To be specific, I have in mind only those rock albums designed intentionally as such, not collections of previously released singles. The creation of an album of rock music is not at all the same as the production of a single, and the implications of this difference are extremely important.

The production of rock LPs became well nigh universal by 1963. Singles became the derivative medium as a consequence (with very few exceptions). Some popular music, in addition to classical, had been recorded on albums prior to this period, but not (significantly) blues, C & W, or rock and roll. These latter were thought (perhaps unconsciously) not to permit such quality treatment. The Beach Boys were the first rock performers consistently to break through the barrier and make it onto the charts beginning with *Surfin' USA* in 1963. (Elvis, Ricky Nelson, Dion, and Chubby Checker had a few entries prior to this, but they lacked the album orientation of the Beach Boys.) Then in 1964, the floodgates were opened with *Meet the Beatles*, the year's top album and the first time a rock album made it to the number one spot. Soon there emerged the "concept album," an LP devoted to the expression of a specific theme. While the Beatles are usually given credit for this development with *Sgt. Pepper*, the practice has become comparatively common among rock musicians today. (Pink Floyd, for example, has done little else.) What is important, however, is not whether an album is intended as a concept album; it is the album medium itself that carries the message of seriousness.

Some clarification is needed. First, seriousness should not be understood to imply dourness or humorlessness or anything of the sort. On the contrary, seriousness can easily encompass humor, joy, pleasure and all sorts of fun. *Talk Show* by the Go-Gos exemplifies this perfectly. True seriousness is merely the opposite of triviality and frivolity, and it need not have been consciously intended as such. What is important is that it be interpreted as such. The vital aspect of messages is not how they're sent but how they're received. Second, as far as possible, I want to focus on the qualities of the $33 1/3$ rpm recording itself, not on the peculiarities of its contents. And third, while what naturally comes to mind is stereophonic sound, or at the very least high fidelity, most of the following can just as easily apply to the early monaural recordings as well.

Individually, these characteristics may seem relatively unimportant, but together they make a pretty convincing case. One has to do with the price of an album in comparison with that of a single. Because of this, it has never been an easy decision to buy an LP; buying a 45 can almost be done on a whim, but buying an album takes some thought. It is not simply a matter of the amount of time spent in deciding; it's more a matter of the source of the decision. Singles are bought mostly as the result of caprice, prompted by forces outside of the deciding agent (usually the force in question is the familiarity created by excessive airplay). Few albums are bought like this. Most are purchased on the basis of reviews, hearing them first, trusting what others say about them, and the artists' past performances. In other words, the decision to buy a single stems largely from external causes, while the decision to buy an album originates internally.

It is also significant to consider where the album is kept once it's purchased. Singles are packed away in those little carrying cases or in some other inconspicuous place. Albums, however, require their own furniture. Hence, even small collections necessarily become part of the home's decor. Because of their size, they can never be an incidental feature of the room; they have to be deliberately placed into their setting (like the sound equipment itself) available to anyone interested in checking out the collection.

Yet another distinguishing quality is the album's artwork. The jacket's size and relative permanence permit some rather elaborate endeavors of various kinds, and there are quite a few books devoted exclusively to album art as a field in its own right. But regardless of the quality of any given album cover, the artist must give some thought to how the art relates to the contents of the album. And since this is "commercial" art (as if there were any other kind), some consideration is inevitably given to the effectiveness of the artwork in selling the album. The art, in other words, is never the product of accident.

A related quality concerns the liner notes. Something has to fill up the back side of the album, if not further art, and the inner sleeve isn't usually allowed to go to waste either. (Cheap repressings are another matter entirely.) As with the artwork, thought has to be given to the notes' relationship with the contents as well as to potential sales; again, nothing is left to chance. Interestingly, the punk movement of the late 1970s and early 1980s quite self-consciously avoided both art and notes, as a symbolic rejection of the kind of image and attitude that had at that time become associated with the album medium. Of course, this very denial was the result of a calculated decision; this too was not done by happenstance.

Thus the decisions as to what will be included on the album require careful thought, aesthetic as well as commercial. Moreover, attention has to be given to which cuts should be released as singles because they will receive most of the airplay. If the singles make the charts, the chances increase that the album will do well too.

The kind of station that's likely to play cuts from the album directly, without relying on singles, is obviously one devoted to AOR (album-oriented rock), and this means FM almost exclusively (despite the fact that FM programming has tended to emulate AM in recent years). This, too, contributes to the connotation of seriousness.

One element common to all these various qualities is thought, or more specifically, the reasoning process. The reasoning may not always be very good, but it is unavoidable, and it is essentially political. Thought, after all, is intrinsically connected with the act of choice, the making of decisions, and choices are nothing other than evaluations: goodness and badness might even be defined as our affirmations and negations. The evaluation of alternatives, to continue, is at basis the political process itself—its heart and soul.

The fact that the kinds of decisions relating to rock albums have been remarkably consistent is obviously significant, and this consistency is largely what this book is about. People who produce and purchase rock albums share certain fundamental values, and as it happens these values are in conflict with the traditional values of our culture. Why this is the case has a lot to do with the historical context, and this will be the theme of the third part of the book.

——— The Counterculture and the Record Store ———

A certain kind of record store epitomizes the dialectical relationship between the values of the traditional culture and those of the counterculture. Some features are obvious. In addition to an emphasis on rock music, there are clothing, books, and magazines, all with an identifiable antiestablishment character. Often such record shops sell drug paraphernalia as well. Virtually every city or town has such a store or a chain of such stores.

What makes them essentially different from other record stores is their attitudes toward the records. On the surface, all record stores are doing the same thing—selling records for a profit. But whereas in the traditional record store the records are merely the commodity to be sold, having only extrinsic value, in the counterculture store the records are regarded as intrinsically valuable. To put it differently, in the former the records exist for the business, and in the latter the business exists for the records. Profit isn't denied; it's just relegated to the status of necessary means for the distribution of records. I realize that this is a bit simplistic, but the idea is nevertheless valid. (As a small caveat, I have in mind the attitude conveyed by the sales personnel and not by the owners, who must in any case be aware of the image being presented.)

Thus understood, the counterculture record store functions as a haven, a sanctuary from the established order. To see this, the observer need only witness the discomfort of ''straights'' who enter this alien environment. If ever there were a litmus test for values, this might be it: a discomfort index for customers. In any case, it is here, if nowhere else, that rock-and-roll recordings can properly be appreciated for what they truly are: the principal means for the dissemination of revolutionary values, the latest form of testimonial.

Film:
A Creative Tension

6

Film is a hybrid medium according to McLuhan, being "a spectacular wedding of the old mechanical technology and the new electric world." Visually, film is closely associated with hot, intense technology and the lineally structured rationality of print; whereas the presence of sound places film squarely within the revolution brought about by electronic technology. This was more than merely an aesthetic development. According to McLuhan, the electromagnetic sound track already forecast the substitution of an electronic implosion for a mechanical explosion.

The inevitable result of all such hybrids is internal tension and the consequent release of energy. The way energy is released, however, depends on the cultural context in which the hybrid develops. In the highly literate West, for example, an electronic implosion must inevitably lead to the steady transformation of fragmentated cultures into ones that are highly interdependent. Nuclear fusion was McLuhan's analogy. Human relationships could be expected to undergo a similar change.

With this idea in mind, there are two key elements to consider about film as a medium for rock music. One is the dichotomy between the visuals and the sound track. The other is the enormous tension produced by film in our highly literate society and the possibility of serious conflict as a result. Rock music has exacerbated this tension and has speeded the transformation along.

The object of this chapter is to investigate the interrelationships among rock music, film, and culture; hence, I'll be concentrating only on those films that have as their thematic content the periods in which they were produced. So there won't be any analyses of documentaries (for example, *Woodstock*), concerts (for example, *The Last Waltz*), retrospectives (for example, *American Graffitti*), biographies (for example, *The Buddy Holly Story*), and nonperiod films using postsynchronous rock music as interpretive of the plot (for example, *Apocalypse Now*). All of these are secondary or derivative; they do not permit us to view the period directly, as if we were actually there. To do this, we have to concentrate on films that (1) portray the period in which they were made and (2) are fictional in their narrative.

The first condition is obvious: self-examinations like this make direct access to the period possible. But it might be objected that no film can do this. All films are the products of the collaborative efforts of everyone involved (writers, directors, actors/actresses, editors, producers, cinematographers, etc.); so they are all necessarily derivative. Obviously, there's a point to this objection; portrayals of events are not the events themselves. This, however, is precisely why I've specified the second condition. For what interests me, and what I find directly revealing of the times, is the collaborative effort itself—as interpretation (not as factual reportage, which it could never be). These film *interpretations* are direct manifestations of the periods in which they took place. Authenticity, not accuracy, is the ultimate criterion for selecting a film for consideration, and the sustained narrative of a fiction film provides the most authentic cultural artifact. With fiction, after all, there need be no attempt to have the narrative correspond with brute facts (even if there were such raw, uninterpreted data); nothing need interfere with the interpretive effort. In short, the interpretation itself is the artifact.

Second, we shouldn't get bogged down with aesthetic criteria. Even if there actually were such standards, and even if they could be determined apart from mere personal taste, they would be irrelevant here. "Bad" films can be just as revealing as "good" ones. Some will always be more revealing than others, of course, but this has nothing to do with their quality.

Third, the time periods I've already suggested will provide the structure for the analysis: the fifties (1955–63), the sixties (1964–74), the interim (1975–79) and the counterreaction (1980–present). Each of these periods is characterized by a certain attitude toward fundamental values, attitudes unrelated to any particular set of emotions. Negation and affirmation can be expressed in a variety of ways, including those that might seem paradoxical.

Finally, by utilizing the dichotomy between visuals and sound, I want to suggest how the revolutionary process has been reflected in film. Basically, each stage of thought and history eventually produces its own negation, which causes internal conflict. This antagonism eventuates in the creation of a new stage, which then undergoes the same process as the earlier stage. And so it goes.

The Fifties

As a period of negation, the prevailing value structure was often attacked with a vengeance. Some of the earliest youth films of this era had the attack itself as the principal theme. Most important were *The Wild One* (1954), *Rebel without a Cause* (1955), and *The Blackboard Jungle* (1955), beginning a new genre, teenage *film noir*. With the notable exception of *Wild One*, they wound up reaffirming the traditional values. The attack was portrayed as superficial, ineffectual, and most certainly evil; the initially appealing bad guys always got what was coming to them, their threats having been thwarted by the reawakened virtue of the established order; society was then returned to its previous state, stronger and wiser for the experience. We need only reflect on the conflict between Glenn Ford and Vic Morrow, the teacher and the teenager, in *Blackboard Jungle*. There was never any doubt as to the eventual victor. Rock music, however, was absent from the sound track of these films (*Blackboard Jungle* being a special case), a fact that called attention to its existence and presence all the more. Nobody was fooled.

When it was explicitly introduced as the focus of the film, an interesting contradiction began to emerge. Support for established values was maintained in the narrative, but the music in the sound track simultaneously called them into question. Some of the more interesting internally divided films include *Rock around the Clock* (1956), *The Girl Can't Help It* (1956), *Don't Knock the Rock* (1956), *Shake, Rattle and Rock* (1956), *Loving You* (1956), *Jailhouse Rock* (1957), and *King Creole* (1958). A scene from *Don't Knock the Rock* illustrates this point beautifully. Ostensibly, the message of the film is that rock and roll is simply the most recent expression of youthful exuberance, no different from that embodied in the dance crazes of earlier generations. Its bad rep is undeserved and based on ignorance, easily enough overcome. Yet, at an impromptu party at one of the kids' homes, while the parents are away no less (the ideal teenage party), the dancers get so carried away with the music that they dance all over the furniture to the strains of Bill Haley's version of "Rip It Up"—not the kind of action likely to carry the film's message very effectively. In *The Girl Can't Help It,* a romantic comedy-satire exploiting the then-common belief that rock and roll was a gimmick of the music industry and a passing fad so simplistic that anyone could perform it, there's a scene in which Jayne Mansfield sinuously sways across a nightclub floor accompanied by the rhythms of Little Richard singing the title song—all the while seeming to ogle her every movement. The narrative suggests the essential harmlessness of rock, but the music celebrates miscegenation, one of America's most fiercely defended taboos.

This kind of tension couldn't last for very long; some kind of resolution had to be effected. One way for this to occur was through a narrative expressing the dangers of rock, thus harmonizing the plot with the dangers implicit in the music. A number of films took this tack. *High School Confidential* (1958) was perhaps the best of the lot, but there were many others, including *Hot Rod Gang* (1958), *Girl's Town* (1959), and *Daddy-O* (1959). Teenage *film noir* was clearly at its nadir. With greater or lesser degrees of artistry (usually the latter), all of these films consistently ground out the idea that rock and roll was responsible for every social evil imaginable (sexual aberration, violence, drug abuse, miscegenation, and laziness). This accord between music and narrative, however, was no less superficial than the films themselves. For whereas the narrative lamented this deplorable situation and the threatened loss of American youth to demon rock and roll, the music was positively celebratory. Who could take seriously all of the horrors attributed to rock when the likes of Jerry Lee Lewis, Gene Vincent, and the Platters were blasting forth with some of the most playfully exciting music of all times? In *High School Confidential,* for example, Jerry Lee comes rolling across the screen, pounding on his piano on the back of a truck. What kind of warning is this? The moods of the music and narrative are incongruous, yielding conflicting messages.

Another attempt to effect a resolution to the internally divided film was to deactivate the music, force it to fall in line with the traditional narrative. Selective use of genuine rock and the production of quasi rock was how it was accomplished, and the result was another seeming harmony between music and narrative. Consider these examples: *Go, Johnny, Go* (1959), *Where the Boys Are* (1960), *Wild in the Country* (1961), *Twist around the Clock* (1961), *Play It Cool* (1962), *Bye-Bye Birdie* (1963), *Beach Party* (1963), *Bikini Beach* (1964), and *Muscle Beach Party* (1964). Although there were legitimate rock artists in some of these films, their role and music were incidental to the narrative. If a musical performance was essential to the plot, we could always count on the Hondells, the Walker Brothers, Jimmy Clanton, Connie Francis, Billy Fury, Bobby Vee, Bobby Rydell and, as epitomes of this kind of musician, Frankie Avalon and Annette Funicello. There was nothing at all threatening about these films; all of the traditional values were strongly supported by the narrative and sound track. The revolutionary essence of rock had been co-opted, defused in order to serve counterrevolutionary purposes. The form was retained, but its substance had been unceremoniously removed. Nevertheless, and this is the internal contradiction, all these films unabashedly glorify youth culture, which by this time was profoundly influenced by rock and roll. The very lack of authentic rock created a striking incompatibility between their portrayal of youth and what the youthful audiences knew to be true. The more these films succeeded, the more they failed.

Both attempts at a resolution had reached an impasse, and both had done so for essentially the same reason. Existing rock and roll had not yet sufficiently distinguished itself from the culture it was negating. Lacking the affirmation of an alternative set of values, the revolution wound up negating itself as well. Self-negation, however, did provide the opportunity for something completely different.

The Sixties

The affirmation of a revolutionary set of values in the sixties resulted partly from the decline of authentic rock music in the immediately preceding period combined with a simultaneous legitimization of the youth culture. It also resulted partly from the fact that, somehow, authentic rock music was preserved throughout this period. Together, these factors helped set the stage for the explosion that followed.

It happened with the release of *A Hard Day's Night* in 1964, a film that coupled this new attitude toward youth with a decidedly positive and far more energetic style of rock (and it was about this time that we stopped calling it "rock and roll," preferring just "rock" instead). From this point on, films having rock culture as their principal textual content were inscribed with the affirmation of new values, making them far more antagonistic to the established order than those expressing the attitude of negation. For by making the conflict clearly evident for the first time, the antagonism was necessarily heightened. Consider these other films: *Help!* (1965), *Blow-Up* (1966), *The Graduate* (1967), *Yellow Submarine*

(1968), *Easy Rider* (1969), *Alice's Restaurant* (1969), *Zabriskie Point* (1969), *The Magic Christian* (1970), *Performance* (1970), *Shaft* (1971), *200 Motels* (1971), *The Harder They Come* (1972), *Five Summer Stories* (1973), *Heavy Traffic* (1973), and *Claudine* (1974). In a list of this diversity, it probably needs to be restressed that the attitude of affirmation does not imply any particular emotional vehicle for its expression. On the surface, the early Beatles films are joyous; however, there is an underlying, subtle anger. *Shaft* tends to reverse this relationship. *Easy Rider* and *The Harder They Come* incorporate a progression of feelings from euphoria and irony to fear and loathing. All, however, are films of affirmation. Closer attention to these films might also help dispel the damaging illusion that the sixties was a period of carefree abandon, Edenic innocence, communal warmth, and utopian zeal. There was a lot of this, of course, but there was also hatred, selfishness, racism, and sexism, both within the movement and in society at large. And, of course, there was the overwhelming presence of Vietnam, international militarism, imperialistic nationalism, and the repressive triple entente of Hoover, LBJ, and Nixon. A period of sweetness and light it was not.

The best of these films were not so naive. Their optimism about a new age was tempered by an acknowledgment of how difficult it would be to actualize it. Opposition from the established order and disagreements from within were coupled with the inevitable problems of bringing into being a completely new cultural orientation. Dustin Hoffman's portrayal of alienated youth in *The Graduate* is a good illustration. Confronted by the incomprehensible and impenetrable world of his parents' generation, Benjamin is immobilized. The enticements offered to him (success: "plastics," and sensual pleasure: "Mrs. Robinson") only make sense in terms of the prevailing value structure. With no clear alternative in mind, and probably unconscious of what he is rejecting, he remains ambivalent to the end (his running off with Mrs. Robinson's daughter notwithstanding). His future is still indeterminate; the film ends, but the problem persists.

The Harder They Come, just as valid a sixties film as any other on the list, actually ends in tragedy. Jimmy Cliff portrays an aspiring reggae musician who finds brief success in the face of establishment opposition (embodied in governmental, criminal, and imperialistic forces). David Ehrenstein and Bill Reed, in *Rock on Film*, describe Cliff's character as "the pop star as cultural guerilla," and with his death in the final scene it is crystal clear that the transformation of culture will not be accomplished easily or rapidly, and perhaps not at all.

No assessment of film in the sixties would be complete without some mention of *A Hard Day's Night*. Aside from representing perfectly the harmonious marriage between narrative and music, this time affirming a new set of values (and doing it so subtly that while pervading the entire film they are never consciously the object of attention), the film's spectacular success served to create an antagonistic reality that would eventually confront all rock films: profit. Surprising to perhaps everyone, including the Beatles themselves no doubt, was the film's unprecedented critical acclaim. When combined with its wholly expected financial success, the result was the sincerest form of flattery—imitation. Some attempts to cash in were so obvious and direct as to border on plagiarism, as with the Monkees. More important, however, was the general recognition that films about rock music and its attendant culture were potentially the most profitable things going.

Imitations of the Beatles' successes continued throughout the sixties; it was inevitable that the film industry would try to capitalize on them. *Head* (1968) was the most blatant example of this trend since it starred the Monkees—the most blatant imitation of the Beatles. But there were others: *Having a Wild Weekend ('65)* with the Dave Clark Five, *Seaside Swingers* (1964) with Freddy and the Dreamers, and *Good Times* (1967) with Sonny and Cher. The cloning was partially successful: many films were artistically and financially rewarding, but they were no longer authentically revolutionary. The form had been retained, but the substance had been subverted. Coinciding remarkably with the end of the sixties, these imitations managed to supplant the real thing almost entirely.

The Interim

Characterized not only by imitation but also by remakes, the avoidance of controversy, and the sublimation or repression of any value that might smack of revolution, the films of this period simply gave expression to the nearly universal exhaustion everyone was experiencing. Nothing was ventured and nothing was gained, but on the other hand, nothing was lost. There exists no better way to describe this than as a holding period, a time for the licking of wounds and the regrouping of scattered forces.

The interim was often referred to as "the me decade," but this little slogan should not automatically be understood as a simple allusion of selfishness. While selfishness was certainly a part of it, a concentration on the self also had reference to psychological survival. Given the traumas of the sixties, it should be obvious that the self was in need of repair. Only if the self is intact can it manifest a concern for others, and recreation is an essential component of keeping it intact. After all, "recreation" means to "re-create." Nothing frivolous about this, and certainly nothing selfish either. Essentially, re-creation is healing, the revitalization of the body and spirit and the opening of the self to the future. A key component in the process of emotional healing is the often underrated dimension of entertainment, literally the pause that refreshes. Looked at in this light, the films of the interim weren't all that bad.

This relative quietus could hardly last for very long. Once the restorative function of this period had its effects on the combatants, the struggle would continue where it left off. Placidity would inevitably produce its own opposite, a renewal of the cultural revolution.

The non- (but not anti-) revolutionary character of this period is evident in both music and narrative, as the following films illustrate: *Mahogany* (1975), *Tommy* (1975), *A Star Is Born* (1976), *Car Wash* (1976), *Saturday Night Fever* (1977), *Looking for Mr. Goodbar* (1977), *The Wiz* (1978), *FM* (1978), *Almost Summer* (1978), *Sgt. Pepper's Lonely Hearts Club Band* (1978), *Thank God It's Friday* (1978), *The Rose* (1979), *Can't Stop the Music* (1980), *Times Square* (1980), and *Xanadu* (1980). The concentration on self is readily apparent in *Saturday Night Fever,* but selfishness isn't all there is to it. John Travolta plays a Brooklyn youth struggling to achieve self-worth in a world that consistently ignores individuals without power or wealth. The quest for self-respect and identity is not selfishness: it's a matter of psychological survival. Tony sees only one way to achieve a worthwhile identity—through dancing. And, as everyone knows, the kind of dancing he does is the much-dreaded disco. Disco, as everyone also knows, is not exactly the music of revolution (and Travolta's character is not exactly a Jimmy Cliff cultural guerilla). Nevertheless, the film is in no way an updated version of the late-fifties beach movies. While the text of the film is hardly an incarnation of the revolution, neither is it a manifestation of the established order, facts which ought not be ignored when disco as a phenomenon of the 1970s is reconsidered. Also part of the disco craze were the aesthetically inferior *Can't Stop the Music* and *Thank God It's Friday,* which were just as non-involved (not to be confused with value-free, since a concern for the self in any understanding is highly evaluative).

Success pervades *Mahogany, The Rose* and *Times Square* as the ultimate goal, but this isn't simple selfishness either. The achievement of personal aims is only incompatible with social aims when the value to be achieved is scarce, when others necessarily become a threat. Neither psychological survival nor self-worth nor success is in any way a scarce commodity. Everyone can achieve them at the same time.

Notice finally the plethora of rehashes: *A Star Is Born, The Wiz, Tommy, Sgt. Pepper,* and *Xanadu.* This hints at an unwillingness and/or an incapacity to venture into something new. There has always been a inclination in the film industry to rely on the successful formulas of the past, but this need not imply only a fear of the new or a lack of imagination. It just might suggest a subconscious need for recapitulation, a desire to make the history of the revolution explicit in the consciousness of individual participants. Each of the five reaches into the past (even the pre-rock past) for its source of inspiration, and by so doing establishes a connection, possibly a healing connection. This shouldn't suggest an attempt at some kind of reconciliation, which can only occur when the parties at odds are clearly manifest. With these films, however, the conflict is suppressed.

Actually, the conflict of values is suppressed in virtually every film produced during this period, resulting in a general lack of direction and an apparent stagnation. But if I'm right, this period did contribute to a renewal of energy; however, the first to benefit from this pause were not the cultural revolutionaries. The first to benefit were the traditionalists.

The Counterreaction

In 1980, with the opposition clearly identifed in the person of the newly elected president, the revolution was also revived. Cinematically, the nonrevolutionary rock films of the interim called forth the only conceivable response: a renewal of negation. It couldn't simply be a reaffirmation of the positive revolutionary values; this would ignore the fact that the established order had meanwhile been rejuvenated. No, the first order of business was to attack the reconstituted establishment and to do so in a relevantly new way.

Hints of the new negation had already been lurking in the wings, as if waiting for the propitious moment. *The Rocky Horror Picture Show,* for example, was released in 1975 but only later achieved its status as the premier cult movie. Its significance for our purposes, however, is the way it has been viewed and interpreted since the election of 1980, as illustrated by a positively brilliant opening sketch done by the cast of "Fridays" (ABC's version of "Saturday Night Live"). As the film begins, the superstraight Brad (''asshole'') and Janet (''slut''), after leaving their friends' wedding, have a flat tire and become lost. They see a light up ahead in the castle of Dr. Frank N. Furter, and proceed to seek assistance. Soon they are confronted by the ''sweet transvestite'' himself, in drag, descending in an open elevator. In the ''Fridays'' version, as Frank N. Furter comes into view, singing ''(I'm a) Sweet Transvestite,'' his net stockings gradually give way to a black corset and finally to the unmistakable face of Ronald Reagan. What follows is a biting satire, completely erasing the apolitical mood of the interim. Understanding the film in this way is a comparatively recent phenomenon.

Another hint was the total *lack* of any rock music at all in the excellent film *Return of the Secaucus Seven*, which concerns the reunion of several close friends from the sixties. The get-togethers are apparently held yearly; this one occurs at the end of the 1970s. The friends still maintain their earlier ideals, and so the striking omission of what would have been contemporary music for them suggests a fundamental incompatibility between the sixties and their present. A still more revealing aspect of this omission is the implicit admission that no music yet exists to carry forth with the cause. The music of the fifties and sixties had accomplished its mission; newer revolutionaries require newer music. Nothing can last forever.

A final cinematic hint, *Rock and Roll High School* (1979), reveals with precision exactly what kind of musical stylings would begin this renewed negation. Culminating with the students' burning their school to the ground, the theme of the film is a celebration of punk rock, specifically, the music of the Ramones, whose music accompanies the burning in an impromptu performance on the school lawn. With the exception of one defector from the teachers, the film portrays the sharp confrontation between two cultures, with little pretense to subtlety. As if to suggest whose music is now in charge of the revolutionary negation, one scene has school authorities comparing various kinds of music on a ''rockometer.'' Naturally, the Ramones are found to be the most destructive, causing mice to explode, but note who follows them (in descending order): the Who, the Rolling Stones, Ted Nugent, Led Zepplin, Jethro Tull, Foreigner, Peter Frampton, Kansas, Donny and Marie, Debby Boone, Pat Boone, and Muzak. In a dream sequence, the *mise-en-scène* includes various records and posters connoting the negation of the fifties and sixties, but P. J. Soles's character conjures up Joey Ramone for the erotic interlude. In both scenes, as well as in the sound track, the music of negation predominates; yet it is completely clear that punk is the new force in rock. Significantly, nowhere in the film was there any reference (except by omission) to the Beatles, the symbol par excellence of sixties affirmation. This just wasn't the time for affirmation.

Again, there was a harmony between narrative and music, and as these three films suggest, the harmony was initially expressed as a negation of the Reaganite sociopolitical program as reflected in the new stylings of punk. (Obviously, much of this new musical form harkens back to the fifties; no development is ever entirely new.) Other films expressing negation include *The Great Rock and Roll Swindle* (1980), *Heavy Metal* (1981), *American Pop* (1981), *Pink Floyd, the Wall* (1982), *Eddie and the Cruisers* and *Footloose* (1984). *The Great Rock and Roll Swindle* seems so negative as to make the expression of anything positive impossible. Starring the Sex Pistols as themselves, in their version of *A Hard Day's Night,* the film takes on the Beatles and Elvis as objects of derision. (Sid Vicious does perhaps the best parody of Elvis ever when he sings "My Way.") On closer inspection, however, it is really just a matter of who is now in charge of the revolution; in no way is *revolution* derided. "Anarchy in the UK" and "God Save the Queen" make this perfectly clear, as if the Sex Pistols themselves didn't. The other interesting film in this list is *American Pop,* because of its attempt to establish a continuity with the past, ranging from vaudeville to the present—and the present is heavy with the music of negation.

Yet if there was to be any hope of continuing the revolution with any degree of success, this negation had to be followed up with a strong reaffirmation of positive, alternative values. *Radio On* ('79) provides the contrapuntal hint in the year prior to the Reagan election. It's a murder mystery set in England in the latter stages of the interim. Although the mood of the film is definitely *noir,* what comes across is the crying need for something positive. The very absence of hope is an effective commentary on the period and serves to prepare us for the inevitable reexpression of revolutionary values. Paul Simon's *One-Trick Pony* (1980) asks the musical question, Can the sixties be revived for the 1980s? It recounts the tale of a sixties rock star trying to rekindle both his personal and his professional life—a kind of parable. Again, the need for affirmation permeates the subtext of the film. On the surface, both these films are depressing, but this is so because they are both self-consciously lacking something.

With *Fame* (1980) we finally get the reaffirmation so desperately needed, and it is the kind of reaffirmation that does not in any way ignore its historical context. The issue of race is a clear example. While the fifties negated racism and the sixties affirmed racial harmony, *Fame* portrays race as an irrelevancy, a reality worth preserving in all its diversity but no longer an issue one way or another. Obviously, this is not *really* the case, but reality is not the point. The film affirms an *ideal,* something specific to strive for. At the same time, the interim's emphasis on personal success is also affirmed.

Three other films of affirmation deserve mention: *Star Struck, Baby It's You,* and *Flashdance,* all released in 1983. The first, a new-wave musical set in Australia of all places, serves to point out the difference in attitude between punk and new wave. It, too, finds value in the struggle for success. *Baby It's You,* although a period piece from the fifties and sixties, illustrates the absurdity of maintaining class and ethnic prejudices in our contemporary American culture, showing them to be hopeless atavisms even then. *Flashdance,* crippled by a thin and often incredible story and weakened further by unconvincing acting, nevertheless links the notion of success with the most energetic and promising of all counterreaction issues—sexism and human liberation. The principal character is a woman driven by a desire to perfect her unorthodox (and apparently untutored) dancing style at a local saloon while supporting herself by working as a welder. Along with both male and female friends, she acquires a lover, using the kind of assertiveness that we all wish we had (firm and sure, without the slightest hint of stridency or resentfulness). Interestingly, the sound track is overwhelmingly comprised of women: Laura Branigan, Donna Summer, Joan Jett, Kim Carnes, and Irene Cara among others. Maybe even more interesting is the film's clear affirmation of eroticism, portrayed without the slightest trace of baseness.

In 1984, there were a series of affirmative films: *Breakin'* and *Beat Street* both celebrated ethnic diversity; *The Big Chill* maintained emphatically that the sixties were far from dead; Prince's *Purple Rain* showed how these same values could be manifest in the eighties in perhaps the most remarkable rock film since *A Hard Day's Night;* and *This Is Spinal Tap*'s satire of ''rockumentaries'' warned revolutionaries not to take themselves with ultimate seriousness.

Affirmation with a subtle, hard edge characterized three films released in 1985. *The Breakfast Club* illustrated that the acquisition of a new, revolutionary set of values must be undertaken anew with each generation, and that the process is often painful. *St. Elmo's Fire* pointed out that holding these new values is no guarantee against the loss of motivation and purpose. And *The Coca Cola Kid,* with its gentle, erotic satire of American imperialism, reminded us that the cultural revolution is implicitly a worldwide phenomenon.

In all these instances, the complementarity of narrative and music is aimed at the affirmation of revolutionary values. Together with the former, negative films, they indicate the general direction to be taken in response to the reawakened embodiment of traditional values.

The Theater as Theater

The most interesting and significant interpretations, the ones that are immediate and not self-conscious, do not occur in the columns of reviewers or in the numerous and thoughtful scholarly articles, nor even in the often lively discussions that take place following a showing. Rather, they take place *in* the theater, during the showing, as the film is in the process of happening. Interpretation is the *way* we have of perceiving something, the mental slot into which we place what we experience. In so doing, we attribute a meaning to that which we are in the act of perceiving. The meaning is not in that which we perceive; the meaning is in the act of perception itself. Not that it is a conscious activity; if anything, it is preconscious. It is the emotional reception that greets the experience on which the later rational commentaries are based.

Recalling McLuhan's claim that the combination of mechanical and electric technologies is analogous to the release of nuclear energy, it just might be that this release occurs in the immediate interpretive process itself. The amount released may even correspond directly with the relationship between music and narrative. The former is cool, and the latter (which McLuhan associated with all the print media) is hot. The locus of their meeting is inside the theater, and that's where we have to look.

With the release of the first movie to make use of rock and roll in the sound track, *The Blackboard Jungle* in 1955, teen audiences went crazy, ripping up the seats (preferably with a forbidden switchblade knife). Audiences viewing many of the later teenage *film noir* continued the trend by cheering the supposed villains, and quite a few of these movies were banned because of how the audiences responded to them. The more musical films prompted audiences to dance wildly in the aisles. None of this should be very surprising, since the essence of the electronic revolution is participation (as it is for all cool media).

The inauthenticity of the beach movies and their kin led to the almost instantaneous decline of participation. Teenage audiences responded to them no differently than to traditional films (which in many ways they were): they sat and watched, lost in their individual thoughts. Commenting on how film was received in highly mechanized Western cultures, McLuhan said: "Typographic man took readily to film just because, like books, it offers an inward world of fantasy and dreams. The film viewer sits in psychological solitude like the silent book reader." Thus ended the fifties on film.

The way music and narrative were interwoven during the sixties led to new depths (or heights) of participation. Rock films were almost always accompanied by the smoking or ingestion of controlled substances; participation had advanced to the state of mystical oneness. Filmmakers, not unmindful of this trend, and being influenced by McLuhan directly, took to producing films that demanded viewer participation: split screens, composite images, stream of consciousness, speed changes, dialogue with the audience (remember *Alfie*?), and the like. *American Graffiti II* seemed so very out of time because of its attempt to emulate this style of filmmaking; George Lucas tried to be authentic to the period in form as well as in content. Not everyone could appreciate his effort, and the film got generally poor reviews.

During the interim, participation ended again. The sound track began to be conceived of as something separate from the film, an entity in its own right. Nothing illustrates this better than the practice of relying on the film to sell the sound track album. Concerning *FM*, Ehrenstein and Reed note that "more people bought the soundtrack than actually saw the movie." Participation continued, of course, but not in the theater; it happened at the disco.

Since the beginning of the counterreaction, there has been a reassertion of participation in the theater, but something new has been added. The midnight cult film has made the theater a social gathering place for various kinds of social "deviants." *Rocky Horror* epitomizes this new style, for not only do audiences come dressed as their favorite characters and dance and sing to the music, they have also developed a counterdialogue, which makes them an integral part of the film experience. Obviously, not all cult films have evolved to this point, yet they all share the same setting—the theater at midnight, the only respectable hour for a cult film. Even if the cult-film phenomenon never becomes very large, everyone knows about it, and this is nothing to be sneezed at. *Fame,* which is not a cult film, includes a scene in which the characters attend a showing of *Rocky Horror,* and they pass around a joint too. This links the small cult audiences with the vast majority of nonparticipants and makes the cult phenomenon more significant as a result. Other linkages have been established with past manifestations of the revolution, for rock films of the fifties and sixties are now being shown at the midnight hour, thus converting them into cult films of the present.

It is impossible, of course, to predict which films will achieve cult status. (It is also impossible to set out to make them deliberately.) But one 1984 release stands a good chance: *The Adventures of Buckaroo Banzai*. In this absurdist, science-fiction satire, the major character is a neurosurgeon, a test-car driver, a physicist, and a rock singer from another dimension. Its ultimate importance may be determined in years to come, at midnight. This may also be the case for another science fiction absurdist satire, *Repo Man* (1984), which toys with the punk phenomenon.

Finally, it's worth noting that, despite its lack of size, the cult phenomenon symbolizes a renewed dichotomy between the cultural revolutionaries and the established order. ''It's just a jump to the left. . . .''

Television: Bringing
It All Back Home

7

The scandal caused by Dylan's apostasy from folk music toward rock at the 1965 Newport Folk Festival is not sufficiently explained by a change in either his style or his lyrical material. What outraged folk purists was the electrification of his music. When he dropped acoustic instrumentation and picked up the electric guitar, his music acquired an authenticity and power it could never have had otherwise. His audience was right in sensing this to be the crucial defection, but they were wrong in accusing him of selling out. On the contrary, what he did was to introduce their common themes to the most radical form possible and thereby brought it all back home where its effectiveness would be multiplied.

In a manner of speaking, this is precisely what happened when rock and roll began appearing on television. No longer was it something that could be safely ignored, something kept securely apart from the family setting and the protection it afforded. Now it was being brought directly into the home, and with an unparalleled seductiveness.

McLuhan's chapter on television in *Understanding Media* is subtitled "The Timid Giant" because of the medium's alleged tendency to avoid or play down controversies and clashes of well-defined and sharply opposing views. While he agreed with this assessment, he was quick to add that this did not imply that television lacked either a value orientation or influence. Its impact is subtle, he observed, but much more thoroughgoing as a result. To understand how this is so, one must keep constantly in mind that the medium itself is the bearer of the message.

Noting some of the technological features characteristic of film and television might be helpful in making some sense of this claim. For unlike all forms of photography (still and motion), the TV image is never still. Rather, it is a ceaselessly forming series of dots (about three million per second), which the viewer mentally (and unconsciously) constructs into an intelligible pattern. Said McLuhan, "The TV image requires each instant that we 'close' the space in the mesh by a convulsive sensuous participation that is profoundly kinetic and tactile, because tactility is the interplay of the senses, rather than the isolated contact of skin and object." The relatively high definition of film imagery, providing an enormous amount of information, requires much less viewer involvement for the picture to make sense; whereas, television's low definition demands that the viewer participate. The result is the creation of a unity between the physical senses and the imagination (which McLuhan called "synesthesia"), a goal that artists have always regarded as unattainable. The effects of this merger have been enormous. As an extension of our central nervous system, television has affected our lives in every conceivable way.

It would be absurd, of course, to claim that everything televised has had the same degree of effectiveness. The "content" does make a difference, with the important caveat that the "content" of any medium is simply another medium. It is the resulting mixture of media that makes the difference. Media more suited to television (the cooler and more electronic ones) are likely to emphasize its effects much more than those less complementary. Television demands a high degree of audience involvement, so the most effective programs are those that require participation—programs that are not whole unless "completed" by their viewers. The portrayal of intimacy requires completion in this respect, for the program is an utter failure unless the viewer becomes deeply involved with the characters. It is especially helpful toward this end if the characters are cool and not very well delineated: "Anybody whose *appearance* strongly declares his role and status in life is wrong for TV. . . . When the person presented *looks* classifiable . . . the TV viewer has nothing to fill in." Similarly, the viewer's participation is necessarily required for programs constructed as a mosaic; otherwise, there will be no unity to the show, and it will appear as no more than a mishmash of disconnected segments. Closely related is the kind of program that makes a viewer's interpretation vital, as when the superficial account (comprehensible and enjoyable for its own sake) contains a deeper meaning which is not immediately obvious. So, broadly conceived, there is a distinction between television programming that requires viewer involvement and that for which the viewer is essentially irrelevant, the former being the more effective of the two in communicating the message of television. It is the difference between the viewer being a participant or a mere witness, and when it comes to a consideration of televised rock and roll, the distinction indicates where we should look for its primary impact.

Without denying this difference, the greater one's exposure to all kinds of television programming, the more it will affect one. McLuhan described its overall impact as "the power to transform American innocence into depth sophistication." This being the case, it is to be expected that the generation that has grown up with television will be the one most influenced by it. Writing in 1964, McLuhan observed,

> The young people who have experienced a decade of TV have naturally imbibed an urge toward involvement in depth that makes all the remote visualized goals of usual culture seem not only unreal but irrelevant and not only irrelevant but anemic. It is the total involvement in all-inclusive *nowness* that occurs in young lives via TV's mosaic image. . . . The TV child expects involvement and doesn't want a specialist *job* in the future. He does want a *role* and a deep commitment to his society.[1]

Since he wrote these words, there have been twenty additional years of viewer experience, and twenty additional years for television to have its way with us. The youth of McLuhan's time are now in their thirties and forties, and only a few of them (the lucky ones) have a role to play. Most are no doubt frustrated to one extent or another—a fact that yields an interesting implication: the greater the exposure to TV, the greater the general level of dissatisfaction in society.

The impact of television may very well be subtle and indirect, but its message is nevertheless revolutionary. With each new television generation, the social discontent will increase, until the bonds of the traditional order snap under the strain. Hence, the great mollifier of controversy is likely to contribute mightily to the overthrow of the prevailing value structure. And it's worth noting that the first television generation was also the first generation to be exposed to the insidious blandishments of rock and roll.

The Viewer as Witness

Rock music and its attendant culture have been the focus of several TV formats, and all of them have reflected the developments within the overall revolutionary process. Some, however, have utilized mixed or nonelectric media as their ''content'' and, as such, have tended to reflect cultural changes more than further them.

The Record Hop

The earliest manifestation of rock and roll on television was Philadelphia's own ''Bandstand'' in 1952, with Bob Horn as the TV disc jockey. Soon after Dick Clark, a local radio DJ, replaced him (allegedly for some impropriety involving one of the young female dancers on his show), ABC began to broadcast it nationally as ''American Bandstand,'' and the rest, as they say, is history. In the wake of its success, every city with television facilities and enough teenagers to pose a threat to civic and gastric peace came up with a clone of its own. With the exception of ''The Lloyd Thaxton Show,'' Clark had no real competitors, and Thaxton was a woefully poor second. ''Bandstand'' was on the air every weekday from three to five in the afternoon, an incredible saturation of the market for then, or any time. Clark's influence was enormous, as much as for whom he didn't invite to lip synch on his show as for whom he did. Whether or not his guest list was suspiciously heavy with those in whom he had financial investments (or those who sang the songs in which he had invested), as some people alleged, the list was certainly comprised of the most sanitized and least threatening performers available. No Elvis, Jerry Lee Lewis, Chuck Berry, Little Richard, or anyone else ''too black'' ever darkened the stage of ''American Bandstand.'' Instead, we got the likes of Frankie Avalon, Bobby Vinton, and Fabian Forte. Single-handedly, Dick Clark virtually defined the essence of ''schlock rock,'' and still today he symbolizes the hard-core sellout. Nevertheless, through his agency, rock and roll was legitimized and brought into our living rooms, and has forever after been accepted as a part of our lives.

''Soul Train'' continued the televised record hop into the 1970s, only in this instance, reflecting later cultural developments, the audience and performers were black. Soul had become a definably separate entity within the rock genre during the sixties, resulting from the militancy and pride of a new black consciousness. The music played on the show was still pretty clean-cut, but black Americans now had access to the nation's living rooms. It didn't make a dime's worth of difference that most whites didn't bother to tune in; what mattered was that the show was programmed equally along with every other show and that it allowed for the expression of black culture as a legitimate component within the larger American culture.

The disco craze of the interim manifested itself perfectly in "Dance Fever," a "Saturday Night Fever" kind of show minus the story. I've never met anyone who has ever watched it for more than a few minutes. Ditto for "Solid Gold," which plays the week's top tunes accompanied by a troupe of interpretive dancers, and they aren't that good either. Perhaps its inexplicable popularity depends more on the dancers' sex appeal than on their dancing.

Cable TV's "MTV" and syndicated shows like "MV-3," "Friday Night Videos," "Music Magazine" and "Black Music Magazine," which rely heavily on the new video technology, are a different matter entirely. Still essentially reflective of cultural change, they tend overwhelmingly toward the many varieties of new music, with the problematic exception of some contemporary black music. Although some people have denied that incipient racism is the explanation for this exclusion, it does seem to stem from their ignorance and narrowness of taste brought about by the separate musical developments over the past several years. And while this is perilously close to racism, I do not anticipate its continuing for very much longer. Musical mergers are already taking place on radio and in recorded music, and this should continue. Aside from this, these video shows are lending strong support to a developing art form: the so-called music videos and video movies (for example, Michael Jackson's "Thriller"). Most of them present some form of interpretive minidrama along with the music, and there are even awards given to the most creative of these productions. The fact that many can be purchased or rented for home use (on recorders or disc players) has led some people to speculate that they will eventually replace the record as the principal means for the transmission of rock music. I doubt this very much: they require too extensive a commitment of time and concentration to appreciate fully. Recorded music allows other things to go on simultaneously; it does not demand the kind of total concentration characteristic of television. Furthermore, records do not restrict the free play of imagination as videos must do in principle. Videos are a separate but related art form—not a substitute.

Despite their apparent diversity, all televised record hops are fundamentally noninvolving. The performers on the set do the dancing, not the viewers at home, who are no more than passive observers.

The Variety Show

The next major manifestation of rock on TV began in 1956, when Elvis appeared on "The Ed Sullivan Show." He had appeared on some other nationally televised show prior to Sullivan, but this one symbolized his emergence as "the King." In terms of significance, his appearance was second only to that of the Beatles not eight years later. The televised variety show has never been an important vehicle for the discovery of emerging talent, but it has been remarkably perceptive in showcasing the current trends, whatever they might be. (Sullivan's indignant statement that "Elvis will never appear on my show" underwent a dramatic conversion to "This is a real, decent, fine boy" when he did appear two months later—after he was smashed in the ratings by Elvis's first TV appearance on "The Steve Allen Show," opposite Sullivan's. It turns out that his entertainment instincts were far stronger than his convictions regarding the protection of traditional values.)

Another show of some significance, reflecting the mood of the sixties, was "The Smothers Brothers Comedy Hour." Heavily weighted toward folk in the music it presented, it had a decided tendency toward the expression of social concerns and protest—factors which eventually led to its demise in 1969, only a little over two years after its debut. When the Smothers Brothers took on America's policies in Vietnam and had as a guest the blacklisted Pete Seeger—who sang the forbidden "Waist-Deep in the Big Muddy (and the Damn Fool Says to Push On)"—cancellation was no less predictable than the sun's rising in the east. An interesting and curious contrast at the end of the sixties was the highly innocuous "Sonny and Cher Comedy Hour," starring the "hip" couple of the sixties. Suffice it to say that nothing more controversial than Cher's navel ever appeared on their show.

All of these variety shows came equipped with a studio audience to whom these shows were directed. The audience at home was necessary for the ratings game, but little else. Interestingly, since the sixties, this format has not been very successful. Almost every attempt to breathe some life into it has failed. This shouldn't be very surprising, since the format is essentially vaudeville, bound to lose out to more electronically oriented programming. In any case, it's still worthwhile thinking back to those first appearances by Elvis and the Beatles on the Sullivan show. What a contrast between them on the one hand and the dancing dogs from New Oxford, Pennsylvania, and the guy from Paramus, New Jersey, who could play the national anthem on his head with wooden spoons! The emergence of revolutionary values was never clearer.

The Concert

Beginning in the mid sixties, live concerts were staged for broadcast, and they were specifically intended to capture the style and flavor of the contemporary scene. Every once in a while, we'd be treated to an "oldie but goodie" (a term which I find as offensive and deplorable as "boy," "the little woman" and "senior citizen," for all of them exemplify a patronizing attitude that the perpetrator seems unable to recognize as such). As can be ascertained from their titles, "Hullaba-loo" and "Shindig" were folkie flavored, but they never completely excluded rock. (This was the sixties, after all.) "Hollywood a Go Go," another mid-sixties entry, catered more to rock-oriented tastes but tended to stress danceable music over anything that might appear to be controversial. As the sixties came to an end, the late-night concert scene began to develop and enjoy a modicum of popularity: "Midnight Special," "Don Kirshner's Rock Concert," "In Concert," and more recently "Rock 'n' Roll Tonight." Their success has depended largely on the shows leading into them—almost exclusively late-night satire. When satire began to decline in popularity, the concert format soon followed. As a participatory medium, the concert is intrinsically flawed; passively watching is about all you can do.

The Film

Films produced specifically for television are different in many important respects from theatrical releases; they differ in terms of structure, concept, theme, technique, and in numerous other ways. My comments will concern the former category only, and I include in it such apparently diverse forms as miniseries and cartoons. Even though all have qualities suiting them uniquely for television, the viewer is nevertheless more of a witness than a participant, comparatively speaking. As such, these programs reflect more than motivate and give direction to cultural change.

TV films about rock music were first produced toward the end of the interim, including "Deadman's Curve" (1978), "Elvis" (1979), "The

Birth of the Beatles'' (1979), and ''The Heroes of Rock and Roll'' (1980), possibly signaling the rebirth of revolutionary fervor. It is significant what meaning is implicit in these films. ''Deadman's Curve'' portrays the tragic and apparent end of Jan and Dean, yet it ends with their tumultuous resurrection after a period of desperate struggle. The analogy with the then-current state of the cultural revolution was striking to say the least. ''Elvis'' and ''The Birth of the Beatles'' were portrayals of the two major symbols of the revolution, each dealing with the earlier part of their careers and each leaving the finale open-ended toward the future. Elvis's negation is clearly reestablished and the Beatles' affirmation is just as clearly revealed as their destiny. The final film is one of the best historical surveys of rock ever done, and significantly it links the music to cultural change (though it tends to overemphasize the present). Interpretations of this kind may seem to be rather far-fetched and more the product of wishful thinking than anything corresponding to the facts. Yet, if the interim is most accurately understood as the result of exhaustion and the loss of an appropriate symbol for the opposition, then a renewal would seem to be the next likely stage following a period of rest and recreation, especially since the established order has again acquired a symbolic head.

The only rock-oriented miniseries I know of is ''Rock Follies'' (1975) and its sequel ''Rock Follies '77.'' Together they illustrate perfectly the various seductions offered by success in the mass market. Authentic revolutionary anger is portrayed as selling out to the allurements of money and fame: rock becomes disco, in other words. Several interesting questions come to mind in conjunction with this theme. Does this account for the decline of rock during the interim? Is a genuine recovery adequately suggested? Is anything significant indicated by the fact that the story centers around a female trio? And most important, where else can you see performing the one and only Rula Lenska (unless you just happen to be one of the friends that she shows around London)?

Television cartoons have obviously catered to the kiddy trade, inducing us to coin the expression ''micro bopper.'' They've included the Archies, the Bay City Rollers, the Monkees, the Jackson Five, and the Beatles. Even though the groups are watered down so as to be unrecognizable except for their songs and visage, the existence of rock is now evident to even the youngest. Further, the Jackson Five and the Beatles continue as a living presence, through Michael Jackson in one instance and legend in the other (the very young learn Beatle songs and stories simply as a part of growing up). The infiltration of rock throughout our culture is, for all practical purposes, complete.

————————— The Viewer as Participant —————————

Television was bound to produce some formats uniquely its own, designed (consciously or unconsciously) to take advantage of the peculiarities of the new medium. As varied as they might be, they all have in common the necessity for an audience; without it, they are unable to accomplish the kind of communication for which they were designed. Some of these formats have been used for the expression of rock music, and the results have been dramatic.

The Situation Comedy

Although this genre is hardly exclusive to television, there are several reasons why the televised version is now much more effective than its predecessor on radio. In every case, this is so because the viewer has become absolutely essential for the completion of the comedy situation. Like television itself (and unlike radio), the characters manifest a coolness, a lack of definition, which the viewer must supplement for the sake of intelligibility. This was only a potentiality for radio, which television has exploited fully. Next, because these series are intended to continue week after week with no specified conclusion, viewers must stick with the show if the events and developments are to be fully understood. This incompleteness produces a fundamental distinction between loyal viewers and all others, a distinction that becomes even sharper when the visual element is considered. Yet since most people watch more than one show, there is no absolute separation between and among various groupings. Finally, because we are able to see the characters (and all of us are seeing the same thing, unlike radio listeners), the intimacy thus created is magnified. Not only do we become more closely involved with the people we meet on the TV screen, but a show establishes a closeness among viewers who meet on the street. The characters necessarily become very real to us, the *same* characters for *all* viewers, and we await their visits with us as eagerly as we would guests or favorite members of our families. (Seeing one of our TV personalities out of character is often distressing to us; it's not at all like seeing a film personality who plays no regular role. Nor can seeing a radio personality be as universally distressing, since we all have a different image of the character in our individual imaginations.)

All of these factors have combined to have an enormous impact on and within the family, and the impact has been both more complex and more effective for its being essentially subliminal. To put it as simply as possible, situation comedies provide us with a series of relationships to emulate, guidance for dealing with problems by means of the comedy paradigm, and a validation for whatever is found acceptable on the show.

When the theme is wholly or even partially concerned with rock music, a sellout is likely to be alleged, as with Dylan at Newport. In both cases, the initial impression is that something authentic has been sacrificed for the sake of popularity and/or money. After all, if someone were to look for the epitome of defanged and declawed rock and roll, the television sitcom would seem to be the first thing to investigate. When the music is considered in isolation from the medium, this is no doubt true; TV executives would probably abandon their hidden expense accounts before risking any advertising revenue by broadcasting genuine, bloodcurdling, revolutionary rock and roll. But also like the Dylan episode, there has been an entirely unanticipated consequence stemming from this alleged sellout: an enhancement of the revolution, for no matter how "schlocky" the music, rock and roll has become an invited guest in the home, brought in by friends whom America had come to trust. No television "family" (and every situation comedy has a family of some kind) was ever threatened by the introduction of rock, so why should the family on this side of the screen be worried? Rock and roll has been consistently portrayed as something the family, the protector of traditional values, need not fear. So, if rock is compatible with the model family, why should its existence within the imperfect but actual family cause any concern? Why indeed?

Here is why. It was the fifties, and the first rock and roll guest to be invited into our homes was none other than Elvis. It wasn't *really* Elvis, of course; it was Ricky Nelson. But we all knew an imitation when we saw one; nobody was fooled, except maybe our parents, who no doubt saw him as the ideal, if irrepressible, son they never had. How could little Ricky do anybody any harm? He was everyone's kid brother; he grew up with us and was probably as much a part of our families as our real siblings. But not only was he safe, he also did what we all wanted to do: he became a rock star. Of course he had a slight advantage over us, since "The Adventures of Ozzie and Harriet" featured his real-life parents as actors, writers, producers, and directors. Somehow they worked him into the show (usually at the end) so that he could sing one or two of his latest songs, and in the process our parents were lulled into thinking that the rock-and-roll phenomenon was nothing more than the latest dance craze.

Significantly, our next important visitors were none other than the Beatles, coming to us in the form of the Monkees (in a show of their own name that was modeled so closely after *A Hard Day's Night* and *Help!* that it's still a wonder no massive suit was brought against them for plagiarism). In terms of making the Beatles acceptable to American sensibilities, these four antiseptic imitators were hardly necessary. By this time the Liverpool originals had become the lovable mop-tops who delighted everyone with their wit, enthusiasm, playfulness, and merry melodies. (They would not remain this way very much longer.) Instead, the Monkees actually preserved a residual hardness and anger to the Beatles' image that might otherwise have been lost. If anyone ever thought that the Beatles had degenerated into mere pap, they had only to look in on a weekly episode of "The Monkees" to recognize the difference. (Later, the Monkees acknowledged their artificiality and tried hard to become an authentic rock group—by actually learning to play their instruments for one thing.) When the Beatles metamorphosed again, into something obviously dangerous, they were already welcome guests in our homes, no longer at a safe distance. But all the while, because of the Monkees, we should have known what was going to happen.

Exhaustion often produces a need for diversion from the source of the exhaustion, so during the interim, the situation comedies ventured nothing and succeeded admirably. "The Partridge Family" and "The Brady Bunch," both with contemporary settings, appealed primarily to the very young and to all those who wished the world contained nothing more threatening than what confronted the characters on these two shows. It might strain credulity to call the music performed on these programs "rock," yet it did serve to introduce a new generation to its form (if not its substance); from then on, American youth would never know a world *without* rock and roll. Every revolution, bar none, has had a problem with the next generation, since only the first generation can possibly experience the beginning and what preceded it. The loss of this element of consciousness has always tended to lessen the passion so necessary for the revolution to continue, for there is no longer any basis for comparison. Hence there arises a dilemma: the new generations must become acquainted with the revolution and its history, yet the spirit and fervor of the original generation are forever lost to them. With these two situation comedies, the demarcation between the generations was established.

"Happy Days" and its spinoffs, "Laverne and Shirley" and "Joanie Loves Chachi," came along next. Set in the fifties, they familiarized this new generation with the idea that rock had a history; not the facts of this history, but the fact of the history itself. This distinction is crucial, and missing it is largely why the significance of these shows (especially the first) has never been properly appreciated. "The Fonz," for example, is in no way an accurate portrayal of a fifties "greaser" (or "drape," as we called them in Baltimore), but the character does accurately indicate that there were such rebels and that they were somehow associated with rock and roll. Moreover, as this generation grew in maturity and sophistication, it was bound to ask why this guy was considered so ominous. He was portrayed as part of the supersquare Cunningham household after all. The more they watched the show, the more this contradiction would gnaw away at them: either Fonzie had to represent a genuine threat, or everyone else on the show was insane. Those interested in what the facts really were just might populate the ranks of today's mods and punks, the inheritors of what Fonzie represented.

As the counterreacton got underway, the networks responded with two critically acclaimed shows. One, "WKRP in Cincinnati," dealt with rock history with surprising accuracy and sympathy. It even portrayed the conflict between traditional and revolutionary values, leaning heavily toward the latter. Yet at the same time there was the clear impression that America's period of cultural unrest was over and done with. (Johnny Fever was a burned-out sixties freak, and Venus Flytrap's continual attempts to be a revolutionary black were laughably and hopelessly outmoded; moreover, both of these disc jockeys wanted *into* the system; they didn't want to change it.) This parody produced a certain energy, which suggested that the reports about the demise of the revolution were highly exaggerated. Though "WKRP" expressed its values murkily if at all, it left no doubt as to where to find them expressed with clarity: in authentic rock and roll. Its undisguised implication was that these values wouldn't be found in anything resembling disco in that contemporary setting.

The other show, "Square Pegs," also with a contemporary setting, was aimed directly at the generation reaching maturity in the early 1980s, just after Reagan's election. Although references to the history of rock were not infrequent, the music was heavily oriented toward new wave (punk being far too negative for the family hour, and probably for any hour). Its portrayal of high school life was egregiously saccharine, but no one has ever accused situation comedies of approaching literal truth too closely. What mattered about this show was its portrayal of a revolutionary response to the counterreaction and the idea that this was linked with the development of new music. The theme for the show was written and sung by the Waitresses, whose commitment to revolutionary values is unquestioned. And Devo actually performed on the show, leaving little doubt as to its orientation. Besides, it was developed by one of the writers for "Saturday Night Live" and a former editor of *National Lampoon*, Anne Beatts, whose revolutionary credentials are impeccable. Both "Square Pegs" and "WKRP" have since been canceled because of low ratings—but then again so was "Star Trek."

Satire

Of the four shows I'm about to mention (all having been cancelled as well), two of them—Rowan and Martin's "Laugh-In" and the original "Saturday Night Live"—presented some of the most innovative programming ever to appear on the tube. The others—"Fridays" and "Second City TV"—while equally good, were essentially derivative (despite "Saturday Night Live" having some roots in Second City's live act). In each case, the format came as close to McLuhan's vision of television's mosaic as anything ever scheduled.

Riding the crest of McLuhan's popularity and influence, "Laugh-In" emphasized the mosaic style to a degree never seen before or since. (Actually, "The Ernie Kovacs Show" came pretty close, winning an Emmy for Outstanding Achievement in Electronic Camerawork for the 1961–62 season, as if to offer a tantalizing foretaste of what was possible. But unlike "Laugh-In" the show never did well in the ratings; Kovacs obviously lived and died ahead of his time.) However, the other three are also best described in terms of a mosaic. Comprised of distinct elements, each one left it to the audience (whether at home or in the studio, and neither "Laugh-In" nor "SCTV" had a studio audience) to establish the connection. The audience was required to integrate and thus interpret what was perceived: The relationship among the disparate parts was not given in the experience. It had to be intentionally supplied. The mosaic is not something visually accessible: "The mosaic can be *seen* as dancing can, but is not *structured* visually; nor is it an extension of the visual power. For the mosaic is not uniform, continuous, or repetitive. It is discontinuous, skew and nonlineal, like the tactile TV image." McLuhan meant here that the viewer must form the pattern, much as a sculptor forms a shape from whatever materials are available.[2]

Not surprisingly, given the similarity of "the materials" made available, the viewers of these four shows came up with similar interpretive patterns or structures. Much of "Laugh-In" was affirmative of something new (mirroring its 1968–73 dates). Its very format told us this

much. Even though there was no recognizable rock music either performed or recorded on the show (it relied instead on some kind of simu-
lated and synthesized rock), its influence was unmistakable and all-
pervasive. Horace Newcomb, in *TV: The Most Popular Art*, attributes
much of the power and popularity of "Laugh-In" to its attack on the traditional values associated with politics, religion, sex, the military, and
the family. All of its segments "were clearly intended to shock, to challenge accepted values, to call certain beliefs into question." Even when
some of the favorite objects of its derision actually appeared on the show
(John Wayne, Billy Graham, and Nixon, for example), the satire was not
thereby lessened or blunted. Yet the attitude of affirmation need not focus its attention, and expend its energy, on an enemies list. It was apparent to cast and viewers alike that there were alternatives to everything
they satirized; for the moment, the opposition could be safely ignored.
(Such naive optimism carries a mixed blessing, since the taste of success
that's so necessary for any social movement tends to be accompanied by a
dangerous underestimation of the opposition.) In any case, some of the
delightfully pointed episodes of "Laugh-In" should be remembered:
The Flying Fickle Finger of Fate Award (given for all sorts of social and
political outrages); the Farkle Family (the many children of which suspiciously resembled the neighbor); Goldie Hawn's writhing, bikinied body
(painted with social, political, and scatological graffiti); the opening
party scene (in which the dancing would stop for short, one-line, commentaries) and Lily Tomlin's Ernestine (whose phone company sketch
was a devastating parody of corporate America).

The rumblings of a new negation began to occur toward the end of the
1970s, and NBC's "Saturday Night Live" captured this mood and encouraged it along perfectly. In its first two or three years, the satire was
positively brutal. Nothing this aggressive had ever appeared on television before, and its anger was directed squarely against the established
order. Playing in the same time slot as "The Tonight Show," "SNL"
underlined the contrast in audience sympathy; very few people watched
both shows, since their points of view were so obviously different. The
focus of attack of "SNL" is plain in a few selected examples: the
Claudine Longet Men's Open Invitational Ski Tournament (the injustice
of the judicial system), Dan Aykroyd's imitation of Jimmy Carter con-
fessing lust in his heart (the stupidity of most sexual restrictions), a
pseudo-union advertisement for the United Marijuana Growers of America, Inc. (the stupidity of most drug laws), Loraine Newman as Squeaky
Fromme (the stupidity of having no effective gun laws), Jane Curtin as
Baba Wawa (the pretentiousness of everyone with status and authority),

Garrett Morris's summer job as a "black boy" lawn ornament (the continued existence of racism), Don Novello's Father Guido Sarducci (the continued existence of religion), Chevy Chase as Gerald Ford (the continued existence of politics), Aykroyd as sexual object in the "beefcake" sketch (the continued existence of sexism), Aykroyd and Belushi as Nixon and Kissinger in "The Final Days" sketch (the continued existence of Nixon and Kissinger), Gilda Radner as Patti Smith, and Lorne Michaels's invitation to the Beatles to appear on the show for the incredible sum of $3,000 (the music business), the Spud Beer advertisement (the medical business), the sketch about the cancellation of "Star Trek" (the television business), Michael O'Donoghue (anything), and John Belushi (everything). Further, only once was there a guest host with an unambiguous establishment orientation, Ron Nessen (Carter's press secretary); most were decidedly of the opposite persuasion, including George Carlin, Richard Pryor, Sissy Spacek, Paul Simon, Buck Henry, Ralph Nader, Lily Tomlin, Eric Idle, Steve Martin, and Jodie Foster. The musical guests were even more obviously cultural rebels, and through the 1979–80 season there had been approximately eighty (with representation primarily from the sixties)—Chuck Berry, the B-52's, Jimmy Cliff, Bob Dylan, the Grateful Dead, the Rolling Stones, Patti Smith, Peter Tosh, and Frank Zappa to name just a few.

The negation of the counterreaction blossomed fully with the satire on "Fridays," as illustrated by the *Rocky Horror* sketch mentioned earlier. Unlike "SNL," it often featured new wave music, with even an occasional punk group invited to perform (slam dancing and all). "SCTV" was always less direct in its satire, and originally it had no musical guests at all. When they finally were added, the emphasis was pretty much a balance between music from the sixties and contemporary music, suggesting an attitude closer to affirmation.

Three of the four shows under consideration were linked in ways not apparent from merely watching what they broadcast. The commonality had to do with the performers' personal lives and how the shows were viewed. First, the persons associated with "SNL," "Fridays," and "SCTV" all knew each other rather well from having a common background, and many were close friends. The similarity among the shows is thus hardly in need of careful investigation. Second, since they were telecast well past the family hour ("SCTV" even followed "SNL" at one time), they were likely to interfere with weekend parties; however, their popularity was such that it was acceptable to interrupt the festivities to watch them. It is probably unnecessary to add that the viewing of these shows was often chemically enhanced, an experience providing yet another dimension to their participatory qualities, to say nothing of their antiestablishment orientation. "Saturday Night Live," of course, lives on in truncated reruns throughout the country, and despite the fact that much of the material is dated, the best of the shows still have a certain zing to them. There is something timeless about first-rate satire, something worth preserving in the best as well as the worst of times. Now that we are without John Belushi, their preservation is all the more important, for he symbolizes better than anyone what these shows were all about.

The Impact of Television

McLuhan remarked that, since the arrival of television, "there is scarcely a single area of established relationships, from home and church to school and market, that has not been profoundly disturbed in its pattern and texture." And he must have meant it. His jumbled list of affected areas is seemingly endless, especially when all the complex implications are recognized. By noting what kinds of values are involved, however, one can bring some organization to his chaotic ruminations.[3]

Among the most important are an appreciation of differences with a corresponding opposition to imposed uniformity, the encouragement of individuality without the corruption of individualism, a unification which recognizes both harmony and diversity, and a deeply committed life instead of a life of fragmented superficiality. If these sound a lot like the fundamental values of the cultural revolution, there shouldn't be any real surprise. The arrival of television as the key electronic medium happened at just about the same time as the release of "Rock around the Clock," and never was television a more unifying medium than in the days following November 22, 1963. At those key points in the development of the revolution, television was there, not only to record but to participate.

Now, maybe some of the manifestations of these values can be perceived and comprehended as the outcome of rock and television's joint impact. Concerning race and sex, McLuhan believed that integration was bound to fail, based as it was on literate culture's positive evaluation of uniformity. The goal was and is the eradication of both racial and sexual differences to achieve conformity. Electronically influenced cultures, on the other hand, have diversity as one of their primary goals. In both the fifties and the sixties, rock music exemplified this latter notion, and it has continued to do so in ever greater depth and complexity, most recently involving itself with the problems of sexism. The repression of normal sexuality he saw resulting from the linear, structured consciousness of literate cultures: Western culture has "fostered the institution of prolonged adolescence by the negation of tactile participation that is sex," which has led to political and moral conformity. The reversal of this is so obviously associated with rock and roll that there is no need to belabor the point. Television's contribution, however, ought not be overlooked. Its emphasis on touch has made the reversal of sexual repression and conformity to sex roles practically inevitable.

In education, the revolution against specialization, selfishness, and materialism was one of the hallmarks of the early New Left. McLuhan saw the "Montessori educational strategy," the "beatnik rejection of consumer mores and of the private success story," and the demand for relevance and involvement as partially the result of television. And, as is perhaps obvious, the New Left was the first television generation. Musically, the dissatisfaction with traditional education has been a major theme in rock, from Chuck Berry's "Schools Days" to Alice Cooper's "School's Out" to Pink Floyd's album and movie *The Wall*. It is a tendency not likely to pass away.

Furthermore, politics (both domestic and international), guided traditionally by nationalism, imperialism, and militarism, has suffered its severest challenge ever. McLuhan claimed that television involves us in a depth experience, but it does not excite, agitate, or arouse, all of which are essential ingredients for the "old politics." Additionally, due largely to television, modern warfare is becoming a morally unthinkable (not, unfortunately, a physically impossible) idea. Along with all the electronic media, television has produced new opinions and feelings that result in our now having instant, global information literally at our fingertips. These new beliefs have to do with political universalism; even modern weaponry, based on electronic technology, serves to make more vivid the unity of the human family. Simply and graphically put, "the electronic techniques cannot be used aggressively except to end all life at once, like the turning off of a light." Nothing says it better than the corresponding imagery of John Lennon's "Imagine," but here again, rock's outrage at "politics as usual" is far too ubiquitous to need documentation.

Among the many other areas affected simultaneously by rock music and television are clothing styles (which reveal a person's musical preferences), automobile aesthetics (highly individualized), books (a preference for paperbacks), sports (football over baseball) and religion (ecumenical and nonideological). Having such an all-pervasive impact, television (especially when coupled with rock and roll) just might deserve all the fear and loathing it so often attracts. For, like Dylan, it has expressed the values of the cultural revolution in the most far-reaching and dangerous of all possible forms.

Revolution and Revelation
Part 3

There's no incompatibility between observing
the world and being tuned into an electric,
multimedia, multitracked McLuhanite world and
enjoying what can be enjoyed about rock & roll.
Rock & roll really changed my life. . . . I really
had a revelation. . . . It seems clear to me that
rock & roll is the greatest movement of popular
music that's ever existed.

—Susan Sontag

Revelation, reveals the truth,
Revelation
It takes a revolution to make a solution
Too much confusion
So much frustration
I don't want to live in the park
Can't trust no shadows after dark
So my friend I wish that you could see
Like a bird in the tree
The prisoners must be free

—Bob Marley & the Wailers

There was something so utterly and disarmingly preposterous about the fiery purges of rock and roll advocated by the Pastors Peters that it is still difficult to appreciate the fact that, in many ways, their fears and anger were fully justified. Ordained by the Jesus People Fellowship of Minneapolis, Minnesota, the brothers Jim, Steve, and Dan, together with their dad LeRoy, comprised the once formidable family ministry of the Zion Christian Life Center in North St. Paul, a family seemingly dedicated to the total eradication of rock music in our lifetime. Recalling some of the religious protests of the fifties, their many campaigns throughout the South and Midwest during 1979 and 1980 led to the roasting of everything from the Beatles and Blondie (which might be expected) to John Denver and the Osmonds (which kind of catches a person off guard). For the moment, it would appear that they haven't yet accomplished their overall goal, but should they falter in their resolve, there are others like them lurking in the woodwork to whom their torch can be passed.

The word *preposterous* is given a whole new dimension by the insistence of such crusades that Satan is somehow associated with rock music. Often the allegation is simply that the musicians have been possessed by demons, the devil's minions. (In this case, the performers wouldn't seem to be evil themselves, merely dupes or victims of the Evil One.) At other times, rock musicians are accused specifically of satanic worship, seen as a most unforgivable offense.

All sorts of evidence is enlisted in support of these and related contentions, much of which is highly esoteric, requiring almost as much blind faith in what the data supposedly portend as that needed to convince one-self of the deity's very existence. Some of the more creative efforts at proof include the various perceptions of "backward masking," all of which declare an allegiance to Satan, presumably for the benefit of those who listen to their records in reverse (the most notorious of the obscure examples being found in Led Zeppelin's "Stairway to Heaven," causing the infamous Black Oak Arkansas among others to lay in a few backward tracks deliberately, as much for the enjoyment of the Peterses and their fellow travelers as for the potential publicity value, I'm sure). Another bit of evidence is the photograph on the interior album cover of the Ea-gles' *Hotel California,* in which a mysterious figure looks down from a balcony—perhaps as an explanation for their ominous warning that "you can check out any time you like, but you can never leave," since the hotel is alleged to be a satanic church. Other works of Satan allegedly include the group KISS (an acronym for Kids in Service to Satan?); the cover of the Alan Parsons Project album *Eve,* which supposedly shows girls with syphilis sores; the ambivalent sexuality of Mick Jagger, David Bowie, Rod Stewart, Elton John, and Boy George; and the non-Christian as well as satanic imagery used by such groups as Blue Öyster Cult, Black Sab-bath, and Ozzy Osbourne, Styx, Rush, and Mötley Crüe. Of course, some authorities trace Satan's influence back to the inception of rock and roll itself. Others find Beelzebub making his debut with the Rolling Stones' "Sympathy for the Devil" (which, ironically, was a forceful plea *against* evil and violence of all kinds) and their album *Their Satanic Majesties Request.*

Aside from these (to be charitable) questionable interpretations, the very idea of Satan only makes sense to believers like the Peterses, who share a certain perspective about the nature of reality—a perspective not shared by any of the people just mentioned. In any case, these accusa-tions have resulted in the destruction of many dollars worth of record jackets; the records themselves can't be burned, since flaming vinyl gives off toxic fumes (no doubt further evidence of Satan's influence).

This state of affairs is as sad as it is humorous, for beneath this paranoia is a genuine anxiety at the prospect of even the slightest amount of change. Like gnostics of all ages, this amorphous collection of sectarians has correctly inferred that to alter or modify perfection in any way is nec-essarily to make it imperfect. For some, perfection is disclosed through reason alone, while for others it comes through revelation; it makes no difference. Change is inherently wrong. This is only a logical point, of course, but if people truly believe that the truth has been granted to them, then any threat to it will inevitably be opposed with all the strength and cunning that can be mustered, and with any and all means available.

The reason for their anger and anxiety is the justifiable conviction that rock and roll is somehow a challenge to traditional religion, especially Christianity (although, in principle, every religion both ancient and contemporary is attacked). All cultural revolutions are, at their core, religious movements, and as such they are struggles and conflicts at the deepest levels of our consciousness (personal and collective). It is not that rock music exemplifies an antireligious state of mind, as its naive critics often assert; rather, its vitality and appeal stems from the fact that it represents and proselytizes for an alternative religiousness. This makes it a much more potent threat to the established order than even its most vociferous opponents believe it to be. Here is the very essence of the cultural revolution taking place in America: the rejection of America's religious heritage and its replacement with something contrary. It is not the devil that's behind rock and roll—it's another god.

Before getting too carried away with this idea, we'd better pause to consider precisely what's involved with religiousness. Far from being describable in terms of a set of generalized concepts, religion is a certain kind of experience, and the best account of it was done in 1917 by Rudolf Otto in *The Idea of the Holy.*[1] His approach was to focus on the seminal religious consciousness prior to the inevitable attempts to comprehend its components rationally. This meant characterizing the experience as a set of nonrational feelings, feelings characteristic of every historical manifestation of religion without exception. These feelings are equally characteristic of the rock experience.

The clearest illustration of this might be to suggest how Otto's six components apply to the typical rock concert. The first is the feeling of insignificance, which Otto called *creature consciousness.* It happens when people are overwhelmed by the knowledge of their utter nothingness, when they sense themselves in the presence of something infinite. For Western cultures, this is most often identified as a god, but it need not be so restricted. Otto preferred calling it the *numinous*—that which is experienced as ultimate. As for the rock revolution, the ultimate is perhaps best understood as the experience of our common humanity and our bond with all other elements of creation. For this is the prime source of the alternative set of values: feelings that combine to negate our sense of superiority and self-importance as individuals and as a species, making us aware of a much larger unity in which everything participates harmoniously. (That's the ideal, anyway.) So what concertgoers experience is a depth dimension of human nature not otherwise available to them in such mass numbers. When you see the throngs swaying together to the music, when you hear them singing along to familiar songs, and when at the end you watch them light thousands of matches in appreciation, it's hard to come to any other conclusion. In many ways, the concert is the paradigm experience which records, disc jockeys, films, and television seek to emulate.

The second is a feeling akin to *awe* or *dread,* which "first begins to stir in the feeling of 'something uncanny,' 'eerie,' or 'weird.'" Being extremely complex, it "*may* indeed be so overwhelmingly great that it seems to penetrate to the very marrow, making the man's hair bristle and his limbs quake. But it may also steal upon him almost unobserved as the gentlest of agitations, a mere fleeting shadow passing across his mood." The experience is not at all unpleasant, producing, instead, enjoyably chilling sensations which the typical rock fan expects from a concert and seeks to reproduce through live albums. Although highly exaggerated, the concert experience does involve an element of risk, especially since rock performers are well known for their physical and emotional exuberance and enthusiasm, often inciting the audience to similar excesses. Usually this doesn't amount to anything resembling actual danger, but that is not the point. What is important is the illusion or imagery of danger in the concert setting—that is what holds the appeal. (Besides, genuine tragedies are exceedingly rare, and often the result of events external to the concert, such as the stampede for thousands of unreserved seats for the 1979 Who concert at Cincinnati's Riverfront Stadium, in which eleven people died.)

The feeling of *being overpowered* by something both mysterious and majestic is the third component. When experienced almost to the exclusion of everything else, the result is mystical absorption. It is a nonrational experience—not to be confused with one that is irrational. The latter is in opposition to reason, while mystical absorption is beyond reason. We need only recall some of the films and photographs taken at Elvis and Beatles concerts to appreciate fully what mystical identification can mean in this context. Obviously, not everyone at a concert succumbs to this extent, but for those who do the experience is nothing short of ecstatic. Others, not able to achieve this degree of identification, tend to resort to artificial means, the point being that the *desire* for absorption is virtually universal among concertgoers.

The fourth component concerns the experience of *energy* or *urgency,* the sensation of being grasped or controlled by a power or force both intimate with and alien to our nature. When this happens at a rock concert, the atmosphere becomes positively electric, charged with an indefinable presence. Often manifested as a surge forward, it is not an attempt to overwhelm the performers but a response to what is felt to be a fervent invitation to participate. A superlative illustration of this was captured on a kinescope taken from a BBC broadcast called "Don't Knock the Rock" (not to be confused with the film of the same name), with Jerry Lee Lewis, Little Richard, the Animals, and a few other lesser-knowns. As Jerry Lee sings "Whole Lotta Shakin' Goin' On," the studio audience gradually but inexorably moves toward him, climbs onto the stage and surrounds his piano—and all the while Jerry Lee just keeps pumping out the rhythms and singing one chorus after another. He plays as if possessed, and the audience responds in kind; the music seems to have a life of its own. The whole scene is reminiscent of an altar call following a fire-and-brimstone exhortation.

Otto believed, as the fifth component, that the source of this rapturous experience is forever beyond our rational understanding. It is *wholly other*. Not only is it beyond our powers of comprehension (which might be a mere difference in degree), its reality is entirely different from ours (which is a difference in kind). In the typically religious understanding of the numinous, this may seem obvious, but the same is true for any experience of an ultimate, no matter how this-worldly it might appear. For non-ultimate or finite beings cannot possibly comprehend that which is ultimate, in principle, even if the ultimate is humanity itself. The only way to express whatever is experienced as ultimate or infinite is through what Otto called "signs," that is, special persons, places, events, and the like. Paul Tillich expanded on this idea in his theory of symbols, and I'll be making extensive use of this theory in the chapters on Elvis and the Beatles. In the meantime, it should be obvious that, as far as events and occurrences are concerned, the concerts at Woodstock and Altamont are signs par excellence. Still today, the "Woodstock Nation" is looked back to as the paradigm of the new order. And Altamont is regarded as the warning of what might happen if Woodstock is taken too literally.

The sixth and final component, *fascination,* creates a paradox, for along with the feelings of dread and horror already mentioned is now added this curiously compelling quality. Fascination, for Otto, was the key for understanding the religious consciousness: "These two qualities, the daunting and the fascinating, now combine in a strange harmony of contrasts, and the resultant dual character of the numinous consciousness . . . is at once the strangest and most noteworthy phenomenon in the whole history of religion. The daemonic-divine object may appear to the mind an object of horror and dread, but at the same time it is no less something that allures with a potent charm." It is precisely this strange harmony of contrasts that ties together the negation of Elvis and the fifties rebels with the affirmation of the Beatles and the new romanticism of the sixties. It also explains how Simon and Garfunkel on the one hand and the Sex Pistols on the other can possibly represent the same thing—to say nothing of Woodstock and Altamont.

Together, in an insoluble unity, these six components constitute the fundamental religious experience; although, depending on the cultural conditions, some are more likely to be experienced more intensely than others. In every instance, however, there will be some symbolic reference to an ultimate. The symbol is the singularly indispensable facet of the religious encounter, for in no other way can ultimacy be expressed. Christianity has its cross and the person of Jesus; Judaism has its Torah and the Wailing Wall; Islam has Mecca and Muhammad; and nationalistic religions have their flags and leaders. This holds true for the rock experience as well; a symbolic reference will necessarily be present. Needless to say, there are many such symbols, some more inclusive, more potent, and more enduring than others. And in the entire history of rock, and thus in America's cultural revolution, there have been but two.

At this point it is necessary to sketch out the bare bones of Tillich's theory of symbols so as to prepare the way for the analyses to follow, and again there are six characteristics.[2] One is that symbols necessarily point to something beyond themselves. Another is that they participate in, are intimately involved with, that to which they point. A third is their ability to disclose aspects of reality that are not available to us through any empirical or scientific means. Similarly, as the fourth characteristic, they can reveal a connection between the ultimate and the depth dimension of our human existence, a connection that just might be an identity. With respect to this depth dimension, Tillich believed that "there are within us dimensions of which we cannot become aware except through symbols, as melodies and rhythms in music." Fifth, they cannot be intentionally manufactured or produced as so many contrivances; symbols are natural developments that must emerge from and be accepted by our collective human experiences. Hence, as the final characteristic, they grow and die only insofar as they elicit or fail to elicit a response. Supposedly "dead" symbols may only be dormant and are thus capable of being reawakened; for symbols always embody in themselves the power and vitality of their original meaning, and that which has been truly meaningful for people can never really die.

My contention is that a symbolic interpretation is the *only* way to understand the Elvis and Beatles phenomena and explain their continued influence. To be clear about this, to acknowledge their symbolic stature does not in any way require an agreement with what they stand for; nor does it imply anything about their validity as symbols. Tillich's test for validity isn't all that helpful, since applying it is intrinsically subjective, a matter of personal opinion. Nevertheless, the test quite effectively indicates the necessary prerequisite for validity, that without which a symbol is intrinsically idolatrous: self-negation. He wrote, ''Every type of faith has the tendency to elevate its concrete symbols to absolute validity. The criterion of the truth of faith, therefore, is that it implies an element of self-negation. That symbol is most adequate which expresses not only the ultimate but also its own lack of ultimacy.'' Faith, for him, was the attitude of ultimate concern, an attitude shared by everyone, differing only in terms of how it's symbolized. Conflicting symbols, then, imply conflicting faiths, and this is by far the most revealing way to understand the cultural unrest in America: as a conflict between incompatible ultimate concerns, each believing itself alone to be valid.

Symbols never appear in isolation, however. ''They are united in 'stories of the gods,' which is the meaning of the word 'mythos'—myth.'' Tillich added that ''myths are always present in every act of faith, because the language of faith is the symbol.'' If taken literally, a myth becomes idolatrous, so here too, self-criticism is absolutely vital if myths are to point effectively beyond themselves; something in the mythic tales must express self-negation. When considering the numerous accounts about Elvis and the Beatles in particular, the perhaps overwhelming tendencies toward idolatry must not be overlooked. Equally necessary, of course, are careful observations of the extent to which self-negation is present. It is most important to remember, however, that neither idolatry nor self-criticism are qualities intrinsic to the symbol or myth; they are qualities of the *perception*—their presence is a matter of interpretation. No matter how many data are available, these qualities are always a matter of what the observer supplies to the experience.

To complete this introduction to the ''religiousness'' of rock, some of the distinctive attributes of mythology ought to be highlighted. In the classic study done by Mircea Eliade, *The Sacred and the Profane,* the religious consciousness is portrayed as regarding every facet of reality (space, time, nature, and humanity itself) as qualitatively different from the way they are experienced by the nonreligious consciousness. This difference, however, is a matter of interpretation; there are no objective measures to determine which is correct. Both perceive the same empirical data, but they see the data as having conflicting meanings. To be meaningful, reality has to be organized and structured in some way, and the religious way of doing this differs from the profane as dramatically as night from day.

Similarly, American mythology is organized and structured according to one ultimate perspective or another. The established order has its perspective, and the revolutionaries have theirs; what's interesting about this conflict is, again, not the data but how the data are given meaning. No one will deny the existence of the personalities, events, artifacts, and history of rock and roll; but a considerable dispute will inevitably arise over what all of this means. Our interest, of course, is in the meaning given by the cultural revolutionaries, and Eliade's description of the structure of myth is of considerable assistance.

Essentially, from the religious-mythological perspective, certain times and places are qualitatively different from all others, for they harken back to The Beginning, the events of which can periodically be recovered and restored through the use of symbols. The entire cosmos, in fact, is understood to reveal the ultimate to those with the proper perspective. The process of human existence from birth to death is also believed to involve a relationship with the ultimate, and the constant human quest is to establish a proper relationship. Only in this way can life have any meaning. The symbolism of various rituals affords humanity the opportunity for achieving a meaningful and worthwhile life. Eliade felt that none of these attributes of the religious consciousness were totally absent in today's profane world; there are vestiges to be found everywhere, and this extends to the ongoing cultural revolution.

In this final section of the book, I'll be utilizing a selection of ideas adapted from the work of Otto, Tillich, and Eliade in order to comprehend the course that the revolution has taken so far. None of the four chapters is intended to be a chronological account; all are conceptual in nature. Nevertheless, they obviously reflect the four major periods of America's revolution and the meaning I believe to be implicit in them. Although the end is still to be written, one thing is certain: the cultural revolution in America has exposed us to a new and disturbing revelation.

Elvis and the Negation of the Fifties

——————————————— 8 ———————————————

Once upon a time, there was no such thing as rock and roll. Oh, there was the music, of course; at least all the necessary ingredients were present in roughly the correct proportions. But it wasn't *called* rock and roll, and the naming of it as such was a momentous occurrence.

Most people attribute the naming to Cleveland disc jockey Alan Freed, whose observations of white teenagers buying rhythm and blues records in 1950 led to his programming this music on his Moondog Show. Called "race" music at the time, Freed tried to avoid the epithet and, no doubt, the accompanying bad publicity and poor ratings, by adapting some of the music's frequent phraseology as a more apt description. (He did, after all, have a large white audience.) Probably the term originated from "We're Gonna Rock, We're Gonna Roll," a 1947 song by Wild Bill Moore or the even earlier, but stylistically different, "My Daddy Rocks Me with One Steady Roll," recorded by a variety of artists throughout the 1920s.

By 1954, the term still hadn't achieved widespread acceptance, but the impact of the music had surely been noticed. In the July 3 edition of *The Cash Box* that very year, Jerry Wexler and Ahmet Ertegun reflected on what they termed "The Latest Trend: R & B Disks are Going Pop."[1] They suspected that it was only a matter of time before the trend would blossom into a full-fledged craze. As evidence they cited reports from the South, where high school and college students had begun dancing to rhythm and blues records instead of those by nationally known artists such as Jo Stafford, Eddie Fisher, Perry Como and Patti Page. They also found it significant that, while "hillbilly fans" apparently initiated the trend, they were quickly followed by the more financially influential "bobbysoxers." When disc jockeys saw which way the wind was blowing, they were not only forced to bring R & B records with them to record hops, they were also forced to change the format of their radio programs. Larger audiences and more advertisers were the immediate results.

After tracing how this music had spread throughout the South and into the North, the Midwest and the West Coast, Wexler and Ertegun made a self-consciously futile attempt to define the kind of music that they were talking about. Resorting to an "ostensible" definition, they listed about a dozen examples, including songs by Lloyd Price, the Clovers, the Drifters, the Crows, Joe Turner, Ruth Brown, Fats Domino and the Chords. Following the southern "hillbillys" and "bobbysoxers," they called it "cat" music. It was music with a beat, with infectious catch phrases and with a "message."

It wasn't long before juke box operators followed suit by putting "cat" records in more and more ostensibly "pop" locations. Record companies responded by having their contracted artists "cover" the new music. In both cases, although Wexler and Ertegun didn't mention it, white kids were beginning to adopt black music as their own, and the mixture was bound to be volatile. They concluded their observations with the conviction that "cat" music was now on center stage in the national music scene. Indeed it was.

In the beginning, white teenagers, initially the outcasts and then later the middle class, began listening to and buying black recordings, music that was expressing an almost total disillusionment with American society and its prevailing values. Underneath the danceable rhythms and high spirits was a mixture of indignation and accommodation, resentment and resignation, none of which was lost on the new white audience. What developed was a curious and potentially explosive conflict, a conflict that could only have arisen under circumstances such as these. For the "message" conveyed by this music was in direct contradiction to what virtually every middle-class white had always been taught about the American dream—equality before the law, hard work leading to success, human dignity for everyone, the guarantee of opportunity, an appreciation of individuality, liberty for all, and the pursuit of happiness. These are all potent ideals, and the more they were believed (consciously or unconsciously), the greater the anger and outrage at being confronted with the fact of their denial to all but the powerful and privileged few. White teens, in massive numbers, were now stricken with a divided consciousness: the ideals they had been taught were being subjected to a complex attack through the music they had come to love. On the one hand, they had to face the fact that, for a significantly large group of Americans, these ideals would never be realized; on the other hand, they had to absorb a whole new set of ideals, some of which violated their accepted beliefs. No other group in America could incorporate this internal dilemma, and, as a consequence, it was from them that the explosion emanated.

When whites started writing and performing this music on their own, not just covering it, there were added subtle new elements—a barely suppressed rage and fury at the hypocrisy to which they had been subjected, and a fascination with hitherto forbidden attitudes and pleasures. With these driving forces behind the music, genuine rock and roll was born.

Its parents were the rhythm and blues of black Americans and the hillbilly sounds of white southern outcasts. Bill Haley put them together with his cover of Sonny Dae's "Rock around the Clock" in 1954, but it took the film *Blackboard Jungle* to catapult the song into national prominence and notoriety and establish it as a lasting phenomenon. Bill Haley, however, with his recently transformed country and western band, the Saddlemen, could in no way exemplify the material they were playing. What was needed was someone who could merge the two musical traditions into something uniquely one, as a direct manifestation of a singular personality. Neither Fats Domino nor Chuck Berry, who were far more talented and who also had hits that year, could do it either. All of them, their music aside, didn't have the kind of basic and universal appeal that might accomplish such a merger, and because it was to be a merger of black and white, a truly charismatic personality would be essential.

As myth would have it, Sam Phillips of Sun Records in Memphis, Tennessee, had been on the lookout for just such a person, and with Elvis Aaron Presley, a part-time truck driver for the Crown Electric Company, hailing originally from Tupelo, Mississippi, he found him. Wexler and Ertegun couldn't have known it, of course, but just three days after their column appeared in print, Elvis was in the studios of the Memphis Recording Service at 706 Union Avenue (a mere stone's throw from the justly famous Beale Street), readying his first single "That's All Right (Mama)" for release. The rest of the story is too familiar to repeat, but it's worth remembering that none of it would have happened had not Elvis been familiar with black music as well as white. (He grew up listening to C & W performers like Hank Williams and Jimmy Rogers, pop singers like Dean Martin and Mario Lanza, blues singers like Big Bill

Broonzy and Arthur "Big Boy" Crudup, and the R & B sounds of Johnny
Ace and Rufus Thomas.)

Because of his debilitating final years and tragic death, there is a tendency to dwell on the weaknesses associated with his arrested
adolescence—his preference for kinky sex, his dependency on a veritable
cornucopia of pharmaceuticals, his perverse pleasure in the martial arts,
his inability to accept anything but toadyism from his employees and associates, and, of course, his savage abuse of carbohydrates. To concentrate on his flaws, however, would be to miss his monumental significance for contemporary American culture. No doubt quite apart from his
conscious intentions, Elvis forced us to confront the repressive sexual
morality so characteristic of our Western religious heritage. Further, his
very success pointed out the outrageous disparity between the quantity
and/or quality of effort on the one hand and the social rewards on the
other; there was no correlation whatsoever, no justice at all. He also
single-handedly transformed America's color from white to black. If this
last claim seems a bit extreme, consider for a moment the racial designation attributed to the children of mixed parentage: never are they desig-
nated white. Such is the power of racism to regard anything nonwhite as a
contaminant. Similarly, the merger of black and white music was perceived by nearly every antagonist to have been just such a "contamina-
tion"; rock and roll, no matter what its actual origin, was deemed to be
black, and everyone knew what this connoted. The premier playing of
"That's All Right (Mama)," on WHBQ's blues program, "Red Hot and
Blue" (hosted by Dewey Phillips, no relation to Sam), was so well received that Phillips had to play it repeatedly all evening, and was finally
compelled to have someone drag Elvis out of a local movie theater for a
live interview. A reception like this stunned everyone involved with the
recording; they apprehended an experience more along the lines of being
run out of town on a rail, after having been unceremoniously dipped in tar
and feathers. Elvis was white, but he clearly sounded black—a heady
brew for the folks at that time.

Dread

Of all the feelings described by Otto, the one most emphatically characteristic of Elvis was the sensation of dread or horror, all the other components of the religious consciousness being colored by this one feeling.

Even those of us who were, openly or secretly, his fanatic devotees found him in many ways terrifying. He wasn't anything like anyone we had ever known or even heard about: he dressed differently, he wore his hair differently, he spoke differently, he moved differently and he sure sang differently. He wasn't black, but somehow he wasn't white either; he was "something else," something to be regarded with extreme caution. Needless to say, if he struck *us* this way, there was no telling the apoplexy suffered by our *parents* because of him.

Today, all of this might seem laughable, but at the time it was pretty traumatic. Elvis was authentic—no *poseur.* His alienness was genuine, as Greil Marcus observes in *Mystery Train:* "Elvis didn't have to exile himself from his own community in order to justify and make real his use of an outsider's culture. . . : as a Southerner and white trash to boot, Elvis was already outside." No matter what became of him later, he would always remain something mysteriously other, unapproachable in some vaguely absolute sense. His self-imposed seclusion within the confines of Graceland obviously contributed to this, but even when he toured, his performances were seemingly intended to perpetuate this image. Even the degeneration of his personal life served to distance him from us, for revulsion, too, is an important facet of Otto's concept of daemonic dread.

His alienness notwithstanding, his attraction for the youth of the nation was overpowering, mystical even. Given that McCarthyism was still a virulent presence in American life, anything as captivating as this was necessarily viewed as a threat. While there were some who alleged a direct connection with "the international communist conspiracy," others, along with Frank Sinatra, believed that rock and roll was "the martial music of juvenile delinquents," with Elvis as their general—leading a pack of black-leather-jacketed hooligans bent on the total destruction of life as we know it.

Elvis was part of, if not the founder of, the whole rockabilly movement, the first fruits of the merger of black and white. In *White Boy Singin' the Blues,* Michael Bane links this movement with the entire history of rock that followed: "It was rockabilly—the music of Sam Phillips and Elvis Presley—that set the tone for rock. Rockabilly, with its balanced exuberance and fury, its tension between blues and country, black and white, plucked a chord that is still vibrating strongly. It was rockabilly that decreed rock and roll should be more than just fun; that rock was a revolution in lifestyle as well." Ultimately, this is what scared the hell out of everyone, the specter of rebellion, of the outcasts arising and losing their chains, the haunting prospect that everything familiar and secure was about to be overthrown. As it turned out, everyone was right.

It is worth remembering exactly what rockabilly was all about, and Bane recaptures its spirit pretty well:

> Rockabilly, at its very bottom, is *mean* music, sung through clenched teeth by red-eyed men who look as if they've seen the wrong end of too many broken bottles. That's something we've lost sight of today. . . . It's easy to forget that beneath the insipid lyrics and the simple rhythms, rockabilly tapped a wellspring of revolution. It dipped below the calm surface of the 1950s to the dark smoldering potential of a generation looking for a voice. . . . With a few decades safely between us and the music, we can manage to overlook the level of violence inherent in it, the shattering of a way of life. Yet the violence walked hand in hand with an overwhelming sense of joy and release. Rockabilly is a statement of identity and a call to battle at the same time. . . . To the kids around Memphis, rockabilly was a revolution deeper and more profound than anything that would happen in the 1960s. . . . What happened in Memphis in the days that followed a certain July afternoon in 1954 was that for a second or two, black and white understood each other completely, on a gut level, and the world rocked.[2]

The pinnacle figure behind all of this was the overpowering presence of Elvis Presley, who in his very person embodied the paradox of violence and joy, anger and release, that Bane notices.

Greil Marcus sees the same kind of paradox in Elvis's music, especially in *The Sun Sessions* (his earliest singles, recorded originally by Sun, but bought and released in 1976 by RCA): "What I hear, most of the time, is the affection and respect Elvis felt for the limits and conventions of his family life, of his community, and ultimately of American life, captured in his country sides; and his refusal of those limits, of any limits, played out in his blues. This is a rhythm of acceptance and rebellion, lust and quietude, triviality and distinction." Coming out of the South was perhaps the only way this revolution could have begun, for it was there alone that race was the singularly most influential, yet wholly unsuppressed, determinant of consciousness; and only in the South was a strain of puritanism both practiced and violated with equal and unashamed enthusiasm. According to Marcus, "[I]f Elvis's South was filled with Puritans, it was also filled with natural-born hedonists, and the same people were both."[3] So, as hordes of unregenerate southern patriots had been awaiting for lo these many years, the South did indeed rise again, but not quite as they had anticipated.

The Man in the Pink Cadillac

Just as Elvis symbolized the initial period of the cultural revolution, the pink Cadillac (convertible) came to symbolize him, and no one was more aware of it than Elvis himself. Immediately after buying one of his very own, as a measure of his newly achieved status, he adapted the lyrics of a black blues song by Arthur Gunter, "Baby, Let's Play House," as an expression of his mixed feelings: "You may have a pink Cadillac/But don'cha be nobody's fool." Marcus believes that "the pink Cadillac was at the heart of the contradiction that powered Elvis's early music; a perfect symbol of the glamor of his ambition and the resentments that drove it on. . . . Elvis sang with a wish for its pleasures and status. Most of all he sang with delight at the power that fame and musical force gave him: power to escape the humiliating obscurity of the life he knew, and the power to sneer at the classy world that was now ready to flatter him."[4] Michael Bane, too, sees the symbolic link between the man and the car. Prior to Elvis, performers were jus' good ol' boys, providing a service for which they were duly compensated; they were not yet "personalities." "The first time Elvis went tooling down the street in his pink Cadillac all that changed. Elvis was more than simply an extension of his audience. He was a figurehead for that audience, a living, breathing symbol of the revolution that all the kids of the 1950s were beginning to feel. He had come from the community . . . but he was no longer part of the community and he never would be again."[5] No observer of contemporary American culture, no matter what his or her personal feelings about Elvis might be, can avoid sympathizing with Greil Marcus's conviction that "Elvis Presley is a supreme figure in American life, one whose presence, no matter how banal or predictable, brooks no real comparisons."[6]

All of this is right on the mark, but it only makes sense when Elvis is correctly understood as a symbol, when his status as such is clearly distinguished from him as a flesh-and-blood person. No matter that his goal was to be another entertainer like Dean Martin, that his songs were written by others (black and white), that he also recorded some of the ickiest glop ever heard, that he eventually became a parody of himself, and that he would always be known in the black community as "the white boy who stole the blues." Of such things are symbols made.

In Tillich's terms, Elvis Presley pointed to a dimension of sensuality and pleasure hitherto forbidden (if not unknown) to whites, and by so doing he smashed the barriers separating the races. It was a level of reality in which he himself lived, not very successfully, admittedly, but the important thing in this is how he was perceived. Sam Phillips may have been looking for just such a person, but it's extremely important to recognize the fact that he *found* him; he didn't *create* him. The distinction is crucial, for if the Presley phenomenon was a deliberate creation, then it could be duplicated. Virtually everyone in the business tried, of course, even Phillips himself, and he tried with some of the very best (Carl Perkins, Roy Orbison, Johnny Cash, and Jerry Lee Lewis). All attempts failed. If anything, the Elvis phenomenon resulted from the unconscious strivings of the vast numbers of repressed American youths who had tasted of the tree of rhythm and blues.

The key element responsible for its working out like this was Elvis's whiteness. A revolution of this character could never have come from those already excluded from a genuine entry into American society. It had to come from those invited inside, from those who were self-consciously benefiting from America's class and racial divisions. In other words, the revolution had to come from the immense, patriotic and religiously conservative middle class. No other group could feel the contradictions in numbers sufficient to threaten the status quo. Comfortable whites would never have been disturbed by the complaints of blacks or even poor whites; as so often in the past, their rumblings could easily have been dismissed as sour grapes or simply ignorance, if not the pure manifestation of laziness. But when they heard these same complaints coming from their own children, who had begun to identify themselves with the sentiments of the outcasts, something was bound to happen. Imagine the internal contradictions these youths must have felt when they first adopted this strange music as their own; it was expressing emotions and attitudes dangerously at odds with everything they had been taught, and they were buying into it in ever increasing numbers. At the very least, it caused them to question the legitimacy of their position and the position of the outcasts in American society; at the most, it caused them to do something about it.

The primary carrier of this infection was, of course, Elvis, the symbol. Were it not for his unique status, he would never have been able to broach the legal and moral fortress the established order had erected to protect itself. Writing from a white's perspective, Michael Bane is convinced that "the final element necessary to turn rock into something other than just another musical fad was the element of rebellion, and that had to come from the whites themselves. Chuck Berry could slyly hint at it, and Little Richard . . . could even shout it out, but the message wouldn't become real until it came from one of *us*, as opposed to one of *them*. . . . A fusion had to take place; a white boy had to sing the blues. There had to be an Elvis."[7] Make no mistake about this. Elvis was no mere imitation; he absorbed the music of both blacks and whites, but what resulted was something never before heard. According to Marcus, "It is vital to remember that Elvis was the first young Southern white to sing rock 'n' roll, something he copied from no one but made up on the spot; and to know that even though other singers would have come up with a white version of the new black music acceptable to teenage America, of all that did emerge in Elvis's wake, none sang as powerfully, or with more than a touch of his magic."[8] We could listen to him and admire him because he was white, but he told us about a world of forbidden pleasures, and when we heard about it, like it or not, we would never be the same.

Some say it all came to an end when he acquiesced to the United States Army's apparently desperate need for his services, although this was years before an opposition to the draft would mean anything. Others mark the decline even earlier, with his leaving Sun Records for the seductive entrapments of the corporate world of RCA. But it really makes no difference; at some point, Elvis, the living symbol, ceased to be. Yet, like a well-known predecessor, he rose again to live on in spirit. The tragic hulk of flesh and blood that Elvis eventually became was committed to the ground at Graceland, but the real Elvis, the symbol, has never died. Shortly before his own tragic death, John Lennon, in a *Playboy* interview, remembered all those years ago when rock and roll became a way of life for him: "I think it was 'Rock around the Clock.' I enjoyed Bill Haley, but I wasn't overwhelmed by him. It wasn't until 'Heartbreak Hotel' that I really got into it." And he was still into it in December of 1980. In the same interview Lennon stressed the distinction between Elvis himself and what he stood for: "The early Elvis records live on without Elvis being a beautiful male animal who swung his pelvis. . . . I didn't see him. I heard the music first. Afterwards I saw that it did come in a package. But *you don't need the package*. With Elvis, the basic thing, the basic energy, is on the records."[9] So it is, but even more it's in our consciousness, ready to be reawakened whenever the occasion arises.

The single most important factor hindering his resurrection for many people is the idolatrous regard in which he has always been held. Perhaps it was unavoidable, but his countless worshippers have never been able to distinguish between the transitory and finite Elvis and the Elvis who is eternal and infinite. In all probability, they've never tried. If so, the only thing remaining to them is the sediment of nostalgia, a dead past. Avoiding idolatry is the only possible way for a symbol to live on eternally, and self-negation is the only means to accomplish this, which is Tillich's criterion for validity.

Despite the fact that many of his fans missed or ignored Elvis's self-negation, there are ample illustrations of how he satisfied the criterion. No doubt he was completely unaware of what he was doing, but his awareness is totally irrelevant. As I've tried to stress so often throughout the book, what matters is how things are perceived, for there is no other reality available to us. For most observers, Elvis's self-negation actually comes closer to self-destruction. The debauchery of his later years seems now as if it were intentionally undertaken to accomplish the necessary self-negation, but the indications were clear even in his prime. Greil Marcus feels "[H]e was implicitly presenting his new successful self as a target for his own resentments. . . . Somehow taking both sides, Elvis could show his listeners just how much, and how little, that pink Cadillac was worth: more and less than anyone would have guessed." And he adds in a footnote, "When he smashed through the contradictions of his career with such music, we have Elvis at his greatest." Marcus, I think, is one of the most astute of all the practicing Elvisologists, but his analysis was done while Elvis was still alive, before all the postmortem exposes and maudlin retrospectives complicated the possibility of intelligent criticism. He saw an Elvis who "parodied his menace," an Elvis whose quintessential performance was

> an overwhelming outburst of real emotion and power, combined with a fine refusal to take himself with any seriousness at all. Finding that power within himself, and making it real, was part of the liberation he was working out in his music; standing off from the power, with a broad sense of humor and amusement, was another. This was the saving grace of Elvis's ambition, and a necessary counter to it. It allowed him to transcend his success and his public image . . .; that casual élan would let him see at least part of the way through the unprecedented adulation he received.[10]

Whether or not this attitude lasted with him to the end can never be known, but what is certain is the fact that he felt trapped by what he had become. This is a sure sign that he was aware of the liabilities of being Elvis Presley.

An episode from his "coronation" (his three appearances on "The Ed Sullivan Show") suggests the presence of self-negation from the very beginning, for anyone who had eyes to see. Only on the third show was he shown from the waist up; for the earlier two, he was merely requested to control his suggestive body movements so as not to offend common decency. During one song, however, he got so caught up in the music that he *apparently* forgot his instructions. When he realized his "wiggling" was beyond the pale, he laughed and crossed his legs at the knees as if to conceal his pelvic parts from the invasive scrutiny of the network censors, knowing full well that the audience would scream with delight. At other times, while singing or during a pause, he would feign a snarl or hint at the possibility of an illicit movement—and laugh at himself. The point is that he knew very well what he was doing, and we knew that he knew, and he knew that we knew that he knew. Ed Sullivan didn't know and our parents didn't know, but we didn't care, and he didn't care either, and we and he knew that too. Under these circumstances, the only people who were taking Elvis with ultimate seriousness were those most distant from him, people who tended to identify the flesh and blood person with what he symbolized. As a result, much of the outrage and adulation was misdirected; attention was mistakenly focused on the swiveling hips of someone who died in 1977 (and thereby calling far more attention to them than even the best efforts of Colonel Tom Parker could ever hope to approximate). Those who knew better, fans and enemies alike, were looking at someone whose presence is with us still.

Recognition of Elvis's significance hinges directly on his symbolic stature, that which Greil Marcus perceptively acknowledges:

> At his best Elvis not only embodies but personalizes so much of what is good about this place: a delight in sex that is sometimes simple, sometimes complex, but always open; a love of roots and a respect for the past; a rejection of the past and a demand for novelty; the kind of racial harmony that for Elvis, a white man, means a profound affinity with the most subtle nuances of black culture combined with an equally profound understanding of his own whiteness; a burning desire to get rich and to have fun; a natural affection for big cars, flashy clothes, for the symbols of status that give pleasure both as symbols and on their own terms. Elvis has long since become one of those symbols himself.[11]

Marcus wrote these words in 1974, three years before Elvis died; he revised the book in 1982, five years afterward, and he chose, quite consciously, to retain the present tense. That says it all.

—————————————— Illud Tempus ——————————————

In the beginning was the music, and the music was with Elvis, and the music was Elvis. So it began.

The fifties began with a new testament. The promises of the old order were now in the process of being fulfilled by that which was at the same time ending the old order. The latinization of "That Time" was Eliade's way of stressing the paramount importance of the Time of Origin, the events of which are always preserved in myth and symbol, making its return and reactualization an eternal possibility. Michael Bane, too, is sensitive to this dimension of the cultural revolution: "The late 1950s mark the beginning of the rock and roll mythology, the gospel according to rock."[12] And forevermore, this would be the essential spirit to be re-captured, the final measure of authenticity, the time before which there was only darkness upon the face of the nation.

None of this should imply, however, that there were no roots that led up to this moment. Any decent history of American music would dispel that impression immediately. But we are not really dealing with facts of this kind; our attention is on the mythic account, *interpreted* facts orga-nized in such a way as to provide a meaning for whatever data actually exist. And there's quite a bit to work from in this case. By now, of course, many of the musicians' names are legend, but many more are known only to those who've devoted their lives to a study of rock's pre-history. Sadder still is the fact that an unknown number of names are lost for good, no one ever thinking that their many contributions would amount to anything worth noting for future generations. In any case, this music has a past that ought not be forgotten.

From its African roots, which took hold in the South and traveled north along the banks of the Mississippi, to its eventual merger with a variety of old-English traditions hidden away in the hills of Appalachia, it was played, sung, and performed by countless musicians of varying degrees of talent and skill. Elvis certainly didn't create his distinctive sounds *ex nihilo*; more accurately, he gave a shape and meaning to the musical tra-ditions he found readily available in the multiracial culture of the South. It was a shape and meaning that the world had never before experienced, something wholly unanticipated.

According to Eliade, "every myth shows how a reality came into exis-tence, whether it be the total reality, the cosmos, or only a fragment. . . . To tell how things came into existence is to explain them and at the same time indirectly to answer another question: *Why* did they come into existence?'' A factual account is obviously important, but far more important for our human existence is the meaningfulness of it all, and this is the overriding purpose of myth. Without providing a meaning, a direction, or an overall scheme, a myth could not fulfill its *raison d'etre*; indeed, it would not be myth. Eliade added that ''[T]he supreme function of the myth is to 'fix' the paradigmatic models for all rites and all significant human activities,'' and he listed such activities as eating, sexuality, work, education, economics, and war.[13] In other words, everything.

As for Elvis, in his very being he showed us how it all came about; he was, after all, a white boy singing the blues, and the message wasn't lost on anyone, least of all our parents. Those old enough may recall the now laughable rivalry between Elvis and Pat Boone. Pat covered some of Fats Domino's songs and, for one brief moment, embodied the ''clean'' (non-black) side of rock and roll. He was one of the establishment's attempts to co-opt something it could neither appreciate nor understand. He was at that time the only safe alternative to Elvis available to the establishment, and his white bucks and ducks seemed deliberately to indicate just a bit more than the color of his favorite beverage. Guess who our parents preferred.

As has happened so often before with the founders of cultural movements, an outcast led the way and became the model for his followers to emulate. If Elvis could walk on what was, for then, the ''wild side,'' then so could we. If Elvis could express uninhibited sexuality, then we'd try it too. If Elvis could regale, to the point of obscenity, in what everyone knew to be wealth and privilege not ''earned'' through hard work, then our attitudes toward work would be transformed accordingly. Our parents worried about our affecting the outward trappings of the Elvis imagery—a black leather jacket, long sideburns, a d.a. (duck's ass) haircut, a certain demeanor of body movement, and a well-practiced, disdainfully cavalier turn of the upper lip. The trappings were important, of course, but the real changes weren't visible; they took place in our consciousness. Even the vast majority who adopted none of the visible signs were irreversibly influenced, and this includes all the ''squares'' who ostensibly hated everything Elvis stood for. No one escaped. Elvis the symbol told us how it all happened and what it all meant. It took some time for everything to sink in, but once it did, we were never the same.

Through appropriate rituals, the mythic time of origin is infinitely recoverable and the founding events eternally repeatable. According to Eliade, every religious festival is based on a sacred event that took place *ab origine* (in the beginning), which is ritually made present. In this way, the participants in the festival can become contemporaries of the earlier mythical event. In his last years, Elvis himself assumed the role of reactualizing his mythic past in the highly ritualized setting of his concerts. (The 1968 comeback special on TV is a notable exception in only one respect: it was superlative, a work of genius.) Somewhere, usually toward the end, he would go through a medley of his early and classic hits, attired, as he always was in his later concerts, in what for lack of a better phrase can only be described as an "Elvis suit": a gold, white, or black sequined monstrosity, girdled with a wide ornamental belt (designed partially to hold in his girth) and a buckle that could stop an artillery shell; accented with a raised collar at least four inches high; framed with an immense, swooping cape that he would unchain with a ceremonial flourish at an appropriately dramatic moment; and intended to reveal an equally ostentatious shirt that displayed every hair that could ever be grown on his chest. During the medley, one of his sycophants would hand him a continual supply of cheap silky scarves, which he would ritualistically pass around his neck and toss out into the worshipful crowd (overflowing with aging men practically dragging their sideburns over their shoulders, and their plumpish wives sporting their own distinctive bleached beehive coiffures).

A sad and tacky exercise in nostalgia? Perhaps. But it was also much more than that, as one of John Lennon's friends found out. "A friend of mine," Lennon reported, "a *big* Elvis fan, *bigger* than I was, went to see him. . . . When he saw him in Vegas, I asked my friend how he was. He said, 'Well, if you sort of half shut your eyes and pretended, it was heaven.'"[14] Ordinary, chronological time doesn't permit this kind of reversal; mythic time, however, demands it. "Religious man," who for Eliade is the only fulfilled human, "feels the need to plunge periodically into this sacred and indestructible time. For him it is sacred time that makes possible the other time, profane duration in which every human life takes its course." It is *not,* however, "a rejection of the real world and an escape into dream and imagination"; on the contrary, "it is at once thirst for the *sacred* and nostalgia for *being.*"[15] More than anything else, Elvis's audiences came to reorient themselves to something they felt to be timeless, the source of everything they had come to be. This was no simpleminded journey down memory lane; this was their attempt to get in touch with their existential roots.

Before Elvis there were rich and vital musical traditions among both blacks and whites, but there was no revolution. Before Elvis there was even something called rock and roll, but there was no revolution. Before Elvis there was rage and alienation throughout the entire country, barely held in check by a dogmatically repressive and subtly authoritarian regime, yet still there was no revolution. Before Elvis there were many people who embodied perfectly the tensions that lay just beneath the surface of the supposedly placid Fifties, but they were neither symbolic nor actual revolutionaries. Hence, as John Lennon observed on hearing about his death at Graceland, "Before Elvis, there was nobody."

——————————— Vignettes of Negation ———————————

If Elvis symbolized the negation of the prevailing attitudes towards sex, race, and work, there were countless others who were living the negation. Two groups in particular were the beats and greasers.

After the Soviet Union's wholly unforeseen triumph in putting the first artificial satellite in orbit around the earth (*Sputnik*), beats came to be known as beat*niks,* to suggest that their leftish leanings did not go unnoticed. A more perceptive appraisal came from *On the Road,* Jack Kerouac's literary tone poem on the American hipster. Aside from virtually defining what it meant to be beat, Kerouac and his North Beach associates named an entire generation. Although the beats were few in number, their influence was staggering. Those who didn't emulate them in some way were frightened by them, but no one could ignore them. In one of those paradoxes so incredibly strange that it necessarily escapes a mind attuned only to the rational, the very people who had the most to fear from what the beats stood for were also the very ones to propagate and popularize the beat movement. The established order devoted far more attention to it than would seem to have been warranted—news coverage, editorial lamentations, sociological and psychological analyses, religious outrage, and, most important of all, commercial exploitation.

Many people, including myself, first encountered the beat movement without meeting a single genuine beat. One guy in high school, for example, affected the style pretty well, and we all went along with his charade, because, well, real beats were hard to come by. On Saturday nights a group of us would hang out at one of Baltimore's hip "coffee houses," the Flambeau, and pretend to be hipper than thou, snapping our fingers to the absurdist poetry and minimalist music while sipping expensive and oddly named herb teas and spiced coffees. Last, and certainly least, was Manyard G. Krebs, TV's picture of the lovable, harmless, and slightly touched beatnik, whose weird and unthinkably wild clothing consisted of dungarees and a sweat shirt. Thus, in the strangest of ways, were most of us introduced to the beat movement, at least its style if not its substance. The idea that a counterculture group *existed* was what was propagated, causing us to wonder what it was all about. And so the movement was spread farther and wider than if the established order had left well enough alone. What we eventually learned from the beats mirrored precisely the messages we were receiving from rock and roll; the only significant difference was the beats' enjoyment of something called marijuana, and of that we would learn more later.

Greasers were another matter entirely. They challenged the same values but in a very different way. The beats were essentially peaceful and nonaggressive, almost to the point of isolationism, while the black-leather-jacket crowd presented the image of violence and terror. Again, this was far more the result of creative publicity than hard, verifiable fact, but the image is what counted. I remember asking my parents for a black leather jacket for Christmas one year; I also remember the consternation that this request caused them, yet they never explained why such an artifact had this effect on them. (My gift turned out to be a rather bulky *brown* leather jacket, which I consigned to my little brother as soon as decency and good taste would permit.) Unlike the beats, who tended to relate to each other in small, amorphous, and ever-shifting groups, the greasers were gang oriented. Everyone needs some kind of support group for the development and protection of personal identity, but a gang gives its members a sense of power as well, which every youth at that time lacked, simply by virtue of youth. Although the greasers were just as small a minority as the beats, their influence might actually have been even more disproportionate; we didn't want to join them, or God knows, even associate with them, but we sure envied them. Marlon Brando and James Dean weren't youth heroes for nothing.

Of the three issues most obviously and intimately involved in the fifties negation, race topped the list. In a very real way, all other facets of the negation were implicit in the toppling of the prevailing attitude toward race relations. What was being negated was the notion that whiteness was equivalent to goodness, both moral and nonmoral, (for example, "That's white (meaning decent) of you," and "If it's white, it's all right"). This equation has been so ingrained in our culture that it wasn't until Diana Ross and the Supremes that white males could openly acknowledge that black women could be just as beautiful and desirable as white women. And still today, it remains the case that "innocent until proven guilty" is much more of an unrealized ideal for blacks than for whites. Yet this disparity is no longer an acceptable part of our culture, as it once was. One of the most interesting illustrations of how this racial equation was negated has to do with Johnny Otis, a white man who self-consciously chose to live black and play the blues. Never before was it so clearly apparent that blackness and whiteness are the result of social conventions, not physical characteristics (except in minor and unimportant ways). For him to "pass" in the opposite way would have been unthinkable without the destruction of the racist equation, at least for him and all those who accepted and admired his "passing." With the inception of rock and roll in the fifties, the destruction began in earnest, an irreversible process that continues to this day.

The second most influential negation concerned sexuality, and again, what was being destroyed was an equation involving goodness: goodness associated with a certain set of sexual mores, notably virginity or abstinence, self-restraint, male dominance, exclusivity, procreation, heterosexuality, all of which were based on the religiously sanctioned monogamous marriage. Sex was unclean, a weakness to be strongly resisted, an understandable drive for men but a craven urge for women; its ultimate (and often singularly) justifiable purpose was to fulfill the divine command to multiply and subdue the earth. Rock and roll's attack on this ideology has been so massive as to be impossible as well as pointless to document. The very term "rock and roll" is sexual in origin, and "dance" is used euphemistically so often that, for all practical purposes, "to dance" is to attack the inherited equation. In the music, sex is portrayed positively, a part of our physical nature to be enjoyed, desirable in and of itself, good for no other reason than that it's pleasurable. Other implications of the attack would have to be worked out in the future (most especially the sexist baggage), but for the moment, it was sufficient to undermine the rectitude of the traditional standards, replacing the fundamental idea that sex is bad with its opposite. After all, the usual reason given as to why rock and roll was so devilishly corrupting was sex, and those who felt (and still feel) this way were pretty close to the mark. An interesting change has taken place, however, since the attack was first engaged. In 1958, at what seemed to be the pinnacle of his career, Jerry Lee Lewis was ruined because of a sex scandal, having married his fourteen (or thirteen, or twelve, depending on the source) year old cousin. The specific charge was incest, but rock and roll was deemed to be the underlying cause. Significantly, this was the last time a sex scandal ruined any rock and roller's career; soon a "scandal" had pretty much the opposite effect.

The third and final activity singled out for negation was the complex set of norms commonly referred to as the Protestant work ethic: the idea that effort, skill, and talent are in some mystical way directly proportional to success and rewards; another idea that work itself was desirable as an ultimate value; and the idea that a morally good person would necessarily be hardworking. So again, there is an equation: work is intrinsically good, both as an end and as a means. Because of the music, however, it was becoming increasingly obvious that work and success were unrelated; not only were the founders of the rock tradition never adequately compensated for their contributions, but luck and aggressive promotion were playing a much larger role than anything else. How else can the likes of Frankie Avalon and Fabian be explained except through the well-financed campaigns of their manager, Robert Marcucci (about whom the film *The Idolmaker* was made)? If hard work wasn't very effective, neither was it desirable. If anything, it was a means to an end, but the end was pleasure. The Protestant work ethic was being confronted with nothing less than the gospel of hedonism, an unequal contest if there ever was one.

The negation of the fifties came very close to what some philosophers have termed "negative freedom," the freedom *from* certain interferences and barriers. The removal of these obstacles was the immediate object, but we must never lose sight of the fact that nothing less than freedom was the ultimate aim. What this meant in positive terms would be spelled out in the sixties, but the sixties could never have happened had the fifties not cleared the way. And if anyone captured the spirit of this negation, and embodied its threefold attack in his person so perfectly that the very mention of his name can evoke its power still today, that person would have to be none other than Elvis Presley.

The Beatles and the
Affirmation of the
Sixties

─────────────────── 9 ───────

The sixties began with a bang, three of them to be exact, all presumably fired from the sixth-story window of the Texas School Book Depository in Dallas, Texas, at 12:30 P.M. on Friday, November 22, 1963. Thus are we provided with the one infallible criterion for identifying the sixties generation: if it has been indelibly etched into your consciousness where you were when you first heard the news (and if Pearl Harbor is not a part of your consciousness in this way), then no matter what your social, political, or cultural allegiances, either then or now, you are a "child of the sixties." Far too much has been made over participation in one or more of the various, highly visible counterculture groups, such as the New Left, the black militants, the hippies, the Student Nonviolent Coordinating Committee (SNCC), the Congress of Racial Equality (CORE), or any number of others, as the distinguishing measure, when everyone was equally affected and permanently changed by the overwhelming reality of the assassination—not in the same way, of course, but just as thoroughly as the Pearl Harbor generation was by its key event.

It was more than a murder, more even than an assassination; it was the destruction of a dream, the hope that a better world was about to happen. Kennedy brought to our national consciousness the belief that we could appreciate the past without being trapped by it, that there was a promising future just ahead. All we needed to do was to work together and all of our national and international problems would eventually be resolved. America was in for a new day in the sun. There you have it . . . Camelot.

No matter that John F. Kennedy was perceived far differently than what the facts can support. Even some of the most sympathetic accounts of his presidency point out that his legislative accomplishments were slight and his innovative proposals more often than not the products of other minds. Moreover, on civil rights, his support was less than wildly enthusiastic, resulting more from political expediency than moral conviction. In foreign policy, the nearly universal opinion that he redeemed himself for the debacle at the Bay of Pigs with his courage and decisiveness in dealing with Khrushchev in the Cuban missile crisis, is an opinion derived undiluted and unaltered from a frame of mind structured by the Cold War. His redemption only makes sense as such to those whose consciousness has been set by the remembrance of Pearl Harbor, those who viewed the war in Vietnam as if it were like our war with the Japanese. Speculation still abounds as to what might have happened in Southeast Asia had Kennedy survived, but this kind of fruitless activity reveals more about the speculators than anything else. What really matters is the meaning John Kennedy had for the American people, not what he did, didn't do, or might have done; his stature as a symbol is what's important.

Looking a bit more deeply into the Camelot mythology, we see that something else was destroyed in Dallas along with the dream of a particular kind of national destiny. It was the unspoken and mostly unconscious assumption that difficult and dramatic changes could be expected to occur in an evolutionary fashion. No radical measures would be required: no fundamental break with the past, no questioning of ultimate values, and certainly no introduction of new and conflicting values. If anything new was necessary, it would be acceptable only insofar as it could be modified and absorbed so as not to threaten the received tradition. This, too, died in Dallas.

The multifaceted consequences of the assassination help partially to explain the magnitude of the shock, disbelief, and outpouring of emotion throughout the nation and the world that followed. Many world leaders followed along behind the funeral cortege. Even Fidel Castro expressed genuine sorrow at the news. More than likely, all of them were experiencing the loss of the unspoken assumption too. We mourned for a shattered future, but also for the peaceful transition that was to take us there. Kennedy had symbolized both, and with his death we were left with a strange feeling of emptiness, a loss of direction and a failure of confidence. "He was a friend of mine," sang the Byrds, "His killin' had no purpose/No reason or rhyme." Such feelings rang true no matter what worth there might be to the many and varied conspiracy theories. Even more to the point was "He never knew my name/Though I never met him/I knew him just the same." All of us, like the Byrds, felt that we knew him but what we really knew was what he meant to us. Years later, and from a very different rock musical perspective, Lou Reed would still recall "The Day John Kennedy Died" as the death of a dream, even when the dream he sang about bore little resemblance to John Kennedy's. Kennedy spoke to something far deeper within us than our political convictions, and he represented something that would never again be.

It was only fitting that all television and radio programming ceased normal operations to cover the martyrdom in its entirety. Despite our divergent religious beliefs, political affiliations, ethnic backgrounds, and patriotic sympathies, we all sat, stunned, in front of the television for the duration. All normal activities had come to a complete halt (even cloistered nuns were released from their religious isolation to watch), as the reality of it all began to sink in. And so for a short time, we as a nation were united. We who had at one time playfully asked "Lyndon Who?" were now prepared to entrust to him our destiny—a national consensus such as experienced by perhaps only one other president (Franklin D. Roosevelt) was his.

But this unity was not to last. Exactly eighty days later, cracks were to appear that would grow ever wider. The process was imperceptible at first, but in retrospect, it was inexorable. For on Sunday, February 9, 1964, America was invaded by the British. To be sure, there were only four of them, but they were carrying ideas and values that were directly at odds with traditional American beliefs, ideas and values that would, for many Americans, fill the void left by the assassination.

When Ed Sullivan's plane was forced to circle London's Heathrow Airport in the middle of the night in order to permit something called the Beatles to land first so that they could be transported safely through thousands of their screaming fans, he decided then and there to sign them for his "reallybig shew." He didn't care what kind of act they were; if they could draw that kind of crowd at that hour, he wanted them. Thus it was, on that Sunday evening in February, that we sat down in front of our TV sets to watch, as we usually did, "The Ed Sullivan Show." When it was over, we weren't quite sure what had happened, other than being introduced to a new prefix for the word *mania,* but one thing was certain: America had just surrendered to these British invaders.

Bob Dylan and I (and probably many others as well) have one thing in common: neither of us would admit at the time how much the Beatles had overwhelmed us. Anthony Scaduto reports, in *Bob Dylan: An Intimate Biography,* that Dylan laughed condescendingly along with his friends at how faddish and juvenile their music seemed, suitable only for the listening enjoyment of those still committed to satisfying their oral fixations with a stick of bubble gum: "We were driving through Colorado . . . we had the radio on and eight of the Top Ten songs were Beatles songs. . . . They were doing things nobody was doing. Their chords were outrageous, and their harmonies made it all valid. . . . But I kept it to myself that I really dug them. Everybody else thought they were for the teeny-boppers, that they were gonna pass right away. But it was obvious to me that they had staying power. I knew they were pointing the direction where music had to go . . . in my head, the Beatles were *it.* In Colorado, I started thinking but it was so far out I couldn't deal with it—eight in the top ten. It seemed to me a definite line was being drawn. This was something that never happened before."[1] I wonder how many of those driving along with him that day were keeping the very same secret, embarrassed or afraid to admit that the times were indeed changing, but perhaps not in the ways they had always anticipated. My guess is that quite a few were keeping it to themselves.

In my own case, I was heavily into the classics, refusing to admit to any interest whatsoever in popular music; not jazz (music for the terminally obscure); certainly not rock and roll (music for the witless); and not even the new folk trend, which was attracting so many refugees from rock who were searching for some way to express a growing uneasiness with American society (music for pseudointellectuals). This was possibly my own way of distancing myself from an increasingly alien society, although I was hardly aware of it at the time. After returning to college from our extended Thanksgiving break (because of the assassination and funeral), I was in the mood for some serious discussion of the impending crises, especially concerning civil rights. (Lyndon Johnson, after all, was a southerner.) My ex-roomies offered the best prospects, since our ethical convictions about society were very similar and were leading us to seminary after graduation. Expecting to hear the latest from Joan Baez or Ian and Sylvia emanating from their hi-fi, folkies that they were, I was startled to find them listening intently to top-40 radio, madly switching stations and barely acknowledging my presence.

Then it happened. "Listen to this!" they insisted, turning the volume up higher. They had come across "I Want to Hold Your Hand" somewhere in the middle of the song. It was something I had never heard before—the harmonies, the bass, the volume, that incredible falsetto on "hand"—chills went immediately up my spine. *Who is this?* I wanted to ask, but didn't. It would have severely compromised my sophisticated detachment, so I feigned uninterest.

"Isn't this different?" they asked, obviously excited, and certainly not expecting any disagreement.

"It sounds just like any other rock and roll to me," I lied, with as much haughty condescension as I could muster up without offending them too much. I had, of course, already heard *about* the Beatles from the news, but I had never actually *heard* them. The music was overwhelming, but I couldn't admit that. It had dredged up those long-forgotten memories of hearing "Rock around the Clock" and "Heartbreak Hotel" for the first time. This time, however, there was an enormous difference: Bill Haley and Elvis Presley had been tearing something down; these guys were building something up; you could hear it in just the first few bars.

It hadn't happened overnight, of course. Ever since The Beginning in 1955, England had been going crazy with hastily formed skiffle bands, one of which was the Quarrymen out of Liverpool. America had imported the rock revolution to England, and in 1964, it was returned with interest. In the meantime, the Quarrymen had paid their dues in dingy little clubs, playing impossibly long hours in the strip joints along the Reeperbahn in Hamburg, losing two of their original members, adding a new drummer from Rory Storm and the Hurricanes, acquiring a devoted and sensitive manager, and, of course, changing their name.

What was about to happen (in England, America, and throughout much of the Western world) was a change of consciousness: the complete reorganization, reinterpretation, and reevaluation of the perception of reality in accordance with a new and contrary set of ultimate beliefs and values. In his *Invitation to Sociology*, Peter Berger describes this as a conversion experience or (to avoid the religious connotations) the process of "alternation," in which people opt for a system of meaning radically at odds with the one they abandon. Most important, a change like this is comprehensive—everything is altered. Within our own consciousness, even the past is "malleable and flexible, constantly changing as our recollection reinterprets and re-explains what has happened." Conversion is thus "an act in which *the past* is dramatically transformed." Most of the time we undergo such alternations unconsciously and haphazardly, stumbling "like drunkards over the sprawling canvas of our self-conception, throwing a little paint here, erasing some lines there, never really stopping to obtain a view of the likeness we have produced." Berger maintains, however, that "there are some cases where the reinterpretation of the past is part of a deliberate, fully conscious, and intellectually integrated activity. This happens when the reinterpretation of one's biography is one aspect of conversion to a new religion or ideological *Weltanshauung,* that is, a universal meaning system *within which* one's biography can be located."[2]

Obviously, not everyone had such a conversion experience, an alternation of *Weltanschauung;* also, when it did happen, it was neither instantaneous nor completely conscious; nor has the opportunity for its happening ceased. The fifties had shaken the foundations of the established order and had left an entire generation expecting something new. The assassination made it clear that the something new wouldn't be forthcoming from those succeeding Kennedy. The problem wasn't just that there was no longer a charismatic leader who could lead the way; rather, people came to the unsettling realization that the prevailing order was intrinsically incapable of providing anything new. It had given us its best and its brightest (as David Halberstam so aptly put it), but these people were sincerely committed to a set of fundamental values that many of us could no longer unquestioningly accept. Along with everyone else, we were shocked into insensibility by the killing that had neither rhyme nor reason, and we mourned Kennedy's passing and all that he meant. Yet those of us whose consciousness had been troubled by the vision of the man in the pink Cadillac, who had heard the voice crying in the wilderness, were ready and waiting for a new beginning. We had been left with no viable alternative to the established order.

Into this void, straight off of their BOAC jet from London, stepped those four lads with their outrageously long hair. Two days later they ascended the very stage that Elvis had ascended eight years earlier and underwent the same rites of coronation that had confirmed him king. That evening Elvis relinquished his crown and even sent a congratulatory telegram, giving substance to a story so often retold, that Brian Epstein was the only manager to claim his group would be bigger than Elvis . . . and be right.

Fascination

Just as dread colored every aspect of the Elvis phenomenon, so fascination was the overwhelmingly pervasive quality with regard to the Beatles. Together, these two feelings create the "strange harmony of contrasts" referred to by Rudolf Otto as the key characteristic of the religious experience. Although both Elvis and the Beatles have given expression to the other's primary sensation as well, their one quality has been so dominant that every other element of the religious experience is subsumed within it.

At this point, an extended reference to Otto is necessary if the Beatles' exemplification of fascination is to be appreciated. Most often present in traditional religions as a quest for some kind of salvation, the feeling of fascination incorporates the desire and yearning for something ultimate. Throughout history this longing has taken many different and seemingly incompatible forms, but

> in all these forms, outwardly diverse but inwardly akin, it appears as a strange and mighty propulsion towards an ideal good known only to religion and in its nature fundamentally nonrational, which the mind knows of in yearning and presentiment, recognizing it for what it is behind the obscure and inadequate symbols which are its only expression.[3]

At its peak, the feelings associated with fascination account for "the unutterableness of what has been yet genuinely experienced, and how such an experience may pass into blissful excitement, rapture, and exaltation verging often on the bizarre and the abnormal." If these comments are divested of Otto's conviction that only something supernatural (the numinous) can possibly provoke such feelings, Beatlemania becomes intelligible as more than a teenage fad: it becomes apprehensible as the phenomenon of mass conversion.

John Lahr wrote in the December 2, 1981, issue of *The New Republic* that "'Beatlemania' was a misnomer. Beatles fans were not so much hysterical as spellbound. The Beatles' music was a form of sympathetic magic, and the Beatles were local divinities who could change the mood and the look of their times by a song, a style, a word." The Beatles themselves were caught off guard by such adulation and were never comfortable with or fully recovered from the role imposed on them. "At first the Beatles didn't understand either their healing power or their shamanistic role," Lahr continued, citing a remark by Lennon in support: "It seemed that we were just surrounded by cripples and blind people all the time. And when we would go through the corridors, they would be touching us."[4] The role had its benefits, of course, but there were liabilities as well, and ever since, they have tried to separate themselves from this mixed blessing. Each of them came to know, more than anyone else could possibly know, how much of a burden being a Beatle had become. They reacted by partially accepting and partially rejecting the burden, using their power to accomplish certain goals, and using it against themselves as well. They had the power to shape popular consciousness, the greatest power there is, but they were trapped; no matter what they did, they couldn't rid themselves of it. In their earlier days, they had often voiced their mutual commitment to make it "to the top," but they had achieved far more. They had become the long-awaited promise for filling the void.

The darker side of the phenomenon was evident from the beginning. The four musicians embodied Otto's paradox so perfectly that religion is the only appropriate characterization for Beatlemania. Their early Teddy Boy image, though not an expression of their fundamental nature, was nevertheless a genuine manifestation of their anger at having been relegated to working-class oblivion. None of them had shown any promise whatsoever of becoming anything different from all their contemporaries, who were similarly condemned. In a fairly rigid class system, such as that in England, the chances of breaking free without showing exceptional promise are practically nonexistent. Knowing this, as each of them surely did, made for a potentially explosive situation. As more recent events in Britain have revealed, the frustration and anger among working-class youths hasn't abated very much in the intervening years, if at all. It is from this repressive social context that the Beatles' negation had its source—theirs and everyone's who saw their lives leading nowhere, inhibited and determined by a political structure that ignored them (at best). The Beatles, of course, broke free, and in so doing they gave voice to the hopes of everyone who was left behind. Perhaps this explains why their anger was so often tinged with the brash and carefree playfulness that we so often associate with them.

Both major biographies (*The Beatles* by Hunter Davies and *Shout!* by Philip Norman), as well as the personal recollection written by their friend, business associate, and manager, Peter Brown (*The Love You Make*), tell the tale far more effectively than needs to be done here. All three document the unresolved and barely restrained tension that's so evident in all of the group's finest music. Examples are legion, but a sample from the Beatles' various musical periods would no doubt include the following: "I Saw Her Standing There" from their first American album, *Meet the Beatles* (which opens with what Greil Marcus believes to be Paul shouting "One, Two, Three, Fuck!"); "Run for Your Life" from *Rubber Soul* (which incorporates a line from an old Elvis song—"I'd rather see you dead, little girl, than to be with another man"); "Taxman" (Harrison's scathing indictment of a government that would tax even the pennies on the eyes of a corpse) from *Revolver* (itself, an interesting play on words); "Baby, You're a Rich Man" from *Magical Mystery Tour* (satirizing the "beautiful people," including themselves); practically everything on the "White Album," so egregiously misused by Charles Manson ("The Continuing Story of Bungalow Bill," "Happiness Is a Warm Gun,'' "Piggies," "Why Don't We Do It in the Road?," "Helter Skelter," and "Revolution"—nos. 1 & 9); and even "Her Majesty" from *Abbey Road* (exemplifying at the end of the Beatles' career the class antagonisms that were there at the beginning). Yet there was also something positive in each of these songs, something promising. The quality of affirmation was never far removed from even the darkest and most negative music, for hidden within was the implicit and firm conviction that salvation could be grasped. John Lahr sees this creative paradox in what I regard as the finest piece of music ever written: "Even the great finale of the *Sgt. Pepper* album, 'A Day in the Life,' is a collage of two moods, which creates at once the sense of escape and the sense of terror. . . .''[5] It is hard to avoid the power produced by the collaboration of fascination and dread, for the power is essentially religious.

The other religious qualities (the sensations of wholly otherness, activity, mystical identification, and creatureliness) are so completely integrated within the paradox dominated by fascination that it would be misleading to isolate them for analysis. Suffice it to say that "A Day in the Life" captures them all in the paradoxical harmony of ultimate tragedy and certain victory. No other song better illustrates the religious import of Beatlemania, and no album symbolizes their numinous qualities more fully than *Sgt. Pepper's Lonely Hearts Club Band.* With anticipation no doubt magnified by advanced publicity, the album had been eagerly awaited as perhaps no other in the history of recording, either before or since. After having spent nearly seven hundred hours in the studio, the Beatles scheduled it for radio release at midnight, Sunday, June 2, 1967, a week before it would be available in record stores. Many a fan stayed awake that night listening to the endless replayings and the disc jockeys' repeated attempts to get one of the Beatles on the phone for a live interview. Such was its initial impact.

In an essay entitled "Learning from the Beatles," Richard Poirier singles out this one album for especially close analysis, subjecting each and every song to his exegetical scrutiny.[6] His overall conclusion is that "nothing less is being claimed by these songs than that the Beatles exist not merely as a phenomenon of entertainment but as a force of historical consequence. . . . Listening to the *Sgt. Pepper* album one thinks not simply of the history of popular music but of the history of this century. . . . The songs emanated from some inwardly felt coherence that awaited a merely explicit design." Peter Berger's "alternation," the present-oriented act of transforming our consciousness of both the past and future in the act of conversion, comes to mind immediately, especially when one considers the collage of historical personalities on the album jacket as an interpretive act. Poirier (who undertakes to examine the meaning of the figure portrayed on the cover of his own book, *The Performing Self*) understands the collage to be ''a celebration of the Beatles themselves, who can now be placed (and Bob Dylan, too) within that tiny group who have, aside from everything else they've done, infused the imagination of the living with the possibilities of other ways of living, of extraordinary existences, of something beyond 'a day in the life.''' Sensing the power of this album to shape our consciousness with the promise of salvation, another commentator, Langdon Winner, maintains that ''the closest Western Civilization has come to unity since the Congress of Vienna in 1815 was the week the *Sgt. Pepper* album was released. . . . For a brief while the irreparably fragmented consciousness of the West was unified, at least in the minds of the young.''[7]

What they revealed to us was a dream, an ideal, and they gave us the promise that it could be realized. The ideal was never portrayed as actual; nor was the actual ever portrayed as ideal. The former would be quixotic, the latter defeatist, and both, absurd. No, the Beatles offered a vision of what *ought to be* as distinct from what *is,* and in so doing, refashioned the past and future into something entirely new. Greil Marcus, in *The Rolling Stone Illustrated History of Rock and Roll,* puts it this way:

> As was so often pointed out in the mid-sixties, the sum of the Beatles was greater than the parts, but the parts were so distinctive and attractive that the group itself could be all things to all people. . . ; this was what had never happened before. And so it began. The past was felt to dissolve, the future was conceivable only as an expansion of the present, and the present was defined absolutely by its expansive novelty. . . . The Beatles seemed not only to symbolize but to contain it all—to make history by anticipating it. . . . The Beatles event . . . intensified not only in momentum but in magnetism, reaching more and more people with greater and greater mythic and emotional power, for at least four years. The Beatles affected not only the feel but the quality of life—they deepened it, sharpened it, brightened it, not merely as a factor in the cultural scheme, but as a presence. The Beatles affected *not* only the quality of life—they affected its worth.[8]

John Lennon was right, of course: the Beatles were more popular than Jesus. Though he was probably unaware of the true import of his controversial observation, which led to record burnings and anti-Beatles demonstrations primarily throughout the American South, he had nevertheless hit the proverbial nail squarely on the head, especially when he added, "I don't know which will go first—rock and roll or Christianity." There it was, for all to hear and contemplate: the competition between two incompatible religious movements, one supernatural and supportive of the status quo and the other immanental and threatening to it. He later apologized for having made these offhanded remarks, but he never recanted their meaning. For the Beatles had become far more than just an incredibly successful group of rock musicians; they had become the symbols par excellence for America's cultural revolution.

The Lonely Hearts Club

The Club has had but four members—additions, replacements, or resignations would be neither possible nor tolerated, its membership being the most exclusive in history. Admission and departure were at one time voluntary, but after the coronation there was no longer any choice. The members were trapped—the four loneliest people on the face of the earth—for with whom can the gods commune?

In recognition of what they had become, and as perhaps their last desperate attempt to separate themselves from it, they created mythic personae of themselves—Sgt. Pepper's Lonely Hearts Club Band. If so, the attempt was futile; it had exactly the opposite effect. The insertion of what turned out to be yet another symbol between themselves and the multitudes not only preserved but actually enhanced their absolute *mysterium*. The art for both the album and the film *Yellow Submarine* is so reminiscent of the iconography of the Byzantine church that this effect is hardly surprising. The Orthodox traditions within Christianity, of which the Byzantine church is one of the earliest examples, have always avoided exact representational religious art as being too crass and presumptuous for portraying the divine. They've preferred a mosaic styling, which seems to have ensured the art's symbolic nature; for who could believe these odd mosaics are exact replicas of the ultimate? At best they can only point to it. As a result, the object of worship has been removed almost entirely from the material world, making the artistic intermediary even more necessary as a spiritual bridge.

This might be exactly what Orthodoxy has always desired, but not so the Beatles. Their elaborate attempt at demystification, due to the nature of symbols, was bound to be counterproductive. Fanciful though they be,

Sgt. Pepper's little troupe serves to remove the Beatles further from us. Yet, in true paradoxical fashion, it also grants us access to them and to what they in turn symbolize.

Any adequate Pepperology must make some mention of the narrative of *Yellow Submarine,* no matter how much tongue needs to be placed in the cheek, for it contains some pretty interesting clues. Basically, it's a straightforward tale of good versus evil. The ultrainnocent people of Pepperland, whose god is Love, are set upon by the infamous Blue Meanies, who wish to deny to Pepperlanders the "pleasures of food and music and perpetual celebration and colorful beauty" (as it's so coyly expressed by the liner notes). Sgt. Pepper's Lonely Hearts Club Band is sent to request aid from the Beatles, who of course are only too willing to comply, and together they inevitably prevail.

There is little subtlety or complexity to this message, but then none is intended. Pleasure is affirmed as the ultimate value, but only insofar as it is provided with the moral guidance of love. Yet the implications of this value scheme are nowhere spelled out or even hinted at. Furthermore, the forces of evil are simply characterized as repressive, having no values of their own; they merely oppose the morality of love and pleasure and are thus, by definition, wrong. However, beneath the surface, there is a message of considerable importance being sent, a message of extreme confidence. By the end of the film, the Blue Meanies have been converted to the Pepperlander's morality, not killed as might have been the case. The message is clear: Human nature is such that a new way of relating to each other and a new world are possible, all based on the new set of values expressed through and exemplified by Sgt. Pepper's music. This degree of optimism about the human character is a key, foundational assumption of anarchism, for only by presupposing supreme confidence in how people would relate to each other without external guidance does anarchism make any sense; and given the assumption, *only* anarchism makes sense. "All You Need Is Love" is another way of putting it. There's nothing you can do that can't be done. . . No one you can save that can't be saved.

Such was their message to the sixties, and at the depths of human existence, it was received. The evidence is in the music, for communication of this kind must occur first at the level of feelings; later it can be expressed at the rational level, after the commitment has already been made. There have been numerous explicit references to Sgt. Pepper in song, but two come to mind as especially revealing of the relationship between the Beatles and the sixties. The first is Al Stewart's "Post

World War II Blues'' from his 1973 album *Past, Present and Future,*
which includes the following lyrics:

> I came up to London when I was nineteen
> With a corduroy jacket and head full of dreams
> In coffee bars I spent my nights
> Reading Allen Ginsberg, talking civil rights.
> On the day Robert Kennedy got shot down
> The world was wearing a deeper frown
> And though I knew that we'd lost a friend
> I always believed we could win in the end.
> Music was the scenery
> Jimi Hendrix played loud and free
> Sergeant Pepper was real to me
> Songs and poems were all you needed. . . .

Sergeant Pepper was real to a lot of people, not because of who they were
but because of what it meant.

Another set of lyrics, from ''Sgt. Pepper's Band,'' written by Joan
Baez, with Lennon's murder fresh in her mind, also highlights the relationship. The chorus goes as follows:

> Now I think I understand
> That it was Sergeant Pepper's Band
> That put the sixties into song
> Where have all the heroes gone?

Heroes, of course, are symbols, and genuine symbols can never die; only
people die. What the heroes symbolize lives on after them. So it is with
the Beatles.

There is no easy way to explain the complex set of values that they
pointed to, and the task is made even more difficult for the fact that some
of the values have been for so long ensconced in American tradition that
they are regarded as unquestioned truths. I have in mind such verities as
freedom, equality, justice, happiness, fraternity, individuality, and community, none of which have been fully realized, and some never attempted. Much of what the Beatles affirmed had to do with satisfying
these ideals, feeling as they did the disparity between the promise and the
reality. The Beatles' push towards fulfillment spoke to many of their gen-

eration, people who had been raised to believe in these values but whose experiences exposed them to the contradictions (first made evident to them in music). It was their inchoate but decidedly disturbed consciousness that the Beatles tapped into, organized, and expressed, and all they were saying was that the time had come to actualize the values and to do so without any further delay.

But there was a lot more to it. A set of ultimate values is just that—a set. Values are interrelated in a complex unity; a set is not some kind of list, from which some values might be added and others subtracted without affecting the others. On the contrary, the relationship is that of an organic whole that is larger than the sum of its parts. The set of values pointed to by the Beatles includes more than those inherited from the tradition, and just as important, it omits some traditional values. The overall result was something entirely new, disclosing a quality of existence not hitherto thought possible—a gestalt that formed the motivation and the goals of the sixties.

Included among the additional values were a pantheistic form of spirituality, anarchism, pacifism, pleasure, individuality, mysticism, sensuality, emotionality, and eccentricity. Eliminated were such values as individualism, nationalism, militarism, imperialism, and traditional religiousness (especially Western). David Pichaske characterizes the decade as a dialectic between ''an angry no'' and ''a transcendent yes.'' Although I might disagree with some of his ideas, I think his notion of a dialectical tension is absolutely correct: ''It is in this context of denial as affirmation that the decade must be viewed. Only by grasping this yes in the no can the high moral seriousness of sixties protest be understood.'' And, ''The yes of the sixties, very different in almost every particular from the angry no, was just as compelling. Rooted in idealism, this affirmation could overlap and encompass both protest marches and liberal politics. . . . The sixties yes was a magic yes, a hidden reality that might break out (or through) in any circumstance, extraordinary in its ordinariness, lunacy, spontaneity, freedom, magic.''[9] This complex set of values amounted to something logically contrary to the prevailing set. But because of this complexity, the new set, symbolized by the Beatles, made for an extremely difficult target. The established order often found itself taking potshots at values that it, too, affirmed. A more effective counterattack would have to wait for the election of 1980.

Interestingly, because the Beatles were not American they might have been all the more effective as symbols. For the tendency to confuse the symbol with what it points to was necessarily blunted: how could a British rock-and-roll band represent revolutionary values for Americans?

The connection just didn't seem to be there. Yet, in some strange way, the four spoke to the deepest part of the American consciousness, and many responded by seeing them as the linkage between their personal selves and their shared ultimate beliefs. In such a situation, idolatry is hard to avoid, and the Beatles phenomenon has had its share—as have all the traditional religions. The kind of idolatry feeding the Beatles' mystique, however, is capable of making a great deal of money for anyone who can replicate it. Attempts to do just this are instructive, since they make perfectly clear the impossibility of deliberately creating a symbol. It didn't work for the Monkees in the sixties, and it didn't work for the Knack in the seventies. While these, along with many others, were manufactured, the Beatles *happened.*

As for satisfying Tillich's criterion for validity—self-negation—the Beatles took the ultimate step: they destroyed themselves. In so doing, they guaranteed immortality for themselves, but more important, they focused attention squarely on what the Beatles have come to mean. John Lennon, in a *Playboy* interview, said, "If the Beatles of the Sixties had a message, it was to learn to swim. Period. And once you learn to swim, swim. The people who are hung up on the Beatles and the Sixties dream missed the whole point." The message was the thing; as far as he was concerned, the Beatles could be dispensed with. Given his iconoclastic sense of humor, especially as it pertained to the Beatles (from which he was forever trying to separate himself), he no doubt would be amused by William Scott's drawing on the cover of Rhino Record's *Beatlesongs!* (a collection of songs about the Beatles). Standing amid tacky Beatles artifacts strewn about the floor, festooned with John-buttons, and holding an autograph book in his fist, is, as George Harrison put it, "the devil's best friend, someone who offended all." Of course this is sick, but it's just this kind of desperate measure they felt to be necessary if they were ever to be freed from the mythology that had trapped them.

Given what they had done, and all their succeeding efforts to preserve their individuality, the numerous calls for a reunion would never have been answered, especially if it would have amounted to a mere nostalgic look backwards. (A creative risk-taking reunion, which looked forward with something new and challenging to say, would have been another matter entirely.) On those occasions when we've been able to avoid the pitfalls of idolatry and think clearly, we've always realized that a reunion (even for a single concert) was not in the cards. And in our exceptionally wise moments, we've even felt it to be undesirable.

For a long time the four knew that the Beatles were more than just another rock group, and their mixed feelings about what had happened made for some of their most creative work. Much of their creativity manifested their efforts to shatter the various images that imprisoned them. The infamous "butcher block" cover made for the first copies of *Yesterday and Today* is an example. It was their attempt to destroy their prevailing image of being decent, innocent, fun-loving, and harmless. Throughout their career, however, self-parody was their usual tactic, and Richard Poirier finds this to be among their finest qualities, preserving them from the kind of self-deception that might otherwise have been inevitable in their case. I agree. One song comes to mind as an exceptional example: "You Know My Name (Look Up the Number)." Originally released as the B-side of "Let It Be," it makes fun of almost everything, especially themselves.

Nothing worked, however, and destruction of the Beatles became the only possible recourse. Having to be the Beatles finally overwhelmed them. It was all too much. Touring and live concerts had to be halted; after a while they couldn't even hear themselves play. Their last performance was an impromptu concert on the roof of Apple Studios, captured for the film *Let It Be*. It is worth seeing if only for the sensation it caused.

In the tenth-anniversary issue of *Rolling Stone* (December 15, 1977), Jonathan Cott reflected on the "Children of Paradise, the Sixties generation," from what he termed "the calculating, mean-spirited perspective of the Seventies."[10] Trying to communicate what he had felt so strongly, he wrote that "[W]e forget that the Sixties impulse to bring us back to where we once belonged was almost single-handedly delineated and symbolized by one rock group from Liverpool." The reader can almost feel him straining for the appropriate analogy: "The group's four members came to be seen and thought of symbolically—like the Four Evangelists or the Four Elements. And in an elementary sense, each of the Beatles—in the way each became defined by his face, voice, and songs—took on an archetypal role: Paul, sweet and sensitive; John, sly and skeptical; George, mysterious and mystical; Ringo, childish but commonsensical—like Sancho Panza." It makes no difference how many people agree with him, or even whether the observations are at all accurate; what matters is the fact that thousands, nay millions, of others have made similar attempts at capsule summaries. Even Brian Epstein was reputed to have offered his own characterizations. The point is that, as individuals and a group, the Beatles reached a generation that was looking for a new set of values to replace those found no longer meaningful. Cott saw them as the perfect archetype of wholeness, musically expressed in "the merging of their singing voices at the conclusion of 'Happiness Is a Warm Gun,'" which for him was "one of *the* inimitable moments in rock history.'' Maybe wholeness is the key; they certainly pointed to it as an ideal, and to the best of their abilities, they tried to live the ideal. ''They presented themselves to us,'' Cott continued, ''as members of a little tribe which provided an example of how each of us could become part of the necklace of Shiva in which every diamond reflects every other and is itself reflected.'' He ended his comments with the acknowledgment that all was not sweetness and light, but ''The values of the Sixties—non-grasping, non-authoritarian, non-invasive—still make sense to me.''

How and why these values can still make sense to people requires a three-part response. First, it has to do with what Tillich called the dormancy of all valid symbols—valid ones can never really die. They can be reawakened whenever the time is ripe. Second, such reawakenings are, according to Eliade, one of the inherent possibilities of mythic time, partially explaining what Tillich had in mind. Third, however, it has to do with the times being ripe, and ripe they are.

———————— The Beatles Forever! ————————

This now-famous slogan seems to promise much more than it can possibly deliver, but this is so only if we lose sight of the basis for a genuine immortality and, instead, substitute a superficial dredging up of nostalgic remembrances. We can never go back, as the pain of nostalgia so clearly implies, just as we can never recapture our youth. In fact, the irreversible process of aging is a pretty good analogy for understanding how the continuing presence of the Beatles can possibly make any sense. Cott has no use for those ''who take the flickering simulacra of the television tube to be reality,'' who either narrowmindedly debunk or unreasonably glorify the period. He also pointedly answers those who accuse sixties people of wanting to live in the past: ''When we were told that we could only get to heaven if we became like little children, we were not supposed to infer that we should remain children forever.''[11] Nor should we infer that our childhood should be forgotten, if this were even possible. Coming to maturity means, among other things, accepting our past and learning from it. For all of us there are certain events, persons, and places that we shall remember all our lives, because they have given meaning to our lives. These are best understood as personal symbols, and though we inevitably change, they are not likely to lose their importance for us unless we radically alter our personal identities in the act of conversion or alternation (for then we abandon them and adopt different personal symbols).

Those who have maintained their personal and social identities as "children of the sixties" can legitimately retain the Beatles symbology as long as it enables them to look ahead to the future with a particular set of values for guidance. If the Beatles are no more than something to look back to, if they evoke only memories, then their symbolic function has been lost if it ever truly existed. They would then function as idols, false symbols, and would be dangerously stultifying. My guess, however, is that for literally millions of people, the dream goes on. The future that the Beatles once pointed to still lies ahead, and the symbolic lens through which we once saw it is still clear.

John Lahr concludes his piece on remembering the Beatles for the *New Republic* by stressing the fact that, though the times have changed, the Beatles endure: "Then, as now, the songs ventilated life with their articulate energy. Familiarity has robbed the music of its astonishment, but the songs still have the power to tap ancient longings. . . . The Beatles' music makes joy; and that joy, once felt, is never easily forgotten."[12] These ancient longings are for what the Beatles pointed to, not them, and examples of attempts to reactualize and regenerate their mythic power are legion. According to Eliade, "religious man assumes a humanity that has a transhuman, transcendent model. He does not consider himself to be *truly man* except in so far as he imitates the gods, the culture heroes, or the mythic ancestors."[13] In this way the Beatles can continue with us as a living presence, fueling the fires that have been smoldering ever since the sixties came to an end.

Consider the following illustration: 1. A radio station in Texas dropped its top-40 format so as to program Beatles music twenty-four hours a day. This is a tad extreme, but it's similar to the special Beatles programs that virtually cover the dial on particular anniversaries. 2. For a few months beginning in July 1983, Abbey Road Studios was opened for guided tours while undergoing some refurbishing. The throngs lined up outside waiting their turn were never ending. 3. The popular stage show, *Beatlemania,* which grew out of and has in turn spawned numerous smaller and lesser known versions of the same thing, seems always to be playing somewhere. I once saw a rather good performance (one of the smaller and lesser-known versions) at an obscure shopping mall in Manassas, Virginia. With no advance publicity whatsoever, the mall became increasingly choked with startled suburbanites who immediately interrupted their shopping to watch. Seeing the costumed performers was visibly unnerving for quite a few of us. 4. The furor caused by Klaatu, a rock group whose emulation of the Beatles sound, coupled with its refusal to be identified by name or visage, stimulated some of the best rumormongering since the Paul-is-dead controversy. Like the Beatles, Klaatu is under contract to Capitol Records, raising suspicions of an eminently successful hype. The group went from obscurity to instant fame on just the vague glimmer of a hoped-for unlikelihood. 5. The film *I Wanna Hold Your Hand,* which re-creates the moment of the Beatles' coronation on "The Ed Sullivan Show," was a surprising critical success, due in large part to its focusing not on the singers but on their fanatic worshippers. Most interesting was the fact that every one of the characteristics of religion described by Eliade is clearly evident, with fascination predominating. 6. The TV special "All You Need Is Cash," starring the Rutles, is the kind of parody that can only be done by those who fully understand what the Beatles were all about. Not only were Monty Python and "Saturday Night Live" people associated with it at all levels of production, but Paul Simon, Mick Jagger, and George Harrison appeared in it as well. 7. One of the more subtle imitations derives from an obscure remark one of the four made in response to a question as to how the group got its name. The reply was something to the effect that "It's just a name. It could have been anything. We could have called ourselves 'the Shoes.'" This was a flagrant lie, of course, as any fan of Buddy Holly and the Crickets would tell you. Nevertheless, as you check out some of the newer groups at your local record store, you'll notice one with the unlikely name, the Shoes. 8. Among the French, rock and roll is still known as "yeah-yeah" music. 9. *Rolling Stone* February 16, 1984, issue was devoted entirely to the twentieth anniversary of the Beatles' conquest of America, and the world. One article describes the new generation of Beatles fans. 10. Perhaps the illustration with the greatest significance is the one most likely to be overlooked. Because of the influence of television shows like "Sesame Street," and because of the prevalence of sixties people in the elementary school classroom, and because the children of today are the offspring of sixties people, the very young are being introduced to Beatles music as earlier generations were introduced to nursery rhymes.

It is important to keep in mind the fact that these are all *contemporary* examples, but the imitative and reactualizing processes actually began shortly after their appearance on "The Ed Sullivan Show." In every case, the implicit reason has been to capture some of the energy and magic that propelled the Beatles from nowhere to the zenith of popular culture and beyond. More than just an attempt to capitalize on their success, this drive is motivated by a yearning for wholeness, meaningfulness, and the indefinable ultimate. Much as the people attending Elvis concerts were doing so for more than simple nostalgia, so too the many recollections and imitations of the Beatles have been more than rock necrophilia. With appropriate apologies for altering Eliade's thought beyond what he intended, he did nevertheless provide an insightful perspective from which we can comprehend all of this: "It is easy to understand why the memory of that marvelous time haunted religious man, why he periodically sought to return to it. *In illo tempore* the gods had displayed their greatest powers. The *cosmogony is the supreme divine* manifestation, the paradigmatic act of strength, superabundance, and creativity. Religious man thirsts for the real. By every means at his disposal, he seeks to reside at the very source of primordial reality, when the world was *in statu nascendi.* "[14] If Elvis symbolizes the mythology of The Beginning, the Beatles symbolize the mythology of The New Beginning. Hence, together, the fifties and the sixties give shape, direction, motivation, and meaning to America's cultural revolution.

The most direct and obvious form of imitation, in music, is the practice of covering. The Beatles have perhaps been covered more often than any other rock group, and possibly more than any other composer or team of composers in history. To be sure, the results have been mixed. "I Call Your Name" by the Mamas and the Papas is one of the best, but nothing can salvage Barry Gibb's rendition of "The Long and Winding Road" (from the equally bad "cover film," *Sgt. Pepper's Lonely Hearts Club Band,* in which the practice of covering reaches a new low). Equally interesting is the apparent *refusal* to cover any Beatles music at all by those who do not find the practice offensive otherwise. For it is precisely this kind of reluctance that can most perfectly acknowledge the Beatles as symbols. Not only is idolatry avoided and concentration focused on what they pointed to, but practically every quality of feeling described by Otto is involved. Symbols need not be loved, and in many ways it is best that they not be loved, since their purpose is to point beyond themselves.

No one, of course, was less in love with the Beatles than the person who said, "Fuckin' big bastards, that's what the Beatles were"; who sang, "I don't believe in Beatles"; and who, in the same song, added,

    The dream is over
    What can I say?
    The dream is over
    Yesterday
    I was the dreamweaver
    But now I'm reborn

> I was the walrus
> But now I'm John

Au contraire, by forcing us to look beyond a transitory group of four individual musicians, John Lennon helped preserve the myth and pass it along to all future generations.

Vignettes of Affirmation

The affirmation of a new set of values symbolized by the Beatles was a living reality for a wide variety of Americans in the sixties, wider than the media and the analysts would have us believe. Collectively, they exemplified the positive dimension of freedom, the liberty to accomplish certain goals both personal and social. Accomplishment, however, should not be understood to be the sole criterion of success. If this measure were used to evaluate the sixties, everything attempted would no doubt be seen as an unqualified failure: absolutely none of the revolution's ultimate values were actualized to any meaningful extent. This criterion might be useful in some instances, but not for the sixties; a stage prior to actualization had to be reached first.

A more appropriate, more revealing, and certainly more accurate approach would be to use a different and more realistic criterion. Given that the prevailing values had become solidly entrenched in American culture, and given that the fifties had been able only to dislodge the unthinking obedience to these values for a relatively small number of people (primarily powerless youths), it would be the height of absurdity to expect the prevailing order to be overturned and a new and conflicting set of values introduced within a few short years. If nothing else, inertia would prevent this from happening, to say nothing of the inevitable opposition. The *most* that could be expected would be for the new set of values to be recognized throughout American society as capable of being realized. In other words, to have them accepted as a genuine possibility, not merely for intellectual contemplation but for actual realization, is a much better measure of success. And from this standpoint, the sixties were overwhelmingly successful.

The most visible, yet essentially amorphous, of the groups manifesting these new values were the blacks, the New Left, and the hippies. In each case, there was a musical expression that reflected as well as shaped the group's consciousness, defining the group as much as anything could.

The activities of black Americans throughout the sixties were obviously an outgrowth of the civil rights movement of the fifties, but something new was added: the implications of the earlier goal of equality were forcefully expressed. More than the acquisition of parity in the social and political marketplace, equality means the establishment of an identity respected by oneself and others; in a word, pride. This, in turn, depends on one's group being considered worthy of respect.

If the rock and roll of the fifties was characterized by a merger of black and white, the sixties saw the gradual reintroduction of separation. This time, however, the separation was undertaken as a positive act, as a way to preserve and perpetuate black identity. First evident in the different direction taken by Motown recording artists under the direction of Berry Gordy, Jr. (the Supremes, the Four Tops, the Temptations, Smokey Robinson and the Miracles, Martha Reeves and the Vandellas, Marvin Gaye, and Stevie Wonder, among others), it matured as soul in the mid to late sixties. This aspect of sixties soul is best personified by James Brown's "Say It Loud—I'm Black and I'm Proud," Otis Redding's "Respect," and Aretha Franklin's album, *Young, Gifted and Black* (to say nothing of her cover of "Respect," which even Otis Redding said he liked better than his own). Whites listened to and could even identify with the earlier Motown sounds, but soul was different; it set blacks apart as a distinct and not entirely comprehensible entity. While it had always been the case that whites were not given access to black consciousness, now whites were aware of how little they actually knew. For the first time, whites were conscious of not holding all the cards; more important, blacks knew it too.

The implications of the Black Pride and Black Power movements of the sixties extended much further than anyone could know at the time. The freedom and necessity for the expression of group pride wasn't limited in principle to race or any other identifiable characteristic. If full equality is contingent on group pride and respect, as the necessary foundation for individual self-worth, as it most assuredly is, then full equality would be demanded by other groups as well: women, gays, ethnics, and the aged among others.

Growing out of an opposition to militarism, the war in Vietnam, and a perceived failure of true democracy in the United States, the New Left was most often allied with the many student movements throughout the country, which had their beginning with the struggles for free speech and relevance in education. Some semblance of unity was brought to this varied assemblage by their collective vision of a new American society, represented by the Port Huron Statement of 1962.

"Participatory Democracy" was a key slogan bandied about by all these varied groups, but its meaning, surprisingly enough, remained consistent: political decisions can only properly be made with everyone's equal and effective participation; unilateral decisions imposed from above are necessarily immoral and must be opposed no matter what they might be. The process of decision making is just as important as the decision itself. Implicit within this seemingly traditional idea is the unequivocal rejection of the principle of majority rule (or popular sovereignty), the notion that political obligation is defined by the will of the majority. The people in the New Left knew, as everyone knows, that mere numbers have never been a sufficient moral criterion; they just simply collapsed the distinction between moral and political decision making, using the former to judge the latter in every instance.

The founders of American constitutional democracy relied on a balance between majority preference as expressed through the legislature and the limitations imposed by universal, natural rights protected by the courts. Majority will and human rights were to be equal bases of political obligation, with the naive hope that a conflict between them would never arise, there being no way to resolve the potential dilemma peacefully and rationally. The founders were convinced that the composition of majorities would constantly be shifting and that there was general agreement that certain rights were inalienable. It was assumed that individual preferences were based solely on self-interest and that rights had to be protected because of this; hence, the necessity for some authority over individuals.

The New Left gave preeminence to the authority of rights and hoped that universal participation would mitigate the unpleasantness of occasionally going against the majority. On the other hand, the majority could be expected to recognize the superiority of human rights over individual preferences. In fact, their preferences weren't expected to violate the rights of others. The vicissitudes of opinion were more the result of a society that structurally encouraged self-seeking than of anything innate to humanity. The belief that such a society could be achieved and actually function was based on the fundamental assumption that moral truths are either innate or the inevitable consequence of people living together freely.

This assumption also explains their opposition to the war in Vietnam. With few major exceptions, the New Left was not a pacifist movement; rather, it advocated selective opposition based on the individual's con-

science. The obvious implication was that the individual's moral authority superseded that of the government, in this and every instance. In other
words, anarchism: there being no authority whatsoever over the individual, a government does not in fact exist.

None of this was well delineated by the New Left, either for itself or for
those on the outside. But for those who had ears to hear, it was all there in
the music. Anarchism and its underlying assumptions were implicit in
much of the protest music of the time, but the focus of this music was
usually on specific events, persons, policies, and the like. A more subtle
and consequently more effective form of music occurred with the merging of folk and rock, called, for lack of anything better, folk rock. Dylan,
the Byrds, Simon and Garfunkel, as well as numerous others made it as
clear as it could be that we don't need this (or any) government to tell us
how to get along with each other. Dylan's "Maggie's Farm" the Byrds'
"Wasn't Born to Follow," and Simon and Garfunkel's "Big Bright
Green Pleasure Machine" demonstrate how effectively political values
can be expressed.

As far as the hippies of the sixties are concerned, a brief glance backwards might provide some needed perspective. For this aspect of the sixties is often regarded as transient phenomenon, an anomaly never before
encountered among civilized people and one not likely to be repeated.
Exactly the opposite is the case: no matter what their guise and no matter
what they might be called, there have always been counterculture groups
in society, and there always will be. In the April 1978 edition of *Head*
magazine, Bruce Eisner discusses "the hippie revolution" in "Looking
Back at Sgt. Pepper." During the course of his essay, he has occasion to
mention briefly the history of such movements. Long before the beats of
the fifties, he says, there were "the agnostic [he probably means the
gnostic] Christian sects in the Greco-Roman world of the second century, the 'cult of pure love' of the twelfth-century Troubadours, the
Brethren of the Free Spirit of fourteenth-century England, as well as the
pre-Raphaelite Brotherhood headed by the Rosettis which existed in England in the late 1800s and evolved into the Aesthetic Movement, the Da-
daist Movement with its absurd style, initiated by the Frenchman Gautier
at the turn of this century, and the Bohemians of the twenties. All of these
displayed aspects of the style which would later be adopted by the hippies."[15]

The hippie style included communal living, "free" sex (that is, sex
uninhibited by conventional morality, *never* licentious—the moral guidelines were simply different), mind-altering drugs (especially marijuana
and LSD), a fascination with all things Oriental, the free expression of

the unique and valuable personality, an emphasis on emotions and feelings, and individuality (the notion that infinite worth resides in each and every one of us, not *individualism,* which values oneself above all others). Many things are implied by this style of life, not the least of which is the assumption that humans are not by nature self-seeking but are rather social and cooperative. This supports the assumption of the New Left and further opposes the psychological egoism of America's founding fathers. Another implication is the notion that the emotional dimension of the person is just as important as the rational and ought to assume its rightful place in our lives (freeing us from the tyranny of reason so long a part of Western civilization). More than providing psychological health, emotional liberation makes us aware of reality in a different way. Drugs assisted in this process and were thus for more than recreational purposes. The Oriental interests supported not only a nascent movement toward an appreciation of the environment and other life forms but also the conviction that everything in reality is intrinsically related in an overall unity. Most of all there was a genuine sense of the possible, including peace, love, and understanding.

Musically, hippies listened to anything that might complement or enhance whatever state of mind they happened to inhabit. Obviously this included the psychedelia recorded and performed by the Jefferson Airplane, the Grateful Dead, the Doors, Jimi Hendrix, and Janis Joplin, but classic black blues and pure folk were just as much a part of the scene. Given such a promising market, all sorts of rock musicians did their best to produce something psychedelic. Even the Rolling Stones made an attempt with "We Love You" and "Dandelion," and if a heavy blues rock band was converted, there's no telling how far the impact extended.

Many others identified with the blacks, the New Left, and the hippies in one way or another and were perhaps even more influential for not having joined in any explicit way. Being on the outside, so to speak, they were in a unique position to see the commonality underlying all of them. What they saw was the harmony and mutual support provided by the affirmation of equality, human rights, and individuality. They were also better able to see the ramifications of these values and how they, too, were interrelated. Although it was certain that the affirmation of this new set of values did not require membership in one or another of these groups, it was equally certain that some kind of action was called for. And such action could, and did, take many forms. Actions of this group are most often overlooked in retrospectives of the sixties, but when their role is properly appreciated, the necessary conclusion is that the adoption of the new set of values was much more extensive than is commonly believed.

Though they will never again perform together, the Beatles are of such enormous cultural significance that anything said about them is necessarily an understatement. For some people they were the chief indication, if not the chief cause, of an irreversible decline in Western civilization. For others, they were nothing less than the pure distillate of all that is hopeful within humanity's many and varied cultures, and an all-too-brief glimpse of a better world. Regardless of how they were evaluated, they could not be ignored, and as long as the dream lives in the consciousness of a single person, they will not be ignored in the years to come.

Perhaps, as Chuck Berry once proclaimed, Beethoven has finally rolled over and given Tchaikovsky the news. But the news is mixed. What seemed so easy and so imminent in the sixties is now viewed with greater realism, but with no less hope. Realization of the dream is by no means impossible, but ''it don't come easy.'' As with all cultural revolutions, success will depend on having symbols to point the way and provide the motivation—symbols that have passed the test of self-negation.

Dormancy and the
Re-creation of the
Interim

————————————— 10 ——

With the Paris cease-fire agreement on January 28, 1973, ending America's involvement in Vietnam, and Nixon's ignominious resignation on August 9, 1974, the sixties came to an end. There were no special news bulletins announcing the fact over radio and television, no celebrations, no offers to join hands again, no peace. Only exhaustion. The capitulation of Saigon in April 1975, being completely anticipated by virtually everyone, occasioned only relief that the last shards of the tragedy had at last fallen to the ground.

America's cultural revolution had entered a six-year hiatus, coinciding almost exactly with the presidencies of Gerald Ford and Jimmy Carter. Such pauses are not uncommon, for it is the nature of cultural revolutions to engage every facet of a culture, and a culture can only endure so much internal tension before some kind of collapse becomes inevitable. Usually, however, neither the revolutionaries nor the old order has crushed the opposition by this point; hence, the conflict will necessarily be rejoined.

During this brief interim from 1974 to 1980, the revolutionary symbols became dormant, creating the impression for many people that the struggle had ended in failure. Meanwhile, the established symbols remained in place, encouraging a strengthening and rejuvenation of the old order so recently threatened. This, too, is typical of cultural revolutions, and in a very real sense, revolutions are won or lost during this period. The outcome depends on whether the revolutionaries can revive themselves sufficiently so as to challenge again the already rejuvenated establishment. Although a renewed struggle is as certain as things can be, the outcome is most certainly not. Nothing is promised by history. There are no guarantees, no assured results, no predetermined destinies. The future is a creature of the present, not the reverse. In situations like this, those in authority and control hold almost all the cards. The very weight of tradition, the nearly universal fear of change, the psychological need for stability, and the simple but powerful force of inertia all combine to make the revolutionaries' task even more difficult than it was at the outset. No longer do they have the element of surprise and the intrigue of something new on their side; now they must fall back on the intrinsic appeal of the new set of values they have proposed, relying on this alone to garner support and carry them through. A culture will discover during this period whether the adherence to the new set of values was merely a passing fancy, or a commitment likely to endure and perhaps even prevail. In short, the revolution must be re-created if it is to continue with any real hope for success.

Recreation is one of those wonderfully ambiguous words that allow us to play around with a variety of meanings, all of which enhance each other. Depending on which pronunciation pops into mind first, diversion, refreshment, and entertainment may seem to capture its fundamental meaning; but restoration, renewal, reformation, and rededication are facets of it as well. I intend all of these meanings. Together they describe the essential character of the revolution during the interim.

Others see this period quite differently. Peter N. Carroll, for example, in his book *It Seemed Like Nothing Happened: The Tragedy and the Promise of America in the 1970s*, sees the decade from 1970 to 1979 as one of decline from the pinnacle of the activist sixties. He concentrates on what was preserved from the initial period of the cultural revolution, not noticing its further developments. His perspective is hardly unusual, and it is mirrored in the many critical observations about the music of the time. In an article from the *Washington Post*, June 10, 1979, titled ''Is Rock Dead or Just Beat?'' the author, Brad Chase, laments that ''Many second-generation rock fans (those who went steady to the Beatles' 'I Should Have Known Better' and became serious with 'Abbey Road') feel the boredom of the 'Me' decade has eclipsed the spirit that once intoxicated the music and its audience in the '60s.'' But both of these pessimistic appraisals overlook the likelihood of a pause in such cultural struggles and, more importantly, the re-creative function it serves.

The process of re-creation is complex, however, for it relates directly to the achievement of self-identity and the desire for self-actualization. Re-creation, in other words, entails self-creation. Jean-Paul Sartre and Abraham Maslow provide some vital clues as to how the restorative and regenerative processes of re-creation occur. A combination of their ideas can help us understand what happened to the revolution during the latter part of the 1970s until the election of Reagan.

According to Sartre, true self-identity can be realized only through the "look" of others, which creates an awareness of the self as an object for others. This awareness makes it possible for the self to "look," in turn, at others and thus know itself as a knowing subject with an identity of its own. "The way to interiority," he wrote in *Being and Nothingness,* "passes through the other person." In his novel *The Reprieve,* one of the characters rejects Descartes' famous dictum "I think, therefore I am" for the more cogent "I am seen, therefore I am." The point is that we can become conscious of ourselves as genuine individual subjects only if others first take notice of us as objects. Having achieved self-consciousness, we may then cast our gaze onto others as a free act of our own. Unfortunately, the inevitable consequences of this process are separation from others and an uneasy conflict with them.

Maslow, on the other hand, would regard this stage as merely the penultimate one in a process of human fulfillment—a goal Sartre would see as forever beyond our grasp. Self-actualization, the ability to realize our potential in cooperation with others, was for Maslow the ultimate itself, the goal for which all of us are striving. Yet in order to reach this goal, we must pass through and satisfy the demands of four other stages. The resultant model is what has come to be known as the "hierarchy of needs." At the first level physiological needs must be met: food, clothing, shelter, and the like. Next are safety needs: assurances that all the more fundamental needs will be met in the future. The social needs for interaction and friendship are at the third level. The fourth, penultimate stage concerns everything Sartre described and more: on the one hand there is the need for self-esteem (self-respect, self-confidence, and competence) and on the other is the need for status (recognition, appreciation, and respect). Only after all these needs have been reasonably satisfied is it possible to entertain the possibility of self-actualization, the realization of our own uniquely personal goals in a harmonious collaboration with others. Given the almost infinite variations in individual circumstances, some are bound to feel a given set of needs more directly than others, but the strongest motivations will always be to achieve the next higher stage, the one just beyond the level currently enjoyed. In other words, until identity has been accomplished, self-fulfillment can't even be contemplated.

Maslow only intended this to be a rough approximation of human motivation, as a heuristic typology; the actual course of human development can never be as neat and orderly as this scheme might imply. Further, he had only individuals in mind; he was a psychologist, not a sociologist. Nevertheless, with a bit of social psychology under our collective belts, and with his same qualifications preventing us from making too much of it, this hierarchy can serve just as well as a device to explain group behavior.

Combining the conceptual highlights from Sartre and Maslow, we can get an insight into the re-creative efforts of several important groups during the interim, some voicing their claims for identity and fulfillment for the first time, others renewing or preserving the claims they had already made. For the remainder of this chapter, I plan to concentrate on how their struggles were reflected in and encouraged by the music, noting along the way how the dialectical attitudes of negation and affirmation were preserved in America's postsixties culture.

Black Americans

Emerging out of the move toward independence evidenced first by Motown and then by soul, black music in the interim continued by achieving an almost complete separation from the various white traditions, becoming an object for their gaze. Few whites were even vaguely familiar with the newer black musicians, and fewer still could appreciate their music. But the music was definably different, most certainly nonwhite; this much was apparent.

Perhaps more than anyone else, George Clinton personified this development. As the major creative force behind Parliament/Funkadelic (one group recording under different names for different companies), he was instrumental in funk's emergence as a significant musical and cultural force in the 1970s. One of the marvels of his wizardry is Funkadelic's *One Nation under a Groove*, a 1978 album that embodies both negation and affirmation in an almost perfect balance. The former comes across with undisguised passion in ''Promentalshitbackwashpsychosisenemasquad (The Doo Doo Chasers)''.

> The world is a toll-free toilet
> our mouths neurological assholes
> and psychologically speaking
> we're in a state of mental diarrhea
> talking shit a mile a minute

or in a state of constipated notions . . . .
And what causes all of this shit?
Ego-munchies
Images doggie bags
Me burger with I sauce on it . . .
a myself sandwich
a personal burger . . .

On the other hand, the title song clearly affirms a greater, all-inclusive
unity as the fundamental human goal. The theme is continued by
"Groovallegiance":

Please come one, come all to the funk
let your feelings grow as one
join this nation, you will see
that we can make you free

The very next song is an allegorical reference to the alienation between
and among the races, primarily black and white. The theme, evident in
the title, is that it can be overcome—"Who Says a Funk Band Can't Play
Rock?" And, it should be noted, the metaphors are musical. Still, the
rejection of a history of racism is an overwhelming presence on the album. In the cartoon collage on the inside cover, for example, a Klansman
is portrayed as trying to steal the "funk." Nevertheless, Clinton is conscious of the separation's achievement; self-identity has been accomplished on black terms, and a reunion, without destroying the valid differences, is being urged. In other words, black self-actualization has now
become a real possibility.

Another funk group with the same essential message is Kool and the
Gang: "Funky Stuff" (1973), "Jungle Boogie" (1974), and "Spirit of
the Boogie" (1975). Notice in these titles that an interesting reversal has
taken place: whereas in the past any reference to the "jungle," especially
in connection with doing the boogie, would be an embarrassment or an
insult, now it's affirmed with pride. Other funk groups from this period
include Con-Funk-Shun, the Bar-Kays, and Rick James.

Although not funk strictly speaking, but close enough to defy any other
description, Johnny Guitar Watson has also made the blend of affirmation and negation into a fine art. It is impossible to listen to his late 1970s
albums without feeling a mixture of anger and joy coming through the
music. Further, on many of his album covers he is pictured in the guise of

a well-to-do pimp, surrounded by several dazzling women, black and white. On his 1977 album, *A Real Mother for Ya*, the back cover adds a shot of him with his mother. The paradox so evident in this imagery is just as clear in his music.

Lest the impression be created that funk exhausted the black musical stylings during this period and that little else indicated the separatist tactic for achieving respect and fulfillment, several other groups ought to be mentioned. The Brothers Johnson, Rufus (Featuring Chaka Khan), and War have all employed a variety of musical stylings as expressions of the struggle, and all have done so with considerable effectiveness. The meaning of "Free Yourself, Be Yourself" on the Brothers Johnson's 1977 *Right on Time* couldn't be more obvious. *Ask Rufus* the same year has one of the most hauntingly beautiful instrumentals I've ever heard, "Slow Screw against the Wall," using nothing but strings (followed by an eighteen-second explosion of funk, "A^b Fry")—a subtle but forceful message that racial harmony is possible. War bridged the sixties and the interim with such depressing songs as "The World Is a Ghetto" (1972) and "Slippin' into Darkness" (1972), but they followed with the more upbeat "Why Can't We Be Friends?" (1975) and "Summer" (1976). But despite their highly appealing combination of soul, funk, and Latin rhythms, few whites found them more than marginally accessible. War was the most accessible of these groups.

Then there was (and still is) Stevie Wonder, whose adopted surname is one of the true understatements in rock. As far as I know, he is the one and only performer whose career has spanned every period of the cultural revolution. His first album (*Little Stevie Wonder: The Twelve Year Old Genius*) was released in 1963. The now-classic *Innervisions* (1973) includes a savage indictment of American society in "Living for the City," but it also has the highly optimistic "Visions." The latter expresses the idea that

> The law was never passed
> But somehow all men feel they're truly free at last
> Have we really gone this far through space and time
> Or is this a vision in my mind?

His last albums of the interim were *Songs in the Key of Life* (1976), a complex mixture that both negated traditional values and affirmed revolutionary values, and *Journey through the Secret Life of Plants* (1979), as enigmatic an album as there is in popular music. I wouldn't venture even a tentative hypothesis toward classifying Stevie Wonder's music, but I have no hesitation in assessing it to be among the finest and most culturally significant ever written. In the years since, his music has continued to reflect and provide direction for black Americans and, increasingly, white Americans as well.

Obviously, this sketch can in no way cover the enormous diversity of black popular music during these six years, but it's not intended to do so. My purpose has been to suggest the *meaning* of what was happening, nothing more and certainly nothing else. (One glaring omission from this list, disco, will be made up for in the following section.)

Finally, while I've concentrated on black music exclusively, symbolically, at least, the black struggle for identity and fulfillment has represented all oppressed racial minorities: Chicanos, Native Americans, and Orientals among them. In a later section, concerning Americans with Third World ties, this same notion will come up.

Homosexuals

Homosexuals and bisexuals have had perhaps the most difficult time achieving self-identity to say nothing of self-actualization. During the interim, however, they came out of their closets as never before, forcing the rest of society to look at them, acknowledge their presence, and accept them on their own terms (to *like* them or to *agree* with them is, of course, another matter entirely, and is not at all implied by Maslow's hierarchy). Their greatest visibility came initially in the resurgent dance clubs, the discothèques found in almost every large American city; although, certainly, not everyone attracted to these clubs was gay. The new dance had its own intrinsic appeal, especially in the dismal wreckage of Vietnam and Watergate. Nevertheless, it was in the discothèque that some semblance of recognition and respect seemed possible, where costumery, performance, style, and showiness were not only expected but vital. "Coming out" could thus become part of the show, and the club could be a place where gays and straights could mingle with equality. On the dance floor, all things seemed possible.

At first, the music played in these clubs was a combination of soul, funk, Caribbean, and slick Philadelphia sounds of artists like Barry White; overwhelmingly black, in other words. Some say the trend began in 1973 with "Soul Makossa" by Manu Dibango, an African who was living in Paris. In any case, it rapidly picked up with music specifically intended for the disco audience. Among the avalanche that followed were "Rock Your Baby" by George McCrae, "Rock the Boat" by the Hues Corporation, "TSOP (The Sound of Philadelphia)" by MFSB, and "Love's Theme" by Love Unlimited Orchestra, all in 1974. The next year the songs included "That's the Way (I Like It)" by KC and the Sunshine Band, "Fly Robin Fly" by Silver Convention and "The Hustle" by Van McCoy. In 1976, there was "Love to Love You Baby" by Donna Summer, "More, More, More" by the Andrea True Connection, "Tangerine" by the Salsoul Orchestra, "Turn the Beat Around" by Vicki Sue Robinson, "I Love Music" by the O'Jays, "You Sexy Thing" by Hot Chocolate, "Play That Funky Music (White boy)" by Wild Cherry, and "Love Machine" by the Miracles. The year 1977 was perhaps the zenith of the phenomenon, capped off by the film *Saturday Night Fever*, which included many disco classics by the Bee Gees, "Disco Inferno" by the Trammps, "If I Can't Have You" by Yvonne Elliman, and "More Than a Woman" by Tavares. Also that year were "Brick House" by the Commodores, "Dancing Queen" by ABBA, "Whispering/Cherchez La Femme" by Dr. Buzzard's Original Savannah Band, and "Keep It Comin' Love" by KC and the Sunshine Band. "Boogie Oogie Oogie" by A Taste of Honey, "I Love the Night Life" by Alicia Bridges, "Jack and Jill" by Raydio, and "Le Freak" by Chic were released in 1978. The gay presence was finally acknowledged by the popularity of the Village People, whose thinly veiled celebrations and spoofs of the distaff life (in which they allegedly participated) were contained in songs such as "Macho Man" in 1978 and "YMCA" in 1979.

In 1979, as the craze was winding down, "Pop Muzik" by M, "Rapper's Delight" by the Sugarhill Gang, and "I Wanna Be Your Lover" by Prince pointed to something new again. With "Pop Muzik," disco and punk were showing signs of merging; with "Rapper's Delight," black music was developing a new social consciousness; and with "I Wanna Be Your Lover," black musicians were renewing their appeal to whites. All these tendencies would be reinforced in the near future.

As with any fad, disco made a juicy target for parody. Rick Dees and His Cast of Idiots had a Number One hit in 1976 with "Disco Duck," but toward the end, the parody became more hostile. Frank Zappa's 1978 *Sheik Yerbouti* was filled with it, including the popular "Dancin' Fool." As the antagonists gained in passion and numbers, involving many of those formerly indifferent to the phenomenon, critics and disc jockeys joined the fray, perhaps sensing fatal weaknesses in their enemy. By the end of 1978, 40 percent of *Billboard's* "Hot 100" were disco albums, as were eight of the top ten singles. One year later disc jockeys were breaking the very same records on the air, record companies were shifting their emphasis back to a more traditional variety of rock, antidisco rallies were being held across the country, and performers were blowing up disco records at their concerts. Aptly dubbed "antidiscomania" by the media, it culminated in the rather nasty "Do Ya Think I'm Disco," recorded by Steve Dahl, then a rock disc jockey on Chicago's WLUP, to the tune of Rod Stewart's "Do Ya Think I'm Sexy":

> My shirt is open, I never use the buttons.
> Though I look hip, I work for E.F. Hutton.
> Do ya think I'm disco,
> 'Cause I spend so much time blowdrying out my hair.

Most radio stations, however, simply decided to follow the movement back to rock without antagonism, feeling that it was either not necessary or not in keeping with the sixties' ideal of freedom of choice and expression. In any case, by the end of 1979, disco had run its course, and so had America's respite from the revolutionary conflict.

No doubt there is a variety of explanations for its demise, but they are likely to fall into one of two radically different categories—one morally acceptable, the other not. For many people, disco (and its sophisticated dance stylings) was just another kind of rock and roll; some of it was good and some of it was bad, pleasing to some, offensive to others. The problem was not so much the music but the media's insistence on programming it over practically everything else, smothering the dial. It was all too much. Their rejection of disco was merely the desire to hear something different for a change.

There were others, however, whose rejection of disco was morally suspect, for theirs was a rejection not so much of the music as of the people involved with it. It was too black, too accepting of gays, too oriented toward the pretentious and upwardly mobile, and not socially or politically aware. Now we might all agree that social and political awareness is a good thing. And we might also agree that nothing's really wrong with being upwardly mobile, so long as the path upward isn't littered with the bodies of those serving as stepping stones for a privileged few, and so long as the path is wide enough to accommodate all who wish to travel it. But an opposition to the battle for equality, identity, and fulfillment for anyone is another matter entirely. This ought not be tolerated.

Disco might not have lasted as long as its aficionados may have hoped, but it did help establish the gay presence in American society as visible and significant. No longer could gays be ignored. Because of this, they have come to symbolize the plight of all social outcasts: if those at the very nadir of social acceptability can achieve some degree of respect, can anyone be left out?

Women

Women have always been involved in rock music, but unlike in the earlier blues tradition and some of its offshoots, they've rarely been able to assume creative control. In those rare instances when they have, moreover, they have not been expected to express the hard edge and toughness of rock, as evidenced best by the singular exception of Janis Joplin. In the interim, this tendency began to change.

The justly famous "girl groups" such as the Supremes and the Teddy Bears were produced by men, Berry Gordy and Phil Spector, respectively. Folk rock had Joan Baez, of course, along with Mary Travers, Judy Collins, and Janis Ian, but there was precious little hard rock in this crowd. Female lead singers (for male-dominated groups) occasionally received a great deal of attention (Grace Slick of the Jefferson Airplane/Starship being the major example), but this doesn't do much to counter the indictment. Moving into the 1970s, Carole King, Joni Mitchell, and Carly Simon achieved considerable artistic independence but, just as before, not in hard rock. Even less effective in countering the restrictive stereotypes were the otherwise excellent feminist singer/songwriters such as Laura Nyro and Holly Near.

Given that the recording industry was male to the core, it is no wonder that sexist stereotypes, male fantasies, and, occasionally, misogyny found expression in rock music. Most notorious, perhaps, were some of the adolescent songs by the Rolling Stones ("Honky Tonk Women," "Under My Thumb" and "Stupid Girl" for example) and some of the imagery in Bob Dylan's work ("Just Like a Woman," "Lay, Lady, Lay," and "Rainy Day Women #12 & 35"). But the Rolling Stones and Dylan were hardly alone.

Aside from the instances of genuine pathology, much of this misogyny is directly attributable to a patriarchal culture. If change were to come, the orientation of the larger culture itself would have to be replaced with one that was nonsexist. There is some evidence that this began to occur even before the interim, since the values affirmed by the sixties challenged patriarchy at its roots (the Western religious tradition) and espoused universal equality. The fact that a nonsexist culture wasn't actualized doesn't deny what was intended. The greatest accomplishment of the sixties was to set the process in motion for the eventual accomplishment of its goals, and a nonsexist society was one of its major implications. To illustrate, on what many regard as Dylan's best album, *Highway 61 Revisited*, released in 1965, "It Takes a Lot to Laugh, It Takes a Train to Cry" has the lines "Well, I want to be your lover, baby/I don't want to be your boss." Seven years later, Helen Reddy's enormously popular "I Am Woman" showed how extensively the feminist implications of the sixties had infiltrated the popular consciousness. Times had already begun to change.

The height of the ERA movement was reached during the interim at the same time that women finally broke into the hard side of rock, equaling in excitement, intensity, and volume anything males had ever done. Their numbers were still small, but the walls of male exclusivity had been breached; in the years to come, women hard rockers would pour through as never before. Black women had begun making some progress with disco and, to a small degree, funk; soon, however, white women were involved with the more raucous styles of rock.

Patti Smith, in my opinion one of the most creative and influential rockers of all times, male or female, deserves special attention. Her style, performance, melody, and lyrics capture everything that rock is about. In her 1978 album, *Easter*, a classic of the genre, is the absolutely devastating "Rock and Roll Nigger." No one can listen to this without sensing every facet of the cultural revolution with such immediacy that neutrality about it is impossible. ("Nigger," by the way, is used to describe anyone outside of society—"Jimi Hendrix was a nigger/Jesus Christ and grandma, too.")

Suzi Quatro's album, with the revealing title *Your Momma Won't Like Me* (1975), includes a song called "New Day Woman" with the lines "God gave us freedom/You know he gave me my Rock and Roll/Come on and join me now." But far more important is her entire demeanor as a performer: she *rocks* with the best of them. The same is true of Ann and Nancy Wilson of Heart; it's their overall style more than anything else that admits them to those areas hitherto restricted to males. So also with Pat Benatar and Joan Jett (the latter first as one of the Runaways and then the lead singer of the Blackhearts); both have exhibited the kind of aggressive, overt sexuality formerly regarded as the exclusive province of men. Finally, it's important to note about all of them that they started young, and they're still active; much more can be expected from them.

Also worth mentioning are Rickie Lee Jones, Chrissie Hynde (of the Pretenders), Donna Summer, and Diana Ross. Although not all of them are noted as singers of hard rock, their status as independent, self-directed women makes them important examples of what developed during the interim as well.

At first glance, the primary musical style of this outbreak suggests more negation than affirmation, yet the fact that *women* were performing it made all the difference. As an illustration of the dialectics of historical change, negation had become its opposite as the role of women began to undergo a dramatic shift.

Despite their numerical majority, women had always been ignored by a male-dominated society, but by the end of the interim this was no longer the case. Further, their essentially subservient role in the cultural revolution was also coming to an end. No longer could they be ignored, and in this, they have come to symbolize all those ignored by society, the helpless, those without any power or voice. The very old, the very young, and the handicapped come to mind immediately as being totally at the mercy of those in power, much as women have been. All those who listened to this new music could hear the changes that were happening and were bound to be affected.

As the revolution moved into its next phase, the women's movement would assume a position of fundamental importance. It is no exaggeration to say that the success or failure of the revolution will depend largely on the support given to it by the women's movement, and the clues will be found in the role of women in rock and roll.

Southerners

Ever since the Civil War, the old Confederacy has not been regarded by the rest of the nation as completely deserving of trust and equality, and certainly not respect. The ostensible reason was the continued evidence of racism in the South, although there was just as much evidence for it everywhere else, the superficial differences notwithstanding. After the war and prior to Jimmy Carter, only three southerners had sat in the White House: Andrew Johnson, Lyndon Johnson, and Woodrow

Wilson. The first two came to the office through assassination; and Wilson purged himself of his regional blemish by moving north, presiding over Princeton University and governing the state of New Jersey. With Carter's election, however, a genuine down-home southerner was in the nation's highest office. At long last, the national divisiveness seemed to be coming to an end, with the defeated Confederacy finally being accorded some degree of respectability.

This movement toward a new self-identity and a more acceptable ideal for self-actualization actually began in Memphis, in 1954, along with the cultural revolution itself. But at that time, it was only the outcasts who were representing the new South. During the interim, a much larger contingent of southerners joined in, expressing their independence in their own unique musical way. Carter's election was one of the manifestations of this new sentiment; but even more important, the revolution gained the participation and allegiance of a body of people who had, in many ways, come to symbolize its opposition.

It goes without saying that only a comparatively small number of southerners were converted to the new faith, yet the defections were significant enough to cause alarm among more traditional southerners, all of which is evident in the music. For country and western music by this time had come to represent the established values so solidly that any deviation from the straight and narrow could not possibly go unnoticed. The "outlaw" deviation was so severe that Michael Bane subtitled his book on the movement "Revolution in Country Music." He was right, but the outlaw revolution concerned more than music; it was part of the larger cultural revolution that had been in progress throughout the rest of the country for at least twenty years. What the "outlaws" brought to it, however, was a much-needed revival of the attitude of negation.

It began with Hank Williams, whose career and life ended tragically in 1953. Williams's influence on country music has been so overpowering that everything since his death has in one way or another been an attempt either to emulate him or to reject him. Elvis, in effect, forced the choice. Country had neither heart nor mind for the rebelliousness of rockabilly; so the softer, pop-oriented "Nashville sound" seemed to be the only available alternative. Abandoning the youth audience to rock and roll, Nashville sought the older and more traditional generation as its audience. Yet the legacy of Hank Williams wouldn't die. His fatalism and sense of the tragic were preserved in the C & W sounds of Nashville, while his hedonism and hell raising were to emerge in the early 1970s as the music of the outlaws from Austin.

In 1972, Waylon Jennings recorded a song written by Lee Clayton called "Ladies Love Outlaws," which soon became the virtual anthem of the movement. "Outlaw" described perfectly the sentiments and the consciousness of the new southern youth, those who couldn't identify with either their parents and their values or the images of hippies, New Left revolutionaries, or counterculture freaks coming from the North. Yet because these southern youths held freedom, pleasure, and sensuality as ultimate values, they found themselves allied with the cultural revolution, if not squarely within the fold. It was only a matter of time before they would self-consciously reject the traditional set of values and join up. And join they did, but in their own way and on their own terms. Thus it was that Willie Nelson, perhaps the symbolic leader of the movement, held the first of many Fourth of July "picnics" in Austin, Texas—with an almost exclusive emphasis on this new southern music. Soon Waylon would team up with Willie to produce one of the most durable duos in any kind of music.

Without any pretense whatsoever of attempting an all-inclusive historical survey of the major outlaw recordings, I do want to suggest some of the breadth and depth of the movement as well as its crossovers to rock. In 1973, shortly after it began, Lynyrd Skynyrd, quite independently, released the electrifying "Free Bird," illustrating that southern rock had an outlaw sensibility too. In addition, the song became a personal anthem for those in all geographical regions who felt a lack of freedom in their lives. Jerry Jeff Walker's recording of Ray W. Hubbard's "Up against the Wall Red Neck Mother" seemed to be a direct rejection of the revolution (including as it does the line "Jes' kickin' hippies' asses and raisin' hell"), but raising hell is certainly not within the traditional value scheme. Paradoxically, this song, too, became kind of an anthem for hippies, no less, albeit with tongue in cheek. On the other hand, a more favorable attitude toward hippies was expressed in Charlie Daniels's "Uneasy Rider" (and in the following year's "Long Haired Country Boy"). "Ramblin' Man" by the Allman Brothers Band, celebrating freedom of a different kind, was another classic crossover from rock and is now a legend.

By 1974, the New Riders of the Purple Sage had entered the outlaw camp. Their "Instant Armadillo Blues" includes a direct reference to the Outlaws' unofficial headquarters in Austin—a defunct National Guard armory called the "Armadillo World Headquarters," used also for numerous Outlaw concerts. Also, an important southern rock anthem was released—Lynyrd Skynyrd's "Sweet Home Alabama," an unabashed celebration and defense of southern culture—in the rock idiom. It became an instant crossover classic.

Country rock, a softer, rock style of outlaw music, was in full swing by

1975. Willie Nelson's *Red Headed Stranger* topped the country charts and forced Nashville to sit up and take notice of what was happening. The Nitty Gritty Dirt Band, Pure Prairie League, and the Eagles all released albums this year. Meanwhile, Commander Cody and His Lost Planet Airmen were keeping the southern boogie tradition alive. Outlaw music had become so broad by this time that it had spawned variations without losing its defining center.

The year following, this variety was fully evident in albums such as these: Poco's *Rose of Cimarron*, ZZ Top's *Tejas* (with such wonderful tunes as "Arrested for Driving While Blind"), the classic Eagles album *Hotel California* (as much pure rock as outlaw), and Bobby Bare's *The Winner and Other Losers*. Bare's collection includes a parody of southern, "born-again" Christianity in "Dropkick Me, Jesus (through the Goalposts of Life)." Also, Moe Bandy did "Barstool Mountain," the meaning of which is obvious, reflecting the ambiguity of drink in the southern consciousness. Finally, another outlaw anthem was released, "Willie, Waylon and Me," by David Allen Coe. His lyrics tie together the outlaw movement with the sixties as no other song has ever done and deserve to be at least partially cited:

> They say the Beatles were just the beginning of everything music could be.
> Just like The Stones, I was rollin' along,
> Like a ship lost out on the sea.
> And Joplin would die for the future,
> And Dylan would write poetry,
> And in Texas the talk turned to Outlaws—
> Like Willie, Waylon and me.
>
> Well, they say Texas music's in the make
> And we've been makin' music that is free.
> Doin' one night stands,
> Playin' with our bands,
> Willie, Waylon and me.

By this time the American consciousness was being inundated by outlaw music as well as disco, an uneasy juxtaposition if there ever was one.

In 1977, outlaw music achieved enormous popularity with Jerry Reed's "Eastbound and Down," which was the theme for the film *Smokey and the Bandit,* and Johnny Paycheck's "Take This Job and Shove It." Together, they illustrate the outlaw's fundamental attitude toward established authorities. Emmylou Harris made it to the top with her *Luxury Liner*, crossing over the other way with a cover of Chuck Berry's "(You Never Can Tell) C'est La Vie." Jimmy Buffett also hit with *Changes in Latitudes, Changes in Attitudes*, with the hedonistic "Margaritaville" making him rich and famous. (Soon after, *Rolling Stone* did an interview with him.) And the Marshall Tucker Band further increased the outlaw presence nationwide with "Heard It in a Love Song."

Townes Van Zandt, writer for many others, released an album of his own in 1978 (*Flying Shoes*); and Willie Nelson, one of the legends of the movement, had another hit ("Whiskey River"). Both illustrate that outlaw music has a mellow side as well.

The son of another legend, Hank Williams, Jr., working hard to maintain his own identity, released "Family Tradition," "Whiskey Bent and Hell Bound," and "Women I've Never Had" all in 1979. Also, Bobby Bare's "Numbers" deserves special attention, since it's one of the few clear indications that outlaws were beginning to sense the new role of women in American society. Although one of the finest songs in the C & W genre about gender equality, it was by no means the first—not by a long shot. Tompall Glaser, one of the Outlaws' founding members, released "The Streets of Baltimore" way back in 1967. Because it told the story of a country girl leaving her husband and going off to the big city to make a living in a rather unsavory profession, he had a lot of trouble getting it recorded and played. Even "Gentle on My Mind," produced by Glaser, encountered the same difficulties (sex outside marriage being its theme).

Numerous others with an outlaw consciousness ought to be mentioned were there time and space enough: Dr. Hook, Rita Coolidge, Jessi Colter, Johnny Cash, and Jerry Lee Lewis to name a few. But the above list should be sufficient to show that the South during the interim had begun to associate with the larger cultural revolution, reinvigorating its sense of negation while giving southern youth a renewed feeling for their own identity, with their fulfillment becoming a live possibility as a result.

The Third World

My interest here concerns the achievement of respect and the hope for self-actualization as they relate to the various Third World communities in America. The music that has both reflected and encouraged this process is the independently revolutionary music from Jamaica: reggae. Interestingly enough, some of its roots can be traced back to America in that reggae evolved out of ska and rock steady, the former influenced by rhythm and blues broadcast from Miami and New Orleans in the fifties and the latter by soul in the sixties. Jamaican musicians, perhaps sensing the drive for liberation contained within this music, concocted an amalgam uniquely suited to their own cultural setting. Ska, possibly deriving its name from the sound produced by strumming a guitar, quickly spread to England, where there was a large West Indian population. America first felt its impact with "My Boy Lollipop," in 1964, by Millie Small. Soul introduced a more upbeat, guitar-oriented sound into Jamaican music, but the resulting rock steady was to evolve further. With the addition of a slower, more complex syncopation and an aggressive, albeit esoteric, political/religious ideology, the transition to what we now know as reggae was virtually complete. In 1968, the Maytals released "Do the Reggay," and a year later Desmond Dekker had the first American reggae hit with "Israelites."

Except for Toots and the Maytals (who have espoused a kind of revivalist Christianity) and Jimmy Cliff (a Black Muslim), most of the reggae artists (Bob Marley and the Wailers and Peter Tosh being the most notable) have been advocates of Rastafarianism. Emphasizing Black Pride, a strong anticolonialism, and a belief that Haile Selassie (the late emperor of Ethiopia, whose common name was Ras Tafari) is the incarnation of God, Rastafarianism symbolizes the plight of all Third World peoples who have been exploited by the primarily white, colonial powers of the West. The downtrodden, represented lyrically as "Trenchtown" (Kingston's poverty-stricken ghetto), are thus portrayed as engaged in a struggle of cosmological proportions with the forces of evil (represented by "Babylon"). The wearing of "dreadlocks," the open and defiant smoking of "ganja," and, of course, reggae music itself are some of the outward manifestations of this revolutionary affirmation. The 1972 film *The Harder They Come,* starring Jimmy Cliff, metaphorically portrays this struggle and has since become a cult classic. The next year, a song written by Bob Marley for Johnny Nash, "Stir It Up," became a hit; yet another dimension of America's cultural revolution was well on its way.

Soon, British and American groups began to incorporate the reggae sound into their own music and thus publicize the Rastafarian movement even further. In 1972, reggae-inspired music included Johnny Nash's "I Can See Clearly," Paul Simon's "Mother and Child Reunion," and the Staple Singers' "I'll Take You There." Led Zeppelin's "D'yer Mak'er" from *Houses of the Holy* followed in 1973 along with Paul Simon's *There Goes Rhymin' Simon* (especially "Take Me to the Mardi Gras"). The trend continued the next year with Eric Clapton's cover of Bob Marley's

"I Shot the Sheriff" and Stevie Wonder's "Boogie on Reggae Woman." In the following two years, War released "Why Can't We Be Friends?" and the Eagles did "Hotel California." Curiously, neither song has generally been recognized as reggae inspired, which they most certainly are. In the following years, with the emergence of punk and new wave, reggae became a fully expected component in contemporary rock (the Clash, the Police, and Elvis Costello, for example).

Most Reggae, of course, came directly from Jamaica: Bob Marley and the Wailers, Toots and the Maytals, Peter Tosh, Jimmy Cliff, and many others less widely known, such as George Dekker, the Peacemakers, Scotty and Lorna Bennett, Rudie Mowatt, Third World, the Heptones, Arthur Lewis, Augustus Pablo, Desi Young, and Burning Spear. By the 1980s, many record stores had added a separate section for reggae, indicating the extent of its increasing popularity.

Reggae, however, has not been the only musical expression of the Third World's struggle for respect and fulfillment. Latin rock had its beginnings with "Donna" (1958) and "La Bamba" (1959) by Richie Valens. A few years later, Cannibal & the Headhunters did "Land of 1000 Dances" (1965), and Los Bravos had a hit in 1966 called "Black Is Black" (the non-Western orientation of the last mentioned is clear, despite the group's having a German lead singer). About the same time (1965), Sam the Sham (Domingo Samudio) and the Pharaohs began producing hits with "Wooly Bully." And with these groups, the viability of Chicanos in rock and thus in the cultural revolution was established. Although never in danger of making it to the top, El Chicano kept the Latin presence alive in the mid 1970s (*Cinco* in 1974, for example). But the biggest Latin group by far is Santana, whose *Abraxas* (1970) has become a rock classic.

In any consideration of Third World music in the United States, the work of Joan Armatrading has to be recognized. Although British by residence, she was born in the West Indies, and her music and consciousness reflect this mixed heritage. Her first album was recorded in 1973, and by her third in 1976 she had become a major artist. Perhaps because of her eclecticism, which makes her music impossible to categorize, Americans have not been overwhelmingly enthusiastic in their purchases. Yet the critics have regarded her as something of a phenomenon. "Love and Affection," for example, from her 1976 album, is paradigmatic of the eclecticism and quality of her music. The albums that have followed have been every bit as good and just as weak in sales. Nevertheless, her presence in American rock ensures not only that the Third World's struggle will have visibility, but that so also will the struggle of women.

Other cultural groups have occasionally been active in rock but not in significant numbers. Link Wray in the fifties was one of the two Native American performers to become successful in the business. Redbone (not Leon) was the other—the only rock band led by Native Americans—with a 1974 hit, "Come and Get Your Love." African groups would have to wait until the 1980s for credible representation, and Orientals are still waiting. Yet largely due to the impact of reggae, all of them have been included in the revolution.

The New Youth

Youth is the only group whose struggle for identity, respect, and fulfillment is their defining feature; for them, the struggle is permanent in principle and can never be accomplished. The very essence of youth is the struggle itself. This being the case, they can provide us with the best possible report on the state of the cultural revolution. If American youth continue to express and respond to the negation of the fifties and the affirmation of the sixties, then the revolution lives. But if they've come to express their struggle in different terms, seeking for example the values of the rejuvenated established order, then the cause is lost. The success of any revolution depends on passing its cause on to the succeeding generation, a process that is by no means automatic, especially if some gains have been made. In such cases there can be no direct experience of the conditions that precipitated the revolution in the first place, and thus the need to continue is not felt as strongly, if it is felt at all. The perennial problem for all cultural revolutions, then, is the maintenance and continuity of a revolutionary consciousness.

Two major criteria measure progress in achieving this objective. One has to do with the instigation of a revolutionary sentiment unique to the new generation; a mere imitation of their parents' consciousness would not only be transparently artificial, it would never last. A genuine revolutionary consciousness has to be a manifestation of the people who feel it; it can't be imposed from without. It has to be a new expression of the revolutionary set of values. The second criterion might seem difficult, if not impossible, to accomplish in light of the first. For there must be a clear linkage with the historical roots of the revolution in the new consciousness of the young. In this case, the fifties and sixties have to be accepted as a living presence in their lives. In my opinion, they have been, but suggesting how this is so will entail a list of staggering proportions.

There were quite a few musical styles within rock during the interim, some almost exclusively negative, others primarily affirmative, and still others expressing a mixture. Except as otherwise noted, all of the following achieved prominence during these six years, and together they should convey an accurate impression of what the new youth were listening to, and more important, what it all meant.

Most evident in heavy metal has been the attitude of negation, with its emphasis on the images of death, satanism, sexual aberration, dismemberment, and the grotesque. In the years 1967 to 1969, heavy metal became an authentic trend with album releases by Blue Cheer, Iron Butterfly, Deep Purple, Steppenwolf, the Velvet Underground, Led Zeppelin, the MC5, Black Pearl, the Stooges, and Grand Funk Railroad. Since then, the theatrical excesses and the decibels have increased to the point where the old banana-in-the-ear joke needs to be updated. ("Pardon me, sir, but are you listening to heavy metal?"/"I'm sorry, you'll have to speak louder; I'm listening to heavy metal.") Some of the more prominent of the genre have included Ted Nugent, Ozzy Osbourne, Van Halen, Black Sabbath, Blue Öyster Cult, Aerosmith, AC/DC, Kiss, Thin Lizzy, Cheap Trick, Queen, Styx, Boston, and Kansas.

My characterization shouldn't be construed to imply that heavy metal is either undesirable or qualitatively inferior, for neither is the case. Negation is absolutely necessary for any change to occur, and the genre *has*, surprisingly enough, produced some rather interesting insights into the human condition: "(Don't Fear) The Reaper" by Blue Öyster Cult (1976) and "Dust in the Wind" by Kansas (1977) are among them. Moreover, the very volume of heavy metal has a unifying effect on its listeners; the differences that tend to divide people are almost literally blown away. Today, as with many of the other musical stylings, allegiance to this kind of music has resulted in a clearly definable subculture among the new youth; its significance has not abated.

Another almost entirely negative style is punk, which began to emerge during the latter part of the 1970s, but with roots reaching back to the fifties and sixties. Its origins were in some of the wilder rockabilly performers such as Gene Vincent, Charlie Feathers, Eddie Cochran, and of course Elvis Presley. The path continued through the Hamburg period of the Beatles and the very early Rolling Stones. Youthful unemployment, the economic hardship of the lower classes amid upper-class affluence, a conservative music industry, an even more conservative political establishment, and a curious but aberrant version of traditional Christianity (the "born-again" movement) all combined to set the stage for a massive, seemingly nihilistic outrage from those at the bottom of society and others who in some way could identify with them. Dr. Feelgood, the Ramones, Blondie, and *The Rocky Horror Picture Show* were some of the earliest manifestations of American punk. The British quickly followed with the Sex Pistols and the Clash, among others. Almost immediately we were hearing from the likes of the Dictators, the Weirdos, the Zeroes, the B-52's, the Fabulous Poodles, 999, and Richard Hell and the Voidoids. Needless to say, since 1980 the punk subculture has not only continued but has expanded, in partial response, no doubt, to the election of a new symbol for the rejuvenated establishment.

Closely associated with punk is the revival of rockabilly (neorockabilly for lack of a better designation) as much a British as an American development. Dave Edmunds and his frequent cohort, Nick Lowe, have been major proponents of the genre, later teaming up formally as Rockpile. Robert Gordon (sometimes in collaboration with Link Wray), the Stray Cats, and Billy Hancock and the Tennessee Rockets have been among the purists in the revival; while Tom Petty and the Heartbreakers and Southside Johnny and the Asbury Jukes have opted for a more modified styling. Even many of the punk and new wave groups have incorporated a few rockabilly songs in their repertoire. It is hard to avoid the conclusion in all of this that the negation of the fifties has been intentionally adopted as a response to a growing perception of the contemporary world.

Another essentially negative style has been maintained in blues rock. In 1974, this was evident in albums by the Rolling Stones (*It's Only Rock and Roll*), Little Feat (*Feats Don't Fail Me Now*), and Van Morrison (*Veedon Fleece*). ZZ Top's *Fandango* and Bob Seger's *Beautiful Loser* came out a year later. Then followed Rod Stewart's *A Night on the Town* (including the sensitive "Killing of Georgie," which portrayed the murder of a homosexual) and albums by Steve Miller, the Blues Brothers, George Thorogood and the Destroyers, Delbert McClinton, and Van Morrison. In 1976, the Rolling Stones released their highly controversial *Black and Blue* album, the issue being misogyny. Although a blues styling might suggest a far greater black representation, the overwhelming majority of musicians in this category are white. But this is rock usage of blues, and besides, black music was then in the process of establishing its independence with something new.

The last primarily negative style has been variously identified as art rock, glitter rock, or simply avant-garde rock. Highly experimental and usually eclectic, involving nonrock ingredients, it has not always been accessible for the mass audience. Avant-garde, however, is necessarily a relativistic description, for what may appear to be so in one period may be considered the norm in another. In any case, the interim had a veritable wealth of such artists. Among them were Lou Reed, David Bowie, Brian Eno, Alice Cooper, and Frank Zappa, and groups such as Roxy Music, Pink Floyd, Jethro Tull, and the Tubes. Although questing for an innovative way to express the alternative set of values, the focus of art rock was an antagonism to the resiliency of the old values so deeply embedded in the American consciousness.

As the obverse of punk, new wave has been imbued with a large dose of the affirmative attitude, espousing values virtually identical to those of the sixties. Elvis Costello's *Armed Forces*, in addition to opposing militarism, includes a song called "(What's So Funny 'Bout) Peace, Love and Understanding" (1978), and the Talking Heads' *Talking Heads: '77* contains the satirical "Don't Worry about the Government" (1977). Both are implicitly anarchistic. Others emerging during the interim include the Police, Ian Gomm, the Cars, Dire Straits, the later Blondie, and even the savage Warren Zevon.

Much of the rock music early in the interim is not easily classifiable, and perhaps for this reason alone, it's worthwhile having a sample. Albums released in 1974 include those by Jackson Browne (*Late for the Sky*), Eric Clapton (*461 Ocean Boulevard*), Linda Ronstadt (*Heart Like a Wheel*), Supertramp (*Crime of the Century*), and ABBA (*Waterloo*). The following year there were albums by Bruce Springsteen (*Born to Run*), Earth, Wind and Fire (*Gratitude*), Fleetwood Mac (*Fleetwood Mac*) and Carole King (*Really Rosie*). Releases of 1976 included albums by Joni Mitchell (*Hejira*), Daryl Hall and John Oates (*Bigger Than Both Of Us*), Jeff Beck (*Wired*), Diana Ross (*Diana Ross*), the Eagles (*Hotel California*), Marvin Gaye (*I Want You*), and the phenomenal live album by Peter Frampton (*Frampton Comes Alive*). By 1977, most of the major releases were beginning to fall into one of the categories already mentioned throughout this chapter. My guess as to why this was the case concerns my admittedly biased observation that the previously mentioned categories are definable as negative or affirmative, while the albums here mentioned are not. As the 1970s came to a close, it became increasingly difficult to produce rock music with neither orientation; neutrality was coming to an end.

The fifties were kept alive by Elvis himself, among others, until his death in 1977, and maybe even more so thereafter. Although much of his later work was of extremely low quality, there were always glimmers of his greatness: "Burning Love" (1972), "T-R-O-U-B-L-E" (1975), "Hurt" (1976), and "Moody Blue," "Way Down," and "My Way" (all in 1977). When the historic *Sun Sessions* album was released in 1976, making his first, revolutionary recordings generally available for the first time, Elvis and the fifties were ensured as a continuing reality in the consciousness of American youth. The 1973 film *American Graffiti* and the TV imitation, "Happy Days" in 1974, had already prepared the way, but Elvis was the real thing. Also real, in a different sort of way, were John Lennon's two interim albums: *Walls and Bridges* (1974) and *Rock 'n' Roll* (1975), comprised exclusively of covers of fifties songs.

The sixties never came close to dying; many if not most of the major sixties performers were still producing new and significant music. Not only was their work enormously popular, it was critically acclaimed as well.

The folk tradition lived on in the music of Al Stewart, Joni Mitchell, James Taylor, Carly Simon, Gordon Lightfoot, Randy Newman, and John Stewart. All had been active to some extent in the sixties, but their major successes came during the interim. Paul Simon, however, had major successes in both periods, even teaming up for one new song with Art Garfunkel in 1975, "My Little Town." It was different with some others. Judy Collins had one major hit in 1978, "Send in the Clowns," but produced little else. Joan Baez began reasserting herself toward the end of the interim with *Honest Lullaby* in 1979, as did Peter, Paul and Mary in their *Reunion* album in 1978. The latter included the song "Sweet Survivor," which concerned maintaining the dream throughout the 1970s. As in the sixties, this newer and revived folk music was overwhelmingly affirmative.

A more complex set of emotions and attitudes accompanied the rock-oriented music of sixties survivors. By this time, the Beatles had gone their separate ways, but they still provided momentum and guidance to the revolution. Despite the 1974 *Walls and Bridges*, John Lennon settled into a self-imposed, semireclusive life, thereby adding to the *mysterium* of the Beatles. Paul McCartney, meanwhile, became increasingly prolific; but, like Lennon, he too was trying to separate himself from a past which had by now assumed mythic proportions. His tactic was a new group, Wings, and a new low profile. To the extent that they succeeded, they solidified the symbolic stature of the Beatles for the future. In 1977, their first (and only) official concert recording was released, *The Beatles at the Hollywood Bowl*, followed two years later by their earliest live recordings ever (at the Star Club in Hamburg in 1962). The enormous efforts taken to restore these crude tapes illustrate perfectly the regard in which the Beatles had come to be held.

Other sixties musicians were active as well: Dylan, with *Planet Waves* and *Before the Flood* (both in 1974), *Blood on the Tracks* and *Desire* (both in 1975), *Hard Rain* (1976), *Street Legal* (1978), and *Slow Train Coming* (1979); the Rolling Stones, with *It's Only Rock 'n' Roll* (1974) and *Some*

Girls (1978); the Grateful Dead, with *Terrapin Station* (1977) and *Shake-down Street* (1978); the Who, with *Odds and Sods* (1974), *The Who by Numbers* (1975), and *Who Are You* (1978); the Beach Boys, with *M.I.U. Album* (1978) and *L.A. (Light Album)* (1979); the Kinks, with *Soap Opera* and *Schoolboys in Disgrace* (both in 1975), *Sleepwalker* (1977), *Misfits* (1978) and *Low Budget* (1979); Crosby, Stills, and Nash, with *CSN* (1977); Led Zeppelin, with *Physical Graffiti* (1975), *Presence* (1976) and *In through the Out Door* (1979); Elton John, with *Caribou* (1974), *Rock of the Westies* (1975), *Blue Moves* (1976), and *A Single Man* (1978); Jefferson Starship, nee Airplane, with *Dragon Fly* (1974), *Red Octopus* (1975), *Spitfire* (1976), *Earth* (1978), and *Freedom at Point Zero* (1979); and the Moody Blues, with *Octave* (1978). While many of these groups might have manifested negation during the sixties, their close identification with the period resulted in their becoming, paradoxically, vehicles of affirmation—so powerful was the mythic stature of the sixties by then.

——————— The Death of Rock? ———————

By 1979, many observers wondered if the age of rock had run its course. Left unsaid, but clearly implied, was the larger claim that the cultural revolution, if in fact there had ever been one, had ended in shambles. Other observers were convinced that after the sixties nothing of worth happened, and contained within was the very same implication: the revolution was over.

Nothing, however, could be further from the truth. Even the briefest of surveys will show that the conflict of fundamental values continued within the course of historical events. Domestically, the "incident" at Three Mile Island fed the fires of the antinuke movement and expanded its focus. The increasing scarcity of natural resources (the energy crisis being the most dramatic illustration) led to a growing environmentalist movement, while other economic crises were manifested in the surprisingly effective "housewives'" meat boycott. Internationally, both the Iranian kidnappings and the capture of the *Mayagüez* prompted a nearly universal outrage among all Americans. Yet the differences in how Carter and Ford handled these two crises occasioned a split response. Although generally ineffective, Carter's emphasis on a respect for universal human rights was regarded positively by those associated with the revolutionary sentiment. Ford's approach, however, was a narrow-minded display of nationalistic macho, and it was not regarded favorably. Both presidents were parodied on "Saturday Night Live"; but while Chevy Chase's impression of Ford was unrelentingly merciless, Dan Aykroyd's version of Carter was much more sympathetic. The difference was not accidental.

Looking back on this period from the vantage of the present, there is reason for confidence. Many individuals departed the scene, but others took their place. Some of the most significant groups disbanded, but they had blazed a trail for others to follow. The social issues assumed a different configuration, but the underlying problems remained. And throughout it all, the music—and the revolution—endured.

Reactualization and the
New Music of the
Counterreaction

11

This chapter, and thus the book, must necessarily remain unfinished, for the denouement of America's cultural revolution has yet to be played out. Although it is true that the future cannot be predicted with certainty, it is nevertheless the case that some reasonably accurate speculation is possible. Based on an analysis and interpretation of the new music (punk, new wave, electro/techno pop, mod, reggae, ska, neorockabilly, neosurf, and, in general, whatever else might be included in the avant-garde) and the continued activity of musicians from the sixties, several observations can be ventured without risk of their being confused too easily with hope.

It seems virtually certain, for example, that a renewal of the conflict between the old order and the cultural revolutionaries can be anticipated. Neither side has slackened its devotion to the set of values it holds most dear; on the contrary, there is every indication that a rededication has taken place on both sides. Less certain, but still highly probable, is the observation that the revolutionaries have undertaken to rejuvenate themselves just as much as the old order has been able to do. Many of the original participants from the fifties and sixties have recovered from their exhaustion, while a new generation has arisen to join them, the latter having developed its own unique identity along with maintaining a strong connection with its revolutionary heritage. Together, they are reengaging the old order with a renewed and revitalized energy. A third observation that can be made with reasonable confidence is that women have opened up a new dimension within the movement, making clear the implicit link between feminism and the larger cultural revolution. Because of the so-called ''gender gap'' (separating women from Reagan) and the fact that women comprise a majority of the population, this new dimension is potentially the most powerful force available for the cause, and more and more people are coming to recognize this, on both sides of the conflict. Finally, it seems fairly obvious that the revolutionary symbols and their attendant attitudes of negation and affirmation have been awakened from dormancy, supplying the revival with its direction and strength.

If it makes sense to characterize cultural revolutions as essentially religious movements, then we have a context in which the process of reactualization can be understood. According to Eliade, "sacred time is indefinitely recoverable, indefinitely repeatable." By participating in the re-creation, it is possible for anyone at any time to become "contemporary with *illud tempus*" (the time and events of the beginning). He was quick to stress, however, that this "is not merely the commemoration of a mythical (and hence religious) event; it *reactualizes* the event."[1] Eliade was not alone. Sören Kierkegaard made a similar claim in *Philosophical Fragments*. Accordingly, whenever an absolute commitment is at issue, a faith commitment in other words, "there is not and never can be a disciple at second hand; for the believer . . . does not see through the eyes of another, . . . he sees only what every believer sees—with the eyes of Faith."[2] All generations are alike in this sense; all are contemporaries. It makes no difference when such a commitment is made—all those who share in it are, by definition, contemporaries.

Like all religious movements in the process of revitalization, America's cultural revolution is now being confronted with the internal conflicts that are inevitably associated with such attempts. Somehow the past must be incorporated into the present in such a way that the primary focus remains on the future. The integrity of all participants (old and new) must be protected and appreciated if the revolution is to continue with any hope of success. Otherwise, the internal tensions, which are so vital as the source of creativity and change, will degenerate into self-destruction. The danger is all the more acute when it's realized that the past and future are simply two different dimensions of the present; they exist together in our consciousness, as remembrances and anticipations. The conflict, in other words, is necessarily internal, and it characterizes the present consciousness of the revolution.

In this final chapter, I'm going to try to suggest the shape of the present conflict and indicate some of its central features. Although the existing evidence allows for only tentative conclusions, it seems to me that the present revolutionary generation has achieved considerable success in establishing a harmonious balance between the demands of past and fu-

ture, while allowing for the continued existence of tensions that are creative. They have begun the difficult process of reactualizing the attitudes
of negation and affirmation in their own distinctive way. The revolution
seems to be alive and well and living in the hearts and minds of those who
are making and listening to the new music.

———————— A Generation in Tension ————————

Without conflict, change is impossible; but without a satisfactory resolution, the changes won't last. It is the overriding task of this current generation of revolutionaries to resolve the potentially destructive conflicts bequeathed to them, while encouraging the healthy tensions. In order to
appreciate the extent to which this is already happening, we first need to
have a rough approximation of the kind of conflicts confronting them.

Analyses of the present are usually notoriously misleading and are
therefore subject to radical revisions, if not outright abandonment, with
the acquisition of greater perspective. Such analyses are basically self-
interpretations, not exactly the kind of thing to inspire confidence. We
can never be sure that all the biases and distortions have been removed,
and there is nothing that can give us this assurance. On the other hand, if
what we're interested in is not a so-called objective and neutral account
but the self-appraisal itself, then we need not fear the intrusion of opinions and assumptions that inevitably color the description. For it is precisely these features that give us an insight into the character of today's
consciousness, presupposing as they do the ultimate values of the persons
performing the appraisal. Perhaps it's a bit of an oversimplification, but
it's not so much *what* these observers see as *how* they see it that's of interest. Their interpretations, in other words, are themselves cultural artifacts worthy of investigation. The new music will yield the most direct
access to the consciousness of the present, but those otherwise intimately
involved with the present generation can offer us valuable insights as
well.

The first and most exhaustive analysis was a seven-part series done by
Dan Morgan for the *Washington Post* (December 27, 1981—January 2,
1982) entitled "Coming of Age in the '80s." His basic conclusion was
that the present generation is internally divided between its allegiance to
many of the ideals of the sixties and its acknowledgment of the practical
demands of the present.

On the one hand he noted that persons currently coming of age are concerned to make the dream of peace, freedom, equality, and justice for all come true, many even suspecting that the sixties rebels have sold out to the establishment. Individual fulfillment is one of their fundamental goals, and it has taken shape in the quest for a meaningful job as well as the search for an all-inclusive spiritual reality. While many have returned to the religion of their parents, others have associated with some of the non-Western traditions, and a well-publicized few have sought the security of a cult. On many social issues (including race, sex, and drugs) they are generally liberal; however, there are also issues on which they are divided sharply (abortion, capital punishment, nuclear energy, pacifism, and America's proper role in the world among them). Mostly, they are patriotic, yet it's a patriotism minus excessive nationalism; they have a pride in what our country stands for, if not always for what it has done. Underlying all of this is a fundamental idealism and a concern for others as well as themselves.

On the other hand, rampant inflation, increasing scarcity, and the ever-present threat of war and ultimate destruction have combined to produce something akin to an obsession with personal security and practicality. This should not be confused with simple greed or egoism, as is so often done. Rather, it is the completely understandable result of this generation's fear for what the future has to offer. Despite having grown up during the 1970s, they uncompromisingly reject any association with what some refer to as the "Me Decade," being suspicious that the appellation actually has no referent at all. From their perspective, they see themselves confronted by a crazy world which has forced them to concentrate their attention on practical concerns to the exclusion of almost everything else. To them, this isn't selfishness at all; it's being realistic.

The resulting dilemma amounts to a conflict between Maslow's second and fifth stages, the need for security and the need for self-fulfillment. For reasons that are not altogether clear, the assurances of the previous generation, that their basic survival needs would be met, have not been successfully transmitted—and not surprisingly, given the present state of the world. The loss of these assurances strikes them as patently unfair, and they want to know why it has happened and who is responsible. They feel cheated. Because of this, all authorities are distrusted, and some even hated. These authorities include parents, politicians, the government and, above all, school (Pink Floyd's *The Wall* has become something of an anthem for them). Curiously, however, they often defer to the very authorities they distrust in their quest for security. Almost universally they exhibit difficulties in handling the freedoms they've inherited from their revolutionary predecessors, and as a result, they tend to reject the very guidance they feel they need.

If Maslow is correct, their struggle for security will have to succeed before they can properly engage in a quest for self-actualization. But the satisfaction of this prior set of needs is predicated on knowing why these assurances have been denied them. More and more they are coming to believe that the rejuvenated establishment is to blame. When and if this suspicion grows into a firm conviction, the renewal of the revolutionary conflict will have begun in earnest.

Mother Jones, an antiestablishment magazine with an ''Old Left'' slant, devoted an entire issue (September/October 1983) to the rising political consciousness of women and their potentiality for wielding enormous political power. While there are many blocs of Americans whose voting patterns have traditionally not been commensurate with their populations, women are becoming increasingly convinced that the rejuvenated establishment is responsible for their present situation, since it sees itself as the protector of the traditional set of values, which are heavily sexist. Although *Mother Jones* didn't dwell on it, the result of their rising political consciousness is a conflict between those wishing to preserve the traditional relationship between the genders (supported by a patriarchal culture) and those who wish to destroy it as repressive. More important than the conflicts engendered by this issue between men and women are the conflicts engendered among women themselves. For, as I've already mentioned, the fate of the cultural revolution in many ways depends on the fate of the feminist movement. More simply, as the women go, so goes the revolution.

Ellen Goodman has pointed out yet another conflict experienced by the present generation, one that's shared with their parents. In a July 1983 article in *Ms,* ''The Turmoil of Teenage Sexuality: Parents' Mixed Signals,'' she discusses the extraordinary tensions created by parents who have adopted the ideals of sexual liberation and gender equality from the sixties, but who, for many psychological and sociological reasons, try to prevent their children from putting them into practice. Inevitably, they must face accusations of cowardice or, worse, hypocrisy, followed by the loss of affection and respect. Since the new sexual ideals generally have been accepted as morally desirable by both parents and children, there is no real possibility of rescinding them; the only real alternative is for parents to support and guide their children in their sexual explorations. Most parents, however, are fighting against two major obstacles: one is their traditional upbringing, which is still a part of them, and the other is a barely suppressed envy for a freedom they never had. Their adolescent children, on the other hand, are rarely capable of empathizing with their parents' dilemma; even rarer are moments of recognition and appreciation of the fact that their opportunities exist only because of their parents' ideals.

It is important to realize that this is not the typical parent-child conflict, for it doesn't derive from their differing levels of maturity. The conflict Ellen Goodman is describing could occur between any two age groups (although the involvement of adolescents certainly complicates the issue). It is a conflict between the espousal of values and their implementation, and because it involves sexuality, it is especially dramatic and visible. Difficult and painful as it must inevitably be to resolve such conflicts, resolution must be attained if the revolution is to have a chance of success.

One of the most provocative of recent observations was spelled out in a "Point of View" column in *The Chronicle of Higher Education* (November 4, 1981). In his guest editorial, H. Bruce Franklin wrote that teaching about Vietnam today is even more subversive than it was in the sixties because students are now learning that the causes of our involvement were not unique, not a one-time thing never to be repeated. The lesson is that it could happen again and the analogies drawn between Vietnam and El Salvador (and by extension the Middle East) are not excessively subtle. Just as important is another effect that this kind of teaching has had: it has served to link the sixties with the present by establishing the historical connection between the two periods and by pointing out that the issues are essentially the same. The bond thus created is doubly solid.

Another journalist, Aaron Latham, was interviewed on the "Today" show (July 23, 1983) about the present whereabouts of the sixties generation. He felt that they were still active. They have come to recognize, however, that the process of change is far slower and much more complex than they had at one time believed. With this accommodation to reality, they have entered the various institutions and professions that they once regarded with scorn. Yet they have found ways to do so with their values intact, making change from within a real possibility for the first time. Latham didn't mention it, but these same people have by this time become parents, with all that this implies.

Finally, I'd like to add a few observations of my own. As a high school student during the fifties, a college student during the sixties, and a university professor from the sixties to the present, I've had the opportunity to observe closely the changing of the generations. (Needless to say, my observations are as biased as those of anyone else.) On the negative side, the present generation exhibits an incredible naivete and ignorance about virtually everything, two unfortunate characteristics that feed on each other. They are manifested in such items as a simplistic patriotism, an even more simplistic religiousness, a lack of critical thinking, and a new kind of illiteracy. (Although they have the *ability* to read and write, rarely do they exercise this ability unless required to do so.) On the positive side, they have developed a complex mixture of idealism and pragmatism that the sixties only dreamed about and the fifties couldn't even imagine. (They see no tension between working in a highly complex and structured society on the one hand and affirming their individuality on the other—even if this occasionally requires breaking the drug laws. In other words, they see no incompatibility between freedom and structure.) All generations, of course, embody negative and positive features; the problem is how to erase the former and encourage the latter.

When I listen to the new music, however, I find some basis for confidence. The angry negation of the fifties and the optimistic affirmation of the sixties have been reawakened, giving substance to their positive side while calling into question the negative. Witness the music.

The Reawakening of Negation

One of the most fascinating and revealing manifestations of the consciousness of musicians is not the lyrics of the songs they write, but rather the names they've intentionally adopted for their groups. Individuals, of course, have adopted stage names, but group names may be more significant. Invariably, they disclose something about the group's overall ideological orientation, whether expressed in straightforward or ironic fashion. Occasionally, the meaning of the name will be disguised, obscure, or arcane, esoteric to all but a devoted few; more often it will be reasonably clear and unambiguous. In what follows, I've tried to include only those names with comparatively obvious meanings. Interestingly, the overwhelming majority of groups playing the new music have adopted names which express the attitude of negation.

Negation pure and simple is the meaning evident in names such as Anti, the Anti-Nowhere League (suggesting the negation of negation), F.U. (Fuck You), Richard Hell and the Void-oids, Mood of Defiance, N.O.T.A. (None of the Above), Suicidal Tendencies, T.S.O.L. (Tough Shit Out of Luck), Void, and, perhaps the best known, X. Other groups have a more specific form of negation in mind, of governmental institutions or the state, obviously suggesting anarchism: Black Flag, the Dictators, Gang Green, Falling Idols, Government Issue, Kilroy and the Anarchists, Law and Order, Manson Youth, MDC (Millions of Dead Cops), My Rules, New Order, No Authority, 100 Flowers (from a speech and policy directive of Mao Tse-tung), Rank and File, the Red Brigade, Red Rocker, Social Distortion, S.S. Decontrol, the System, the Vandals, and Vox Populi. Similarly, there are many groups whose names imply an antiwar theme: Agent Orange, the Clash, Electric Peace, Gang of Four, Ground Zero, Die Kreuzen, Modern Warfare, the New Marines, Spandau Ballet, War Zone, and White Flag.

Negation of a more social nature is directed against religion (mainly Western and Roman Catholic) by groups such as Bad Religion, Battalion of Saints, Catholic Girls, Christ Child, Christian Death, Christian Lunch, Crucifix, the Damned, Doo Doo Church, Last Rites, Lords of the New Church, Moslem Birth, 999 (the "mark of the beast" inverted), Sisters of Mercy, Stepmothers and Nuns, and Shattered Faith. Protestantism and Catholicism are symbolic targets; all religions are implicitly being rejected. Traditional sexuality and the morality that supports it have also been attacked: the Buzzcocks, Naughty Women, the Sex Pistols, Sham 69, the Slits, Sin, Sin 34, Violent Femmes, and X Offenders. Continuing with negation of a social nature, some of the most amusing names concern the middle class and all its trappings: Barbie and the Kens, the Jones (despite this probably being their real name), Jerry's Kids, the Microwaves, the Middle Class, Suburban Adventure, Suburban Blight, the Suburban Lawns, the Suburbs, Television, and the Young Home Buyers. The status and condition of today's youth yield names for still other groups: the Adolescents, Dead Youth, the Misfits, Musical Youth, Wasted Youth, Youth Brigade, and Youth Gone Mad. Even the technological bent of contemporary society is negated, especially insofar as it has a dangerous tendency toward dehumanization: Channel 3, Devo, Essential Logic, Four out of Five Doctors, Modern Industry, and Saccharin Trust.

Sometimes these new musical groups have chosen to express not so much their ideological stance as their relationship with a particular part of the past. Since negation was emphasized by the fifties, the references to this period are especially interesting. At least three have Elvis in mind: Elvis Costello and the Attractions, the Elvises, and Kid Creole and the Coconuts. (Actually, any name of the form "_____ and the _____" has the fifties in mind.) The German group Matchbox takes its name from a song by Carl Perkins, and there's an increasing number of groups using the term "cat"—all having reference to the wild rockabilly (or "cat") music of the period, of which Carl Perkins was a prime example. Hence, there are the Alley Cats, the Pole Cats, the Rockats and the Stray Cats. Some groups have a specific historical event in mind (the Red Scare, the Payolas, and the Body Snatchers); while others seek to evoke the mood of the fifties with names such as the Beatnik Flies, the Chesterfield Kings, Switchblade, and Klark Kent.

New music includes far too many songs evidencing negation to catalog here, but I do want to cite one category of songs that has recently emerged—songs about Vietnam (implying, as they often do, an antiwar message). Robert Hilburn noted in his column for the *Los Angeles Times* (October 3, 1982) that "pop music was a haven in the '60s for anti-war expression," and he mentioned the Beatles, Dylan, and Joan Baez among others, "but musicians were mostly silent during the '70s about the emotional scars left by the nation's Vietnam involvement. They've only recently begun to reopen this delicate wound."[3] His examples, however, were the Charlie Daniels Band's "Still in Saigon," Stevie Wonder's "Front Line," and Billy Joel's "Goodnight Saigon." All of these are excellent examples, no question. But Hilburn took no notice of the same trend in new music (Warren Zevon's "Roland the Headless Thompson Gunner" and the Dead Kennedys' "Holiday in Cambodia," for example). And even Don Henley's "Them and Us" and Randy Newman's "Song for the Dead" should be included as well. All of these are stark portrayals of the horrors of war, both the fighting itself and its aftermath. In the years to come, we should expect more songs of this kind and more about Vietnam in particular.

In this connection, we shouldn't overlook the direct involvement of musicians in protest activity. The MUSE Concerts held in Madison Square Garden (September 19–24, 1979) were especially significant. Sponsored by Musicians United for Safe Energy, there was no doubt of their antiwar sentiments. The performers represented a wide variety of musical styles, including folk-rock (Crosby, Stills, and Nash), jazz fusion (Gil Scott-Heron), blues-rock (Bruce Springsteen), and funk (Chaka Khan). This, and the ethnic mix, foreshadowed the racial mergers to occur a few years later.

It is also becoming increasingly clear that, among the new musicians at least, Reagan is seen as the primary symbol of the revitalized established order, illustrating clearly the antagonism between the traditional values and those expressed in the new music. The antagonism isn't very subtle either. The cover of the October 30th issue of *1981*, an alternative newspaper published in Washington, D.C., was satirically emblazoned with a cropped photo of Reagan taken from one of his patriotic World War II movies. Bedecked in uniform, it shows him with a serious and determined expression, sporting a red Mohawk (courtesy of *No Magazine,* a punk fanzine from Los Angeles). *Flip Side,* another punk publication, reported in its issue number 37 (no date) that the winner of its annual poll for Asshole of the Year (1982) was none other than our president. Other interesting data include an anti-Reagan album entitled *Let Them Eat Jellybeans,* a savage satire of Reaganomics called, simply enough, "Poverty" by Relentless Cookout, and a group that has deigned to name itself Jody Foster's Army. The conclusion is obvious: Ronald Reagan is now the *bête noire* of the cultural revolution.

Also worth noting is the fact that today's youth groupings (not gangs) largely define themselves in terms of the music they listen to. Hence, punk, new wave, mod, and reggae all refer to groups as well as music; while head bangers (or Hessians) and Soshes (or preppies) have their music allegiances as well, heavy metal and top-40 respectively. Very often their musical tastes overlap, making identification somewhat difficult for all but the participants, but clothing, hair, and language are other indicators that help set them apart. Despite their mutual antagonisms, many of which stem from the fact of their youth alone, they are nevertheless in remarkable agreement concerning the various facets of negation (even many Soshes are highly critical of the traditional values). Given their musical affiliations, these groups are best understood as direct manifestations of the revolutionary attitude of negation, much as were the various youth groupings of the fifties.

As a final slice of negativity, it should be recorded by someone that a wide spectrum of Americans was present at the August 1983 ceremony honoring the placement of a new star in Hollywood Boulevard's "Walk of Fame." It reportedly attracted a larger crowd than all previous ceremonies of this kind. The subject of interest was the Three Stooges: Larry, Moe and Curly (recently celebrated in the novelty hit "The Curly Shuffle," by Jump in the Saddle.)

Some people will no doubt wonder what all of this has to do with rock and roll. If so, I'd probably respond that, if they need to ask this question, then they are perhaps still wondering what James Dean has had to do with rock and roll.

—————— The Reawakening of Affirmation ——————

Focusing on the sixties will be unavoidable in this section, since affirmation was that decade's predominant attitude. A word of caution, however: I'm not at all interested in a simple, backward-looking nostalgia—a sentiment that has its rightful place, but not here. Rather, I'm interested in the attempts being made to recover the affirmation of the sixties so as to provide the present generation with impetus and direction for the future. The difference might be subtle, but it's still important.

I see at least three major facets to the reawakening of affirmation: one concerns the sixties survivors themselves (and it's interesting how often the term "survivor" is used to refer to them), a second concerns the new musicians of today, and the third concerns the reactualization of certain key values.

Sixties Survivors

Since the election year of 1980, many of the musicians from the sixties who had, for one reason or another, ceased performing have reentered the music scene. Some have done so as individuals, while others have reformed with their original groups.

Of first importance was John Lennon's reentry. Himself the foremost symbol of the most symbolic group of all times, he further ensured by his respite from "playing the game" that, when and if he emerged, he would be noticed. He was. His and Yoko Ono's album, *Double Fantasy,* was an incredibly forceful affirmation of the direction the revolution must take in the future—namely, like Lennon himself, it must undergo the difficult and often painful process of self-examination so that it might achieve a maturity consistent with its ultimate values. Quite apart from the murder committed shortly after its release, the album has been regarded as one of his best efforts. It signaled a new beginning for the revolution and a new role for himself within it.

Anguish over the loss of his potential was registered far and wide, and the yearly memorials held on December 8 throughout the world make certain that the loss will not be forgotten. As time passes, however, I would expect that the focus of these occasions will more and more be on his dreams for the future. Perhaps this process will be assisted by the final Lennon/Ono album, *Milk and Honey,* which was almost completed before his death. But the anguish will always remain, and so it should.

Ellen Goodman expressed the tragedy for us all in her syndicated column written just after hearing the news:

> The Lennon I'll miss isn't the brilliant Beatle of the sixties with his hair
> "rebelliously" grown below his ears. That John Lennon exists on my records. The man I'll miss is the one I just met again, the man of the eighties,

moving in new ways, making new sounds. Five bullets wiped out this father, husband, musician—human work in progress. . . .

The new record he made with his wife, Yoko Ono, *Double Fantasy,* was the work of a survivor. "You have to give thanks to God or whatever is up there (for) the fact that we all survived—survived Vietnam or Watergate, the tremendous upheaval of the whole world," he said in an ironic prelude to his death. . . .

In a way he was talking to and for his own generation. "I'm saying, 'Here I am now, how are you? How's your relationship going? Did you get through it all? Wasn't the Seventies a drag, you know? Well, here we are, let's make the Eighties great because it's up to us to make what we can of it. . . .'"

You can't kill what a man has already done. You can only kill what might have come next.

The antique John Lennon had already been preserved. Dammit, it's the promise that's gone.[4]

The three remaining Beatles obviously felt Lennon's loss in a personal way; yet, being public figures and musicians themselves, they inevitably revealed their grief to us. They did so, however, in such a way as to preserve his legacy and the legacy of what the Beatles have come to mean. Harrison's "All Those Years Ago," McCartney's "Here Today," and Ringo's album cover of *Stop and Smell the Roses* (showing him weeping while holding three remaining roses) have, together, created the reunion so many had sought for so long.

Also of considerable significance is the Simon and Garfunkel reunion, initiated at their free concert in Central Park in September 1981. In an interview with *Rolling Stone* immediately following the concert, which attracted over a half million people, Simon remarked that there were really only two big reunions possible. "And now," he said, expressing visible emotion, "one of them can't happen. And I think they probably would have done it too, eventually." Since then, Simon and Garfunkel have toured Europe, Asia, and the United States.

Peter, Paul and Mary have also reunited and have also toured the country, releasing a new album aptly titled *Reunion.* They also appeared at the twentieth anniversary of the civil-rights march on Washington (August 27, 1983), just as they had in 1963. Others attempting the comeback trail include the Animals, Chad and Jeremy, the Everly Brothers, the Hollies and (with a revised membership) the Mamas and Papas.

Many other sixties musicians have simply remained active, with greater or lesser degrees of success. Among the most successful have

been the Rolling Stones, the Kinks, and Pink Floyd. Not only have they
continued to produce quality material, they have developed an enormous
following among the present generation. The Beach Boys have come up a
bit short on new material, but their popularity at concerts seems to be
holding. (The death of Dennis Wilson may affect this adversely.)

A few Motown groups have also remained active, some with their
original members intact (as with the Four Tops) and others with a succession of replacements (as with the Temptations). Some of the major solo
artists, such as Stevie Wonder, are of course still active (as was Marvin
Gaye until his death in 1984). And many former lead singers have become soloists—Diana Ross, Eddie Kendricks, and Smokey Robinson,
for example. As for soul, James Brown and Aretha Franklin, among
many others, appear occasionally, but distinctively black music had begun to emerge as something different during the interim.

To the extent that sixties musicians have been able to accommodate to
newer forms and adjust their message to a different time, they have been
quite successful; otherwise, they have been relegated to the inferior and
degrading status of playing nothing but ''oldies but goodies,'' which is
where many persons and groups both black and white have found themselves. Concerts comprised of oldies are often fun, but they offer nothing
new, no challenges for the future.

Reunions and reentries are one thing, but to regain significance these
musicians have to reactualize their capacity to make significant music as
well. To be sure, this is incredibly difficult, especially for those in danger
of becoming trapped in their own mythology, so it's surprising how
many have pulled it off. My interest, however, is in a particular kind of
music they've been making, music intended as a commentary on the
times—specifically, the transition from the sixties, through the interim,
and into the counterreaction.

John Lennon's ''(Just Like) Starting Over'' is a fitting beginning for
this list, since his purpose was to comment not only on his relationship
with Yoko but also on the status of the cultural revolution itself. ''Hard
Times Are Over,'' a song by Yoko from the same album, contains a
similar double message. McCartney's 1982 album, Tug of War, is one
of his best, and many critics think it excels all his previous solo output
by far. It not only includes his personal remembrance of John, ''Here
Today,'' it also expresses his pessimism about the prospects for economic recovery given the present political structure (''The Pound Is
Sinking''), his hopes for a genuine improvement in racial relationships
(''Ebony and Ivory,'' sung with Stevie Wonder), his homage to the fifties (''Get It,'' sung with Carl Perkins), and his vision of freedom

("Wanderlust"). No simple nostalgia exists among any of these songs.

Returning to Simon and Garfunkel, they have done more than merely reunite for a series of concerts. One of Paul Simon's recent songs has to do with the senseless deaths of Johnny Ace (an R & B singer from the fifties), John Kennedy, and John Lennon—"The Late Great Johnny Ace." Even more significant is his addition of a new stanza to "The Boxer":

> Now the years are rolling by me
> They are rocking evenly
> I am older than I once was
> Younger than I'll be
> That's not unusual
> No it isn't strange
> After changes upon changes
> We are more or less the same. . . .

The times may change, in other words, but the human condition remains the same.

Just before Simon and Garfunkel's 1983 tour of the United States, Simon was asked why he thought there was such an overwhelmingly positive response to their reunion. His answer points out that the reawakening of affirmation has become a widespread need: "I feel we've been living in just brutalizing times and any time you come across any public figure or figures that represent the opposite, they become very important."

Continuing in this vein, though Peter, Paul and Mary's *Reunion* was released in 1978, it includes one song in particular, "Sweet Survivor," which could almost be an anthem of sixties survivors:

> You have asked me why the days fly by so quickly
> And why each one feels no different from the last
> And you say that you are fearful for the future
> And you have grown suspicious of the past.
>
> And you wonder if the dreams we shared together
> Have abandoned us or we abandoned them
> And you cast about and try to find new meaning
> So that you can feel that closeness once again
>
> Carry on my sweet survivor

Carry on my lonely friend
Don't give up on the dream
Don't you let it end
Carry on my sweet survivor
Though you know that something's gone
For everything that matters
Carry on

You remember when you felt each person mattered
When we all had to care or all was lost
But now you see believers turned to cynics
And you wonder was the struggle worth the cost

Then you see someone too young to know the difference
And the veil of isolation in their eyes
And inside you know you've got to leave them something
Or the hope for something better slowly dies

Carry on my sweet survivor
You've carried it so long
So it may come again
Carry on

It would be hard to imagine a more insightful portrayal of the consciousness of the revolutionaries just prior to Reagan's election and the consequent period of reactualization.

Joan Baez's *Honest Lullaby* was also released before the election, in
1979, and as with Peter, Paul and Mary, her reflections and sentiments
ring true. The chorus of the title song goes: "And I look around and I
wonder/How the years and I survived/I had a mother who sang to me/An
honest lullaby." The clear implication is that it's now time to pick up
where we left off. Actually, Joan Baez herself has never stinted in her
dedication to the causes of peace, freedom, and justice throughout the
world (through her organization, Humanitas International). Despite the
fact that she has had difficulty recording some of her more relevant songs
("Sergeant Pepper's Band" and "Children of the Eighties" among
them), she continues to be a credible activist. What makes it work is her
dedication, and the fact that it has endured is evident to everyone.

I'm not really sure whether Crosby, Stills, and Nash have reunited, or
whether they were ever a group to begin with. In any case, their 1982 album,
Daylight Again (a title that says something in itself) includes their feelings
about the times in "Wasted on the Way." Written by Graham Nash, who

has since returned to the Hollies, it has such lines as "Oh when you were young/Did you question all the answers/Did you envy all the dancers/Who had all the nerve," and "So much time to make up (So much love to make up)/Everywhere you turn/Time we have wasted on the way."

Regarding the Hollies, their new album includes a cover of the Supremes' "Stop in the Name of Love." What's interesting about it is the video they've made to accompany it: "stopping" refers to warfare and all the militaristic and nationalistic posturings associated with it. Pink Floyd's *The Final Cut,* Neil Young's *Reactor,* Elton John's *Jump Up* (which has his remembrance of John Lennon, "Empty Garden") and the Kinks' *Give the People What They Want* are all oriented around similar antiwar and antiviolence themes.

Other facets of America's cultural malaise have been expressed by some more recent survivors. Bruce Springsteen's *Nebraska* explores the effects of loneliness and the loss of hope. Don Henley's *I Can't Stand Still* is a painful reminder that society has failed us ("Johnny Can't Read") and has unfeelingly invaded our lives ("Dirty Laundry"). Bob Seger's *The Distance* focuses on the people most injured by the economic disasters of the present. And Billy Joel's *Nylon Curtain* includes a little bit of all of the above.

New Musicians

When one looks at some of the names that these musicians have given their groups, their intentional recovery of the sixties and what it affirmed becomes immediately obvious. They include Catch 22, the Dead Kennedys, the Insect Surfers, Kent State, the Pranksters, the Rutles, the Shoes, the Surf Punks, and U2. Despite the hostility evident in some of these names, it is not directed against the sixties per se; it is directed against those who would preserve the past at the expense of the present. U2 in particular has manifested a sixties-like antiwar/antiviolence message in songs such as "I Will Follow" and "Sunday Bloody Sunday." Big Country and R.E.M. exemplify this dual message as well, although their names hardly suggest it. Nevertheless, it is clear that the past, including its outrages, must be preserved in the present's consciousness if genuine progress is to be made.

There are some interesting references to the past in the lyrics as well. Philip Lynott (formerly of Thin Lizzy) reveals his personal bond with the fifties in "King's Call," a song about how Elvis's death affected him.

But his personal bond has functioned as a paradigm for how it affected many contemporary musicians. Lynott also wrote "Talk in 79," about how transitory the new wave is likely to be. This suggests, by implication, that no new symbols are to be expected from the present; the basic symbols already exist.

The Ramones' "Do You Remember Rock 'n' Roll Radio?" recalls, among others, Ed Sullivan, Alan Freed, Murray the K, T-Rex, Jerry Lee Lewis, and John Lennon. They sing about "the end of the 70s" and "the end of the century" and include the plea "We need changes we need it fast/Before rock's just a part of the past/'Cause lately it all sounds the same to me." This call for the revival is necessarily to the past, since the Ramones represent the present; a genuine revival must gather its force and direction from its roots, but the present must make use of it.

An even stronger call for a revival, based on an affirmation of the sixties, comes in Blondie's "English Boys":

When I was 17
I saw a magazine
It had those English Boys
who had long hair

When I was on my own
they moved into my town
and I just called 'em up
and they'd be there

In 1969
I had a lousy time
I listened to the songs
read letters sent from Nam

Now peace and love were gone
the tired soldiers home
Ideal society
gunned down the 70s

Does it feel the same to you?
Why do you act the way you do?
Pack it up or pack it in
There's no excuse

Could the hands of time reverse
Would we wake or take the ride

And again speak with one voice

We knew each other well
Although we never met
Messages passed to tell
Equal respect. . . .

It takes little imagination to realize that the "English Boys" being referred to are from Liverpool.

Affirmation is also evident in some of the rather unexpected musical
developments. Most curious is the apparent synthesis between punk and
country evident in groups such as the Alarm, Blood on the Saddle, Jason
and the Scorchers, Lone Justice, Rank and File, and the all-female
group, the Screamin' Sirens. Equally interesting is the development of a
viable Latino rock, as with the Brat, the Cruzados, Los Illegals, Los Lobos, and Tierra. A neopsychedelia (also known as the paisley underground) has also begun to emerge with groups such as the Bangles, the
Long Ryders, Rain Parade and the Three O'Clock. Then, of course,
there are groups whose music defies description, as is perhaps evident in
their very names: Tupelo Chain Sex and the Fibonaccis. All of the above
groups are genuinely new, and this in itself is affirmative.

Covering the music from the past is yet another form of affirmation,
even when the originals are from some period other than the sixties.
When it's done for reasons other than pure profit, the act of covering
someone else's music is necessarily an acknowledgment and acceptance
of the past, the incorporation of it into the present. It is the recognition
that movement into the future cannot be successfully accomplished until
the present has achieved its self-identity, and this is contingent on its having accepted its origins.

The table on page 226–27 shows some recent covers. Though a much
more extensive compilation is certainly possible, I think these examples
clearly convey the idea that this generation knows where it came from
and where it's going.

Key Values

Among the values being reaffirmed and reinforced are those concerned
with interracial respect, feminism, and the primacy of the human individual over the artificiality of national differences. In many ways, the ulti-

Recent Covers

Title	Origin/Date	Cover
"Forever"	Little Willie John/'56	The Cramps
"Blue Suede Shoes"	Carl Perkins/'56	Toy Dolls
"Breathless"	Jerry Lee Lewis/'58	X
"Rockin' Robin"	Bobby Day/'58	Nine below Zero
"Johnny B. Goode"	Chuck Berry/'58	Peter Tosh
"Poison Ivy"	The Coasters/'59	The Avengers
"Nobody but Me"	Dee Clark/'59	The Pranksters
"Doggin' Around"	Jackie Wilson/'60	Click
"Theme from 'Psycho' "	Soundtrack/'60	The Fibonaccis
"Money"	Barrett Strong/'60	The Flying Lizards
"Stand by Me"	Ben E. King/'61	The Clash
"This Train (Conductor Wore Black)"	Peter, Paul & Mary/'62	Rank and File
"Something's Got a Hold on Me"	Etta James/'62	David Lindley
"Pipeline"	The Chantays/'63	Agent Orange
"Heat Wave"	Martha & the Vandellas/'63	The Jam
"Louie Louie"	The Kingsmen/'63	Black Flag
"Ring of Fire"	Johnny Cash/'63	Wall of Voodoo
"Pipeline"	The Chantays/'63	The Wedge
"Wipe Out"	The Sufaries/'63	Z'Ev
"You Really Got Me"	The Kinks/'64	Oingo Boingo
"Needles and Pins"	The Searchers/'64	The Ramones
"Glad All Over"	The Dave Clark Five/'64	The Rezillos
"Viva Las Vegas"	Elvis Presley/'64	The Dead Kennedys
"Tell Me"	The Rolling Stones/'64	Stiv Bators
"Oh, Pretty Woman"	Roy Orbison/'64	Van Halen
"Land of 1,000 Dances"	Cannibal & the Headhunters/'65	David Himes
"Midnight Hour"	Wilson Pickett/'65	The Jam
"I'm Down"	The Beatles/'65	Adrian Belew
"Satisfaction"	The Rolling Stones/'65	Devo
"Dirty Water"	The Standells/'65	The Inmates

Song	Artist/Year
"19th Nervous Breakdown"	The Rolling Stones/'66
"Time Won't Let Me"	The Outsiders/'66
"Sloop John B."	The Beach Boys/'66
"Tomorrow Never Knows"	The Beatles/'66
"Under My Thumb"	The Rolling Stones/'66
"I Fought the Law"	The Bobby Fuller Four/'66
"Somebody to Love"	The Jefferson Airplane/'67
"Higher and Higher"	Jackie Wilson/'67
"Getting Better"	The Beatles/'67
"Little Bit o' Soul"	Music Explosion/'67
"Mr. Soul"	Buffalo Springfield/'67
"Purple Haze"	Jimi Hendrix
"I Had Too Much to Dream"	The Electric Prunes/'67
"Helter Skelter"	The Beatles/'68
"Dear Prudence"	The Beatles/'68
"Mony, Mony"	Tommy James & the Shondells/'68
"Spooky"	The Classics IV
"Everyday People"	Sly & the Family Stone/'69
"Gimme Shelter"	The Rolling Stones/'69
"Na Na Hey Hey Kiss Him Goodbye"	Steam/'69
"Hawaii 5-0"	The Ventures/'69
"Tears of a Clown"	Smokey Robinson & the Miracles/'70
"Truckin'"	The Grateful Dead/'70
"Who'll Stop the Rain"	Creedence Clearwater Revival/'70
"Riders on the Storm"	The Doors/'71
"Jealous Guy"	John Lennon/'71
"Thank You for Talkin' to Me Africa"	Sly & the Family Stone/'71
"Ziggy Stardust"	David Bowie/'72
"Forever Young"	Bob Dylan/'74
"Live for Today"	Sweet/'77
"My Way"	Frank Sinatra/'70 and Elvis Presley/'77

The Pop
The Modsters
Mike Querico
Phil Collins
Social Distortion
The Clash
Agent Orange
Blue Riddem Band
The Question Men
The Ramones
Dream Syndicate
The Fibonaccis
The Thought
Mötley Crüe
Siouxsie & the Banshees
Billy Idol
Lydia Lunch
Joan Jett & the Blackhearts
Sisters of Mercy
Bananarama
23 Skidoo
The English Beat
The Pop-O-Pies
Heaven 17
Annabel Lamb
Roxy Music
Magazine
Bauhaus
Missing Persons
Lords of the New Church
Sid Vicious

mate success of the cultural revolution depends on how the conflicts associated with these values are resolved.

As practically everyone knows, black and white music underwent a dramatic separation during the interim, both reflecting and encouraging the same kind of separation throughout American society. This has been in some very important ways beneficial, in that it has enabled blacks to achieve the kind of self-identity that was impossible while seeking the goal of integration. Now that self-identity has largely been accomplished, a continuation of this separation (by choice or by force) would be unjust. (It has already worked a financial hardship on black artists, and the media are only haltingly beginning to correct the imbalance in programming that reinforces their inferior status.) The evidence suggests, however, that a merger is beginning to take place, this time on the basis of mutual respect and equality.

Black musicians are beginning to do the kind of rock and roll usually associated with whites. Among the best representatives of this trend are the Bus Boys. Not only are they producing some of today's finest rock music, they are quite self-conscious about what they are doing. "Johnny Soul'd Out" says it perfectly: "Johnny was known as the King of Soul/He was a brother had it under control," and "James Brown was his cousin/Little Richard was his friend." Then they continue, "I saw him do the jerk/I saw him do the twist/The next thing I know/He was acting like this." The chorus follows with "Johnny soul'd out, I tell you Johnny soul'd out/He's into rock and roll and he's given up the rhythm and blues." Their debut album, *Minimum Wage Rock and Roll,* has two other songs that add a little bite to this theme. In "KKK" they intimate that being an American should allow them access to every nook and cranny of society, the Klan as well as rock and roll. And while the point of "Respect" might be obvious, it includes the proclamation "If you don't like rock 'n' roll music/You can kiss my ass," a message intended for everyone, black as well as white.

Prince's *1999* and *Around the World in a Day* also include songs in an ostensibly white style, as does Michael Jackson's *Thriller.* The latter includes the Paul McCartney duet "The Girl Is Mine," and "Beat It," with Eddie Van Halen on guitar.

Other black performers doing white rock include Irene Cara, Junior, the Pointer Sisters, Prince, Terry Scott (whose debut album was sent to program directors in a blank jacket to disguise his race), and Donna Summer. As the media begin to open their minds and doors to this possibility, more crossovers will emerge. After all, to paraphrase Funkadelic, there's no reason why a funk band can't play rock and roll.

To further paraphrase them, there's no reason why a rock band can't play funk, and several are beginning to do so. One of the earliest was M, with its 1979 hit "Pop Muzik," which many perceived as a blend of disco and new wave. Actually, this assessment isn't too far off the mark, since funk has comprised much of the disco sound, and new wave has been mostly white. More recently, the blend can be heard in Blondie's "Rapture," David Bowie's "Cat People" and "Let's Dance," the Clash's "Rock the Casbah," Haircut One Hundred's "Love Plus One," Pete Shelley's "Homosapien," the Thompson Twins' "In the Name of Love," and many others. Ex–Sex Pistol John Lydon (a.k.a. Johnny Rotten), in his new group Public Image, Ltd. (PiL), has "foreshadowed much of the current punk/disco merger by extending the moody, highly textured aural-cinema tradition of bands like the Velvet Underground," according to Robert Hilburn in the *Los Angeles Times* (June 5, 1983). Hilburn has also remarked that "far from the annoyingly repetitious and vacuous records associated with the disco fever of the late '70s, today's dance music benefits from a healthy blend of early disco energy and wry, new-wave spirit.'"[5] One of the finest, yet generally unknown, examples of this blend is an album by the Was brothers (David and Don) called *Was (Not Was)* (1981), especially on "Out Come the Freaks" and "Carry Me Back to Old Morocco." Their adopted surname might imply the past, but their music definitely points to the future. Their album *Born to Laugh at Tornadoes* (1983) has borne this out.

It follows, of course, that if blacks and whites have begun playing each other's style of music, the chances are pretty good it's because each finds something they like in the other's music. Changing radio formats, diversification of video programming, and the new twelve-inch discs all seem to reflect this growing mutuality of interest. Whites are finding that they can identify with the music of artists like Grandmaster Flash, Gloria Gaynor, Eddy Grant, Michael Jackson, Rick James, Prince, Donna Summer, and Stevie Wonder. Blacks, on the other hand, have always been familiar with white music, since fewer than three hundred of the more than eight thousand radio stations in this country have a black-oriented format. One record promoter, Randy Cunningham, feels that the divisions between blacks and whites are now breaking down: "The club jocks are helping to bring cultures together. They realize people are interested in dancing to good music, not just 'white' music or 'black' music. Radio is starting to pick up on what's happening out there, and we should see some changes on that level, too." It should be emphasized that this mutual interest is not in music modified to appeal to their individual tastes (as happened in the fifties); on the contrary, interest today is in the original music itself. Their differing styles are being appreciated for their differences.

As if to underscore this merger, the twentieth anniversary of the march on Washington (August 27, 1983) had a considerably larger white participation than in 1963, bringing it closer to equality. Significantly, the march's theme was not integration as it was twenty years ago, but peace, freedom, justice, and economic security for all. Differing racial cultures are no longer being seen as an obstacle to harmony but rather as a prerequisite.

Perhaps before too long we will see an end put to the odious divisions implied by the three and sometimes four music charts (pop, R & B, C & W, disco). Because of the overwhelming similarities between the pop and R & B charts in the fifties, *Billboard* (and others) discontinued the latter for a short period, only to revive it again with the emergence of soul. But this isn't what I foresee happening; nor do I think it ought to happen. Instead of the music becoming increasingly similar, I envision a diversity of musical styles appealing to and being respected by an increasingly diverse assemblage of people. The result: one chart with many styles represented.

The influence of feminism on the American consciousness is continuing to grow, despite the failure of the ERA in 1982. As mentioned in the previous chapter, women have begun to take an increasingly active role in those areas of rock hitherto regarded as the sole province of males. Among those I've already mentioned are Debbie Harry, Joan Jett, Grace Jones, Diana Ross, and Donna Summer. Others include Laurie Anderson, the Bangles, the Belle Stars, Kate Bush, the Flirts, the Go Go's, Lisa Hartman, Cyndi Lauper, the Leather Angels, Lene Lovich, Lydia Lunch, Madonna, the Roches, Tin Angel, Vanity 6, and the Waitresses. Among this diverse listing is an anomaly, the Waitresses. Although only two of the group's six members are women, the group's overall message is nevertheless an advocacy of full and complete gender equality. Best known for the satirical "I Know What Boys Like," the group's debut album, *Wasn't Tomorrow Wonderful* (1982), also includes "No Guilt." This song portrays a woman's gradual struggle from dependency on a man to full independence: "I've done a lot since you've been gone" and "I'm sorry but I don't feel awful/It wasn't the end of the world/I'm sorry I can't be helpless." In a similar vein, Grace Jones's "Nipple to the Bottle" has a line stressing that she will neither give in to male pressures nor feel guilty about her independence. As a final indication of how things are proceeding, the Leather Angels, from Southern California, are one of the first heavy-metal bands comprised entirely of women—studs, chains, leather and all. The next time around, the ERA won't fall prey to the sentiments expressed in Charlene's reactionary "I've Never Been to Me." Next time, the victorious sentiment will most likely be that expressed in Donna Summer's "She Works Hard for the Money."

A concern for individuals over national allegiances should not be confused with "internationalism," which regards the existence of the nation-state as justified and beyond question. Genuine individuality, on the other hand, considers the nation to be an artificial construct and a dangerous threat to the possibility of self-actualization—and the sooner it's abolished the better. Hence, "non-nationalism" would be a more accurate way to describe what's implied by individuality.

The increasing popularity among Americans of rock music from around the world is a manifestation of the as-yet-inchoate sentiment of non-nationalism. I don't include music from the rest of the English-speaking world in this survey (especially Britain), since ours and theirs have been so closely intertwined from the beginning of the cultural revolution. It would be impossible, and pointless, to attempt an isolation of their music at this point in order to ascertain its impact on us.

Rock music from continental Europe is another matter. When Americans hear rock music performed by people whose native language is other than English, the impression is unavoidable that there is something that unifies all individuals and all cultures, something deeper and more profound than the nationalistic peculiarities that force us apart. Those Americans most closely associated with the revolution are coming to discover that people from vastly different cultures all have certain fundamental values in common, values very similar to if not identical with those of the cultural revolutionaries. Once this is recognized, nationalistic conflicts will be revealed as artificially induced and thus intolerable.

Idealistic? No doubt. But if the medium of music is in any way also its message, this may be an accurate assessment of future developments. In any case, music is expressing this ideal far more effectively than any discursive ideology could ever hope to do. A small sample from the import bins includes bands from Austria (Falco), France (Dün), Germany (Nena, Peter Schilling, the Scorpions, Spliff, and Toten Hosen), Holland (Taco and Vasmak), Italy (Il Volo), and Sweden (Von Zamla). Some of the German groups have, perhaps more than some of the others, expressed antinuclear and antiwar sentiments, for example, Nena's "99 Luftballoons" and Peter Schilling's "Major Tom (Coming Home)."

One European group that most of us are unlikely ever to hear is, surprisingly, a group from the Soviet Union, Time Machine. In a nation so paranoid and defensive that it can be suspicious of, and thus shoot down, an unarmed, civilian passenger plane (killing well over two hundred people with no apparent remorse), it comes as something of a shock that the authorities would permit a rock-and-roll band to exist, much less allow it to perform. According to the *Washington Post* (April 17, 1982), Time Machine was selected as the most popular ensemble of 1982 by the Young Communist League. A few weeks later, these same musicians were denounced by the government as un-Russian, unmusical, and given to the expression of dangerous ideas. It was felt that, along with blue jeans, sweatshirts, and beards, popular music is responsible for spreading degenerate Western influences throughout the Soviet Union. Some of Time Machine's disturbing lyrics were the following (unfortunately, not identified according to song):

I do not believe in promises and will not do so in the
future / There is no point in believing in promises any longer.

Tell me, why are you happy? / Wait, look back, and see how the
fallen leaves decay / How a crow circles where once a garden bloomed.

You have to wear masks, wear masks / Because only under the
mask can you remain yourself.

I am calm only for the fact that now nobody can deceive you /
And you are now prepared to do things for yourself.

One sunny day when millions of young men died / With
song on their lips.

No wonder they're in trouble. Could it be that this presages the reactualization of the authentic Russian revolution? We can only hope.

Along with the increasing popularity of reggae among blacks as well as whites in America, Americans are also beginning to respond favorably to some of the rock music being produced by several of the African cultures. There are at least five anthologies worth listening to in order to get a pretty good sample: *Assalam Aleikoum Africa* (West Africa), *Rhythm of Resistance* (South Africa), *Sound d'Afrique* (Central Africa), *Soweto* (South Africa), and *Viva Zimbabwe!* (East Africa). Albums by individual performers include King Sunny Adé's *Juju Music* (Nigeria), Juluka's *Scatterlings of Africa* (South Africa), Fela Anikulapo Kuti's *Black President* (South Africa) and Prince Nico Mbarga and Rocafil Jazz's *Sweet*

Mother and *Free Education* (Nigeria). Africa, of course, is one of those areas where injustice exists in paradigmatic dimensions, so good and evil are not so difficult to distinguish (at least for the cultural revolutionaries in America). Hence, the music is likely to have a great deal of popular appeal, especially the music from South Africa.

Underscoring rock's cognizance of the worldwide implications of the cultural revolution and the ultimate meaninglessness of nations were the 1980 Concerts for the People of Kampuchea. Sponsored by Paul Mc-Cartney, they involved an interesting variety of groups. Aside from Mc-Cartney himself, there were the Clash (punk), Elvis Costello (new wave), the Pretenders (new wave), Queen (heavy metal), Rockpile (neorockabilly), the Specials (mod/ska) and the Who (classic mod). The implication following from this breadth is that nationalism and ethnocentrism are scorned universally throughout the rock community. More recently was the Live Aid concert, held jointly in Philadelphia and London on July 13, 1985, in order to help feed millions of drought-stricken Ethiopians. It brought together a far larger assemblage of performers, representing styles from the fifties to the present. Other countries participated through live and taped means: Australia, Austria, Japan, and the Soviet Union. The message was clear: national boundaries are not only less important than the people they enclose, but are in fact obstacles. And the message was not only in the music, it *was* the music.

The more Americans incorporate this diversity of music into their consciousness, the sooner total reactualization will be accomplished.

1984 and Beyond

In this final chapter I've been discussing trends, and trends only. Before departing the scene, however, I'd like to offer a few minor tidbits to accompany these speculations. As is perhaps apparent to anyone who has eyes to see and ears to hear, clothing and hair styles are beginning to have political import again. So also is smoking marijuana (no doubt as a partial response to the renewed opposition to the practice by the present administration); recreational smoking isn't declining, but it's taking on this added dimension. Perhaps most important of all, the sexual and gender relationships among the younger generations are beginning to show a degree of equality and mutuality unheard of in the past.

To be sure, these are only small matters, and it's hard to tell what it all means. Yet sometimes the smallest things reveal the most. And what these tidbits reveal is that the major trends discussed throughout this chapter are indeed under way. The ultimate outcome is, of course, unpredictable. But whatever it is, we should hear it first in the music—the music we now call rock.

California:
The Shape of
Things to Come

——————————————— Epilogue —

The introduction of novel fashions in music is a
thing to beware of as endangering the whole of
society, whose most important conventions are
unsettled by any revolution in that quarter.
—Plato

Something is happening here but you
  don't know what it is,
Do you,
Mister Jones.

—Bob Dylan

When people become caught in the throes of confusion and exasperation, tossing up their hands and crying out to whatever gods remain to hear them, "What next?!" it should be of some comfort to them that, no matter what it is, it will happen first in California. Californians, of course, go stumbling merrily on their way, blithely unaware of their tendencies to participate in whatever is new—simply because it's new.

Obviously, there's no way to verify or falsify these simplistic beliefs, but there are many times when I sure feel like they're true. Apparently, I'm not alone, for Theodore H. White, in *America in Search of Itself,* makes a similar observation about this strangest of all the fifty states:

California lay at the sunset rim of the westering impulse, where Americans came to set themselves free from whatever past bothered them back East. To be free meant not simply political freedom. California had always stood for that—indeed, the very first Republican national candidate, in 1856, had been a Californian, John C. Fremont, demanding free soil. Liberation in California in more recent times meant the freeing of behavior from custom, of the individual from the family, of men from neckties, of women from aprons. It meant a freedom of life styles which would eventually, sweep east to undermine older American life styles—a freedom of sex from marriage, of mating from social conventions, of voters from party affiliations, of blacks from the white power structure, and later, for Third World emigrants, a liberation from awe at the world of the white

man. The piston push behind California's rise to national eminence was
. . . demographic, for . . . those who came from afar were divorcing
themselves from old values.[1]

More than a geographical region, California is a state of mind, a condition of consciousness—a place of refuge from the past and openness to
the future, with freedom its defining essence. It may not be that everything happens in California first. But it might very well be true that whatever is currently happening is more clearly revealed in California and the
California experience. This makes more sense.

The reason why California can function in this capacity follows from
the fact that the tensions present everywhere throughout America are
more emphasized here, its freedoms far more blatant. In any case, California has been blessed and cursed with virtually every paradox imaginable. Physically, the state is an incomparable paradise as well as a veritable pit of desolation, the two often existing nearly side by side. It is a
haven for both preservationists and developers, and the distinction between them isn't always too clear. Its political makeup is an impossible
blend of moderation and extremism, with the two ends of the political
spectrum frequently merging, making the moderates seem equally extreme. The conflicts between young and old, rich and poor, black and
white, men and women, straights and gays, hippies and bikers, upper and
lower classes, and so on are both more destructive and more creative than
anywhere else in the world. The most incompatible religious and antireligious sentiments exist here in relative harmony, in the midst of some of
the most rabid apathy imaginable. The state's support for education is
rivaled only by its seeming insensitivity to those students who wish most
to take advantage of it. Its laws allow for an unheard-of degree of freedom in personal matters, yet at the same time they exhibit the kind of
moral oppression that threatens to obliterate the very possibility of meaningful personal action. And the most "laid back" of Californians are often the very same people who are "living in the fast lane." Tensions like
these give California its highly visible energy and vitality. Nothing in this
state is stable after all, including the ground, so movement and change
would seem to be the inevitable consequences of succumbing to this state
of mind.

America's cultural revolution is thus more evident in California than
anywhere else, revealed dramatically in its conflicts and in its attempted
resolutions. Because of this, it's worth taking a final look at the revolution by narrowing our focus to the "Golden State" and in this way trying

to understand present conditions. In keeping with the basic thesis, of course, I believe the best way to appreciate the California experience is to see it through the rock music indigenous to California.

There are really two aspects to look for in this or any revolution: its internal dynamics (in this case revealed by the conflicts intrinsic to California) and its relationship with the established order (revealed by California's encounters with the outside world). The former might help disclose what it means for the very same people to have elected both Ronald Reagan and Jerry Brown governor. The latter might help us understand the meaning behind all those predictable jokes about California. (For example, someone must have tilted the East Coast up, because everything loose fell into California. And, Q: Why is California like granola? A: Because it's filled with fruits and nuts.) Somehow the elections and the jokes relate to the underlying values of the California experience, and these link it with the cultural revolution, establishing an analogous relationship between the two (or so it seems). As long as this approach isn't pushed too far or understood to be a literal identity, an exploration of California through its rock music just might provide a few interesting insights as to where we are and where we might be headed as a culture.

As a theoretical context for this analogy, I've found that a Hegelian structure helps to explain the internal dynamics and a Kuhnian structure the external relationship.

The Internal Dynamics

Hegel offers a way to understand the process of historical change. It's not the only way, of course, and it's certainly not the clearest. But for the purpose at hand, it has three distinct advantages. First, change is portrayed as the very nature of reality; it's not something accidental or induced from the outside. Second, change is oriented toward a particular goal—freedom; every stage of the process brings it closer. And third, the process occurs in our consciousness and then necessarily manifests itself in concrete historical events.

In his lectures collected in *The Philosophy of History*, Hegel said that "universal history shows the development of the consciousness of Freedom on the part of Spirit, and of the consequent realization of that Freedom. This development implies a gradation—a series of increasingly adequate expressions or manifestations of Freedom, which . . . it successively transcends."[2] The dynamics of this process result from the continuous conflict between "being" and "nothing," which produces "becoming." Every stage of this process is characterized by explosive interplay. Although Hegel certainly believed this triad to be the actual, fundamental component of reality, I intend it only as a metaphorical way of understanding historical change.

Being

The thing to keep in mind about pure being is its undetermined immediacy, the fact that there are no differentiating features either within it or between itself and the outside, pure "is-ness" with no particular knowledge about it possible. "It is pure undeterminateness and emptiness."

Perhaps the purest, undifferentiated representation of California's revolutionary consciousness occurs in the music of the Beach Boys, specifically in the third part of "California Saga," a trilogy written by Mike Love and Al Jardine. Called simply "California," Jardine's contribution so perfectly expresses the state's geography, climate, history, idealism, and freedom that nothing else about California is granted any reality at all. The song captures the listener's attention so totally that, for its duration, no other place can exist either: California is all there is. The power is in more than the lyrics, however; the music alone has the same effect. Its emotional impact is simply overwhelming; nothing other than the singers' image of California is permitted to enter the listener's consciousness. On later reflection, of course, this image is recognized for what it is: empty of all the content that would give it genuine reality.

Nothing

Similarly, pure nothingness has no determinateness with respect to itself or to anything else. It is the complete and total absence of "is-ness," the negation of being. Its reality in our consciousness is not simply "no thought," but the "thought of nothing." In other words, it makes sense to speak of the reality of nothingness.

Given that the Beach Boys portray the pure, undifferentiated fullness of California's revolutionary consciousness, the complete and pure negation of this image is best represented by the Doors (especially Jim Morrison). Everything the Beach Boys are, the Doors are not; everything the Beach Boys advocate, the Doors reject. A more perfect opposition would be difficult if not impossible to find. In "L.A. Woman," the city (which metaphorically represents the state) is personified as a whore whose hair is burning and whose wanderings are confined to freeways, midnight alleys, and topless bars. The imagery is as dominated by the dark as the Beach Boys' is by the light; neither gives any promise of ending. Also, there are no references to geography, climate, history, idealism, or freedom in "L.A. Woman." On the contrary, we are confronted with the unmistakable indications of destruction, disease, disaster, and disillusionment. As with the Beach Boys, however, the overwhelming purity of the Doors' portrayal is expressed in their music as well as in their lyrics. The Doors' use of a minor key contrasts so sharply with the major key used by the Beach Boys that there is no way to escape the Doors' undifferentiated mood of negation. Their vision of the California experience is as bleak as the Beach Boys' is positive, and as a result, it, too, is necessarily devoid of the content that would give it genuine reality.

Becoming

Insofar as reality is concerned, pure being and pure nothing have the same characteristics; so neither alone can accurately portray the truth about reality. For Hegel, what is truth is neither being nor nothing, but rather that *each* immediately *disappears in its opposite.* Their truth is thus this *movement* of the immediate disappearance of one in the other: *becoming.* But everything real contains both.

Neither the Beach Boys nor the Doors can truthfully represent the actual revolutionary consciousness of California, since their portrayals of the positive and negative elements within this experience are pure abstractions. Reality is always a mixture of the positive and the negative and the various processes occasioned by the mixture. So it is with the California experience.

"Hotel California" by the Eagles expresses both the mixture and the resulting processes more clearly than perhaps any other song written about California. The "hotel" is obviously a metaphorical reference to California and the state of mind that accompanies it. After checking in for the night, a traveler comes to the realization that "this could be Heaven or this could be Hell"; it turns out to be both. On the one hand it's "such a lovely place," but on the other "we are all just prisoners here of our

own device." While "some dance to remember, some dance to forget."
Inevitably, the resulting conflict dislodges the visitor from any possible
static complacency; some kind of movement must occur:

> Last thing I remember, I was
> Running for the door
> I had to find the passage back
> To the place I was before
> "Relax," said the night man,
> "We are programmed to receive,
> You can check out any time you like,
> but you can never leave."

Notice two things about this final stanza: one is that movement backward
is ruled out, and the other is that movement elsewhere is ruled out. The
California experience can invade the consciousness so completely that
forward motion is only conceivable in terms of this experience. So it is
also with the cultural revolution; once involved in it, other alternatives
cease to have any power or meaning.

Musically, the Eagles have created a song that suggests a combination
of major and minor harmonics. Even more important, however, is their
use of reggae rhythms as an expression of the paradoxes so often encountered in this state. For while Jamaica couldn't be farther away from California and still be within the scope of American culture, the revolutionary sentiments of reggae are right at home. All in all, the song is a
remarkable combination of seemingly opposite tendencies, and anyone
lured into its seductive melodies is bound to come away changed.

Revolution

If, as Hegel suggested, reality is always comprised of a mixture of being
and nothingness (the positive and negative), and if the tension between
them is the fundamental source of change (becoming), then it would
seem that the greater the tension the greater the processes of change. Furthermore, if the conflicts are as severe throughout the rest of the country
as they seem to be within the state of California, then the kind of movement that's under way can only be characterized as revolutionary. The
energy being released by the dynamics internal to this situation is too
great to be described in any other way.

——————————— The External Relationship ———————————

Thomas Kuhn's justly famous book *The Structure of Scientific Revolutions* has stimulated thought in so many diverse fields that it would be a shame not to use some of his ideas to help examine cultural revolutions as well. Actually, quite a few others have already delved into this area, as evidenced by a book of essays devoted to the application of Kuhn's thought (*Paradigms and Revolutions,* edited by Gary Gutting). Especially interesting is the way Kuhn's conceptual scheme lends itself to an analysis of the relationship between a given revolution and the established order. In this regard, the following four themes seem particularly appropriate.

Paradigms and Normalcy

"Paradigm" is undoubtedly the key concept of Kuhn's theory, and the issue of its clarity has provided the grist for an apparently endless flow of scholarly articles, including Kuhn's reply to several of the more serious criticisms. Without getting bogged down in this debate, a paradigm is essentially a perceptual model which is comprised of basic assumptions about the world, procedural norms for understanding it, criteria for assessing truth and falseness, beliefs about the meaningfulness of reality, the ultimate values implicit in any investigation of its nature, and a language designed to express all of this (the Ptolemaic, Copernican and Einsteinian views of the universe, for example). Usually, the commitment to a particular constellation of beliefs captured (often loosely) by a given paradigm is shared by many people; otherwise it would be of little interest and receive even less attention. When those sharing it hold power, the paradigm assumes the status of normalcy—and is understood, consequently, as the unquestioned truth. Rarely do the inevitable anomalies occasion more than passing notice. Eventually, however, a new paradigm arises which can successfully explain the anomalies better than the prevailing scheme, but since the new paradigm is necessarily incommensurable with the old one, a conflict results. Notice that the location of this conflict is in human consciousness, and while it may be manifested in physical violence, this is not inevitable. Fundamentally, the conflict is between incompatible ideas, and the battleground is within the mind. Since the two paradigms entail two different (but usually overlapping) languages, communication between their respective proponents is exceptionally difficult, not the least because this difficulty is not often recognized and/or appreciated.

An amusing but still deadly serious illustration of such confrontation occurred in 1983, when former Secretary of the Interior James Watt refused to allow the Beach Boys to perform their traditional Fourth of July concert on the grounds of the Washington Monument. He alleged that the Beach Boys (and rock music in general) attract the wrong kind of people. Given Watt's state of consciousness, however, his attitude and decision made perfect sense. They were completely consistent with the paradigm he held to be unquestionably true. (By the way, to illustrate the fact that life is a bit more complex and not nearly as neat as any conceptual scheme might suggest, the Reagans, like many others, were upset with Watt's decision, even though they certainly shared the same paradigmatic perspective.) Fans of the Beach Boys and rock music were not only angered but bemused by Watt's action, since the Beach Boys aren't even close to being as outrageous as some contemporary rock groups; they aren't like the Circle Jerks or the Dead Kennedys after all. But this incredulity derives from their having a vastly different perspective on reality than does Watt; neither is really capable of understanding the attitude of the other.

Paradigm Shifts and Revolutions

Essentially, a revolution occurs with the replacement of the established (normal) paradigm by another: an alternation of world views. Such replacements occur suddenly and all at once, in the sense that an evolutionary transition from one to the other is not empirically or even logically possible; the paradigms themselves prohibit this. A more appropriate analogy, one which Kuhn himself uses, is a conversion experience: one paradigm must be completely abandoned in order for another to be accepted; in other words, a total reorientation takes place. Needless to say, the resistance to this kind of change is enormous, and it may take quite a while for the shift to be completed. As the process is under way, the personal and societal crises can achieve considerable intensity and become enormously distressing. Every attempt is made to shore up the defenses of the status quo, and this usually involves some form of repression. Anomalies are either ignored or forced uncomfortably into the existing patterns of thought; alien paradigms are simply given no official recognition and are discouraged in every possible way. What this amounts to is a counterreaction, launched by those most threatened by the new paradigm.

A shift of paradigm is revealed by the Mamas and the Papas' "Twelve-thirty (Young Girls Are Coming to the Canyon)," a song that traces their own conversion experience when moving to California: "I used to live in New York City/Everything there was dark and dirty." Then follows,

> At first so strange to feel so friendly
> To say good morning and really mean it
> To feel these changes happening in me
> But not to notice 'till I feel it

Their entire world view had undergone a change. To call it a revolution of consciousness is not an exaggeration. Other transplants to California have described their feelings in a similar way: Joni Mitchell (from Canada) in "California," America (from England, Florida, and Texas) in "Ventura Highway" and "California Revisited" and the Starland Vocal Band (from the East Coast) in "California Day" among them.

Knowledge and Authority

Kuhn recognizes that revolutions of consciousness are often indistinguishable from ordinary, normal day-to-day events. For this reason, he devotes an entire chapter to an analysis of their invisibility. The principal reason for this problem has to do with the fact that all knowledge is dependent on the prevailing paradigm. Hence, what is taught throughout society is restricted; the institutions that educate the young (schools, families, churches, media, governments, etc.) purvey a notion of truth that derives from the official paradigm, and this alone. It is not so much that other paradigmatic ideas are deliberately and consciously excluded (although this certainly happens); it's more the case that these other ideas are not even entertained in thought. Thinking about something new isn't possible within the prevailing system. The meaning of truth and its criteria are thus based on a fundamental commitment to a particular world view; whatever doesn't fit the pattern is ignored and/or disvalued.

The controversies surrounding the Byrds' rendition of Dylan's "Mr. Tambourine Man," the Association's "Along Comes Mary," Creedence Clearwater Revival's "Proud Mary," and the Jefferson Airplane's "White Rabbit" illustrate how far apart the perceptions based on different paradigms can be. It is not a question of whether or not these particular songs refer to drugs (which they do); it's a question of how drugs are regarded or valued that's important. In *The Story of Rock*, Carl Belz sees such thinly disguised drug references fundamentally as an expression of an alternative life-style: "Those who knew the jargon used it to distinguish themselves from those who did not. It became a method whereby young people defined their personal world and excluded adults from it."[3] Although Belz sees the conflict primarily in generational terms, he's essentially correct. These songs, and others like them, place a different truth value on the use of drugs (and, as I've noted earlier, a clear differentiation is made among various drugs concerning their desirability).

Similar examples could be cited regarding sexuality, the war in Vietnam, the military, the government, and virtually everything else at issue between the revolutionaries and the established order. None of them are capable of empirical or logical resolution, for they have to do with ultimate values. A resolution could only occur if one side were to convert to the other's world view, and even this would not obviate a revolutionary transition, for this is precisely what's entailed by a conversion.

Relativity and Justification

The implication that would seem to follow from this is that truth is logically dependent on the acceptance of a given paradigm. Since there are no external criteria (based on a metaparadigm, perhaps) on which to base an assessment of competing paradigms, truth must necessarily be relative. Kuhn, however, is reluctant to follow his ideas this far; he feels that some kind of pragmatic judgment is possible. It is useful, in other words, both to preserve the existing paradigm for as long as possible as well as to encourage the development of new paradigms. Yet this is hardly a sufficient substitute for the idea of absolute truth: pragmatism must either accept epistemological relativism or concede that it presupposes certain absolutes as a matter of faith. Kuhn, in fact, seems to acknowledge that science, in some ways, is clearly distinguishable "from every other creative pursuit except theology." For both, the final appeal is always to some kind of authority—not truth. Actually, the only social system consistent with the unfettered pursuit of truth is anarchy, for the pursuit of truth and an appeal to any authority are incompatible.

How, then, is it possible to assess the comparative truth of the cultural revolution and the established order if truth can only be decided from within each paradigm? Is the answer no more than a matter of taste? Like Kuhn and virtually everyone else, I am uncomfortable with this solution, yet there doesn't seem to be any way to settle the issue without begging the question (for choosing among competing justifications involves an infinite regress).

The only way out of this impasse, it seems to me, is neither logical nor empirical. Rather it is the act of commitment itself, a Kierkegaardian leap of faith. That to which a commitment is made is secondary to the act itself. It doesn't "prove" anything, of course, but a genuine leap of faith certainly authenticates the commitment as having as much validity as any similar commitment. This, I think, is about the most we can say about justifying one paradigm against another.

Commitments like this can be shown in a variety of ways, but surely one way is for people actually to live the life they propose as desirable for all. As far as California rock music is concerned, examples abound, but as a paradigm of commitment, we need look no farther than the Grateful Dead. Not only did they choose to live communally in the Haight (before its discovery by *Time* magazine), they embodied virtually every other trait of hippiedom, including giving many free concerts. Their performances were (and still are) literal manifestations of the "trips" they frequently took, "trips" for which they were occasionally busted. Some might conclude that they were unable to separate themselves from the world view they revealed in their music, but this would be to denigrate their choice without any reason other than a distaste for it.

The Dead are not the only ones to have made a commitment to this degree, nor is hippie life the only possible form that such a commitment can take. Another exemplar, with virtually nothing in common with the Grateful Dead other than sharing the same revolutionary values, is Randy Newman. More than anything else, his commitment is manifested in the risks he takes in his music. In *Mystery Train*, Greil Marcus sees him this way: "Laconic, funny, grim, and solitary, Randy Newman is a . . . man who does not like what he sees but is wildly attracted to it anyway, a man who keeps his sanity by rendering contradictions other people struggle to avoid. . . . His real task is to make his burden ours."[4] With the success of "Short People" (and his earlier but less successful "Sail Away"), he has partially accomplished his aim. Listening to him assume the role of a bigot and a racist, we cannot ignore what he is portraying. For his portrayal is no parody or satire; he really assumes the role! In so doing he risks exposing his most cherished values to the grossest of misunderstandings (of having others believe that he is actually advocating what he so ardently opposes). He fools around with America's tenderest wounds and forces the listener either to stick the knife in deeper or to pull it out forever.

No commitment, no matter how strong or sincere, can establish the truth of a paradigm and the set of fundamental values that's implied by it. Nevertheless, by putting a commitment on the line, its authenticity can be established, and no more can be asked of anyone.

The State of Rock

Some of the comments made about rock and roll in *Rolling Stone's* tenth anniversary issue (1977) are remarkably similar to the kind of commentary that is appropriate to the state of California today.

Chet Flippo maintained that rock and roll has always meant more than music: "There are books and movies and people and events and attitudes that matter more to a rock and roll way of life than do many records that are labeled rock and roll. Jack Kerouac was rock and roll; Bobby Rydell was not. Tom Robbins is rock and roll; Andy Gibb is not. *Star Wars* is rock and roll; *A Star Is Born* is not."[5] To continue his list, California is rock and roll; Alabama is not.

Jon Landau wrote that "Elvis Presley's rock and roll was a frontal assault on Fifties America. It was a unique expression of people trying to transcend the traditional social and emotional limits of their lives. . . . Sixties rock transformed Presley's unconscious impulses into a self-conscious rebellion. . . . The Fifties rebels without a cause became the Sixties rebels with a cause—and a vengeance." But it was a vengeance with a purpose too. "Great rock not only defines what is, but suggests what might be."[6] These remarks are reminiscent of those made by Theodore H. White, cited earlier, a fact worth pointing out, since Landau wasn't thinking about California and White wasn't thinking about rock and roll. (At least I don't think they were.)

The late Ralph Gleason, one of the founders of *Rolling Stone*, always believed in music's ability to change our lives. He wrote that rock and roll "plays a role unlike anything in history, yes, even including religion. . . . As societal glue, as educational system, as emotional, mind-expanding experience and a view-realignment mechanism, music is now in the process of changing the ways in which things are seen. In the process it is changing ways in which this generation will relate to everything and, in the ultimate, it will change the nature of our society.'' Gleason's optimism might seem a bit naive today, but only insofar as he expected the change to happen quickly. Despite this, he had a grasp on the essential truth about rock and roll: It ''is the new educational system for reform and the medium for revolution. Its importance is impossible to overemphasize.''[7] As it is with the state of rock music and the cultural revolution, so it is with the state of California: what begins on the West Coast will eventually travel throughout the nation, a prospect which some regard with hope and others with trepidation. Both feelings are no doubt correct.

For those of you who say that you want a revolution, it should be carefully noted that all of us want in our own way to change the world. Some speak of evolution. Most of us, after all, are rightly ambivalent about destruction. Nevertheless, there is good reason for confidence, quite apart from those with alleged plans offering us a solution (and requesting a contribution). More often than not, their solutions merely yield an increase in hatreds, which we can well do without. The basic strategy must always be to change people's consciousness first—not constitutions and institutions. Further, a successful revolution must emerge out of and speak directly to the culture that's involved; the revolutions from elsewhere can never be imported. No one will listen.

Regardless of whether or not America's cultural revolution succeeds or fails, America will never be the same again. The changes already begun are irreversible. The process of negation set in motion by Elvis and all that he represented is still alive, as is the process of affirmation instigated by the Beatles. Neither Elvis nor the Beatles have survived the years. But in a larger sense, they're still with us whenever you turn on the radio. They're in every song you hear, every rock-and-roll record you play, no matter what the style, no matter who the artist. Were it not for Elvis Presley and the Beatles, the music of today and the revolution would not exist. And were it not for rock and roll, we would not be able to look at America today and imagine.

Bibliography

American Culture

Carroll, Peter N. *It Seemed Like Nothing Happened: The Tragedy and the Promise of America in the 1970s.* New York: Holt, Rinehart and Winston, 1983.

Dickstein, Morris. *Gates of Eden: American Culture in the Sixties.* New York: Basic Books, 1977.

Goodman, Ellen. *At Large.* New York: Summit Books, 1981.

Halberstam, David. *The Best and the Brightest.* Greenwich, Conn.: Fawcett, 1973.

Holman, Sona, and Lillian Friedman. *How to Lie about Your Age.* New York: Collier Books, 1979.

Medved, Michael, and David Wallechinsky. *What Really Happened to the Class of '65?* New York: Ballantine Books, 1976.

Moment, Gairdner, and Otto Kraushaar, eds. *Utopias: The American Experience.* Metuchen, N.J.: Scarecrow Press, 1980.

Obst, Lynda R., ed. *The Sixties.* New York: Rolling Stone Press, 1977.

Pichaske, David. *A Generation in Motion: Popular Music and Culture in the Sixties.* New York: Schirmer Books, 1979.

Reich, Charles. *The Greening of America.* New York: Random House, 1970.

Roszak, Theodore. *The Making of a Counter Culture.* Garden City, N.Y.: Doubleday, Anchor Books, 1969.

White, Theodore H. *America in Search of Itself.* New York: Harper and Row, 1982.

Wills, Garry. *Nixon Agonistes.* New York: Mentor Books, 1971.

Wofford, Harris. *Of Kennedys and Kings: Making Sense of the Sixties.* New
     York: Farrar, Straus and Giroux, 1980.

Media

Dexter, Dave. *Playback.* New York: Billboard Publications, 1976.
Ehrenstein, David, and Bill Reed. *Rock on Film.* New York: Delilah Books,
     1982.
McLuhan, Marshall. *The Gutenberg Galaxy.* New York: Mentor Books, 1969.
_____. *Understanding Media.* New York: Mentor Books, 1964.
Newcomb, Horace. *TV: The Most Popular Art.* Garden City, N.Y.: Doubleday,
     Anchor Books, 1974.
Norback, Craig T., and Peter G., eds. *TV Guide Almanac.* New York: Ballantine
     Books, 1980.
Sklar, Robert. *Movie-Made America: A Cultural History of American Movies.*
     New York: Vintage Books, 1975.
Tebbel, John. *The Media in America.* New York: Mentor Books, 1976.
Whetmore, Edward. *Mediamerica.* 2d ed. Belmont, Calif.: Wadsworth, 1982.

Philosophy

Arendt, Hanna. *On Revolution.* New York: Penguin Books, 1965.
Barrett, William. *Irrational Man.* Garden City, N.Y.: Doubleday, Anchor
     Books, 1962.
Berger, Peter L. *Invitation to Sociology.* Garden City, N.Y.: Doubleday, An-
     chor Books, 1963.
Blacking, John. *How Musical Is Man?* Seattle, Wash.: University of Washington
     Press, 1973.
Brinton, Crane. *The Anatomy of Revolution.* New York: Vintage Books, 1965.
Eliade, Mircea. *The Sacred and the Profane.* New York: Harper and Row, 1961.
Freud, Sigmund. *Civilization and Its Discontents.* New York: W. W. Norton,
     1962.
Gutting, Gary, ed. *Paradigms and Revolutions.* Notre Dame, Ind.: University of
     Notre Dame Press, 1980.
Hegel, G. W. F. *The Philosophy of History.* New York: Dover, 1956.
_____. *Selections.* Edited by J. Loewenberg. New York: Scribner's, 1957.
Kaufmann, Walter. *Hegel: A Reinterpretation.* Garden City, N.Y.: Doubleday,
     Anchor Books, 1966.

Kierkegaard, Sören. *Philosophical Fragments*. Princeton, N.J.: Princeton University Press, 1962.

Kuhn, Thomas. *The Structure of Scientific Revolutions*. 2d ed. Chicago, Ill.: University of Chicago Press, 1970.

Langer, Susanne. *Philosophy in a New Key*. New York: Mentor Books, 1948.

Marcuse, Herbert. *The Aesthetic Dimension*. Boston, Mass.: Beacon Press, 1978.

_____. *Counter-Revolution and Revolt*. Boston, Mass.: Beacon Press, 1972.

_____. *An Essay on Liberation*. Boston, Mass.: Beacon Press, 1969.

Maslow, Abraham. *Motivation and Personality*. New York: Harper and Row, 1954.

Otto, Rudolf. *The Idea of the Holy*. New York: Oxford University Press, 1958.

Poirier, Richard. *The Performing Self*. New York: Oxford University Press, 1971.

Sartre, Jean-Paul. *Being and Nothingness*. New York: Pocket Books, 1966.

Sontag, Susan. *Styles of Radical Will*. New York: Farrar, Straus and Giroux, 1966.

Tillich, Paul. *Dynamics of Faith*. New York: Harper, 1958.

Tucker, Robert. *The Marxian Revolutionary Idea*. New York: W. W. Norton, 1969.

Rock Music

Bane, Michael. *The Outlaws: Revolution in Country Music*. Garden City, N.Y.: Doubleday/Dolphin, 1978.

_____. *White Boy Singin' the Blues*. New York: Penguin Books, 1982.

The Beatles. *Beatles Lyrics*. Introduction by Richard Brautigan. New York: Dell, 1975.

Belz, Carl. *The Story of Rock*. 2d ed. New York: Harper Colophon Books, 1972.

Blackford, Andy. *Disco Dancing Tonight*. London: Octopus Books, 1979.

Burt, Robert, and Patsy North. *West Coast Story*. Secaucus, N.J.: Chartwell Books, 1977.

Cohn, Nik. *Pop from the Beginning: A Wop Bop a Loo Bop a Lop Bam Boom*. London: Paladin, 1972.

Davies, Hunter. *The Beatles*. Rev. ed. New York: McGraw-Hill, 1978.

Denisoff, R. *Sing a Song of Social Significance*. Bowling Green, Ohio: Bowling Green University Press, 1972.

Eisen, Jonathan, ed. *The Age of Rock: Sounds of the American Cultural Revolution*. New York: Vintage Books, 1969.

Fong-Torres, Ben, ed. *What's That Sound?* Garden City, N.Y.: Doubleday, Anchor Books, 1976.

Golson, G.B., ed. *The Playboy Interviews with John Lennon and Yoko Ono,* conducted by David Sheff. Playboy Press, 1981.

✗ Guralnick, Peter. *Feel Like Going Home: Portraits in Blues and Rock 'n' Roll.* New York: Vintage Books, 1981.

Herman, Gary. *Rock 'n' Roll Babylon.* New York: Perigee Books, 1982.

✗ Hopkins, Jerry. *The Rock Story.* New York: Signet Books, 1970.

✗ Jahn, Mike. *The Story of Rock.* New York: Quadrangle, 1973.

McCabe, Peter, and Robert D. Schonfeld. *Apple to the Core.* New York: Pocket Books, 1972.

Marcus, Greil. *Mystery Train: Images of America in Rock 'n' Roll Music.* Rev. ed. New York: E. P. Dutton, 1982.

Miller, Jim, ed. *The Rolling Stone Illustrated History of Rock and Roll.* New York: Rolling Stone Press, 1976.

Norman, Phillip. *Shout! The Beatles in Their Generation.* New York: Fireside Books, 1981.

Preiss, Byron. *The Beach Boys.* New York: Ballantine Books, 1979.

Roxon, Lillian. *Rock Encyclopedia.* New York: Workman, 1969.

Shaw, Arnold. *Dictionary of American Pop/Rock.* New York: Schirmer Books, 1982.

_____. *The Rock Revolution.* New York: Crowell-Collier Press, 1969.

Stambler, Irwin. *Encyclopedia of Pop, Rock and Soul.* New York: St. Martin's Press, 1977.

Stein, Kevin, and Dave Marsh. *The Book of Rock Lists.* New York: Rolling Stone Press, 1981.

Young, Jean, and Michael Lang. *Woodstock Festival Remembered.* New York: Ballantine Books, 1979.

Notes

Part 1. Music and Culture

Introduction

1. John Blacking, *How Musical Is Man?* (Seattle, Wash.: University of Washington Press, 1973), 25, 53, 58, 104, 115–16, 191.
2. Susanne Langer, *Philosophy in a New Key* (New York: Mentor Books, 1948), 191.
3. David Pichaske, *A Generation in Motion* (New York: Shirmer Books, 1979), xix.

Chapter 2. What Is Rock Music?

1. Herbert Marcuse, *Counter-Revolution and Revolt* (Boston, Mass.: Beacon Press, 1972), 79-82, 87, 93, 99-100, 116.
2. William Barrett, *Irrational Man* (Garden City, N.Y.: Doubleday, Anchor Books, 1958), 41-49, 56, 64-65.

Part 2. Medium and Message

Introduction

1. Marshall McLuhan, *Understanding Media* (New York: Mentor Books, 1964), x, 21, 30-32, 63, 71, 224, 243, 266-67.

Chapter 4. Radio: The Creation of a New Community

1. McLuhan, *Understanding Media,* 261-68.
2. Ibid., 266-67.

Chapter 5. Records: The Newest Testament

1. McLuhan, *Understanding Media,* 247.
2. Robert Hilburn, "The 12-Inch Record on a Hot Roll," *Los Angeles Times* (Feb. 13, 1983), 66-68.

Chapter 7. Television: Bringing It All Back Home

1. McLuhan, *Understanding Media,* 61, 273-76, 278, 282, 288.
2. Ibid., 292.
3. Ibid., 272, 275, 294, 297, 300.

Part 3. Revolution and Revelation

Introduction

1. Rudolf Otto, *The Idea of the Holy,* trans. by John Harvey (New York: Oxford University Press, 1958), 10-31, 143.
2. Paul Tillich, *Dynamics of Faith* (New York: Harper Torchbooks, 1957), 43, 48, 90.

Chapter 8. Elvis and the Negation of the Fifties

1. Jerry Wexler and Ahmet Ertegun, "The Latest Trends: R & B Disks Are Going Pop," *The Cash Box* (July 3, 1954), 56.
2. Michael Bane, *White Boy Singin' the Blues* (New York: Penguin Books, 1982), 119-21.
3. Greil Marcus, *Mystery Train,* rev. ed. (New York: E. P. Dutton, 1982), 155, 173.
4. Ibid., 190.
5. Bane, *White Boy Singin' the Blues,* 129.
6. Marcus, *Mystery Train,* 141.
7. Bane, *White Boy Singin' the Blues,* 101.
8. Marcus, *Mystery Train,* 166.
9. G. B. Golson, ed., *The Playboy Interviews with John Lennon and Yoko Ono,* conducted by David Sheff (New York: Playboy Press, 1981), 48, 108-9.
10. Marcus, *Mystery Train,* 191-92.
11. Ibid., 208.
12. Bane, *White Boy Singin' the Blues,* 129.
13. Mircea Eliade, *The Sacred and the Profane,* trans. by Willard Track (New York: Harper Torchbooks, 1961), 97, 98.
14. Golson, *Playboy Interviews,* 71-72.
15. Eliade, *The Sacred and the Profane,* 88-89, 94.

Chapter 9. The Beatles and the Affirmation of the Sixties

1. Quoted by Greil Marcus, "The Beatles," in *The Rolling Stone Illustrated History of Rock and Roll* ed. by Jim Miller (New York: Rolling Stone Press, 1976), 174.
2. Peter L. Berger, *Invitation to Sociology* (Garden City, N.Y.: Doubleday, Anchor Books, 1963), 54, 57, 61, 62.
3. Otto, *Idea of the Holy,* 36.
4. John Lahr, "The Beatles Considered," *The New Republic* (Dec. 2, 1981), 22-23.
5. Ibid., 23.
6. Richard Poirier, *The Performing Self* (New York: Oxford University Press, 1971), 137, 139.
7. Quoted by Marcus, "The Beatles," *The Rolling Stone Illustrated History of Rock and Roll,* 176.
8. Ibid.
9. Pichaske, *A Generation in Motion,* 92, 93.

10. Jonathan Cott, "Children of Paradise," *Rolling Stone* (Dec. 15, 1977), 37, 41, 43.

11. Ibid., 43.

12. Lahr, "The Beatles Considered," 23.

13. Eliade, *The Sacred and the Profane*, 99-100.

14. Ibid., 80.

15. Bruce Eisner, "The Hippie Revolution: Looking Back at Sgt. Pepper," *Head* (April 1978), 37.

Chapter 11. Reactualization and the New Music of the Counterreaction

1. Eliade, *The Sacred and the Profane*, 68-69, 78, 80-81.

2. Sören Kierkegaard, *Philosophical Fragments*, 2d ed., trans. by H. Hong (Princeton, N.J.: Princeton University Press, 1962), 128.

3. Robert Hilburn, "Pop Breaks Vietnam Silence," *Los Angeles Times* (Oct. 3, 1983), 1.

4. Ellen Goodman, *At Large* (New York: Summit Books, 1981), 204, 205.

5. Robert Hilburn, "John Lydon: Fed Up with Pop Anarchy," *Los Angeles Times* (April 17, 1982), A23.

Epilogue: California—The Shape of Things to Come

1. Theodore H. White, *America in Search of Itself* (New York: Harper and Row, 1982), 64.

2. Georg Wilhelm Friedrich Hegel, *The Philosophy of History*, trans. by J. Sibree (New York: Dover, 1956), 63.

3. Carl Belz, *The Story of Rock*, 2d ed. (New York: Harper and Row, 1972), 171.

4. Marcus, *Mystery Train*, 136.

5. Chet Flippo, "A Style is Born," *Rolling Stone* (Dec. 15, 1977), 21.

6. Jon Landau, "Rock Ages," *Rolling Stone* (Dec. 15, 1977), 33.

7. Ralph J. Gleason, "What We Are and What We Ain't," *Rolling Stone* (Dec. 15, 1977), 27.

Index